FEMALE STUDIES VI
CLOSER TO THE GROUND
WOMEN'S CLASSES, CRITICISM, PROGRAMS--1972

Editors: Nancy Hoffman, Cynthia Secor, Adrian Tinsley

prepared for the Commission on the Status of Women

of the Modern Language Association

The Clearinghouse on Women's Studies
THE FEMINIST PRESS
Old Westbury
New York

The MLA Commission on the Status of Women:

Sidonie Cassirer, Mary Anne Ferguson, Elaine Hedges, Nancy Hoffman,
Carol Ohmann, Elaine Reuben, Catherine Stimpson, Adrian Tinsley

Manufactured in the United States of America.
Printed by The Faculty Press.

Second Edition, 1973   ISBN: 0-912670-26-6

Cover design by by Gilda Kuhlman

CONTENTS

CLOSER TO THE GROUND: WOMEN'S CLASSES, CRITICISM, PROGRAMS--1972

INTRODUCTION

Closer to the ground. The image suggests not theory, but more particular practice, and that is its intent. Female Studies IV, Teaching About Women, which appeared one year ago in December 1971, contained seven essays about women's studies courses most being taught for the first time at established four-year colleges by credentialed faculty. The overwhelming message of these essays was that teaching about women, women writers, women's history, psychology, sociology, was indeed justifiable, both to ourselves, and to the traditionalists in academia; that surprising, even shaking occurrences of a personal nature inevitably happen in classes where the focus is female experience; and that a likely consequence of women's studies classes is the generation of more women's studies classes, of affirmative action, of community resource centers, of general curriculum review -- in short, the generation of feminist activists, writers, thinkers, scholars. The essays in this year's volume contribute little to justifying women's studies; most writers already assume an audience persuaded of the rightness of feminism as an established perspective on the world. Though often highly personal in tone, anecdotal, validating of the "I" and "we" voices of writers as well as those written about, the pain and invigoration of being personal is no longer a subject in itself, but is embedded in differing degrees in each paper. The third message then from last year's volume emerges here with clarity; here are some of the consequences of first women's studies courses, the ideas, the actions generated. Those consequences, more particular descriptions of classes, feminist criticism, and a profile of one women's studies program, each comprise a section of the volume. "Women as Liberators" by Ginny Foster which opens the collection provides a framework for the year's work, and for the years to come.

In the classroom, women and a few men are writing from a perspective of joining, thus deepening an already vital movement. This particularity evidences itself in two changes from last year: first, teachers can be initially feminist, pro-woman, and need not convince men and women that women are justified in taking themselves as a subject of study; and, second, feminists studying, unlike some others in experimental education, have been able to move on from questions of method, structure, and form -- how to study -- to content, studying itself. Women's classes this year immediately and directly ask what has been women's experience, what can it be. For example, Melanie Kaye who taught the first women's studies course in Berkeley's department of comparative literature does not catalogue in her essay the events of the two years it took to establish her course, nor does she agonize about structure. In women's studies, both have become routine. When she calls her tone interrogative, she means that books by women, and women's lives raise the questions. Similarly, at a community

college, a male teacher, confidently feminist, makes the lives of students and one poem by Anne Sexton intersect in a complex project
analyzing an eternal triangle. Or women who have been too abruptly
"de-schooled" come back into contact with books and minds in a self-
taught literature class saying they are doing neither consciousness-
raising, nor studying the women's movement. They too have come to
an institutional place beyond the circle of domesticity to read and
discuss women writers, using their own lives to support ideas about
books. Only in Aleta Wallach's description of overhauling the UCLA
Law School, countering its sexist practices, and giving a women's
course, must we acknowledge the quantity of energy necessarily deflec-
ted outward, aimed at creating an atmosphere in which women can work
and think.

Our teaching essays showed that experiments in and out of the
classroom had gone far beyond the introductory course which often
focused on male's images of women. This year's Current Guide to Female
Studies lists such woman-centered courses as George Eliot, Virginia
Woolf, The Woman in Renaissance Spain, Emancipated Women Writers,
Black Women Poets. Feminist criticism shows, analagously, that we are
no longer revising the male critics, but are writing as feminists
on women's issues. Any of the critical papers in Section III gives
examples of how women solve problems as diverse as whether there is
a female sentence, how to answer and understand a noted woman writer
who attacks feminism, how to interpret Doris Lessing's relation to
time, place, and history, when we know that she herself, Martha Quest,
and we, are children of war, "children of violence." Indeed, the
basis upon which we chose these critical papers was not that they
demonstrated the brilliantly argued thesis, or for that matter, were
examples or models of feminist criticism for the future -- we are
still unsure what that will be, but rather that each is an activist
paper in its way. Each woman raises her specific intellectual questions, solves her specific problem, because she, the writer of the
essay, is first a thinking woman, then a practicing critic. From
that vantage each woman necessarily challenges the institution of
criticism which has taught us to analyze character, to identify stock
figures, to codify thematic patterns, even to discuss the class of
a writer or a figure in a novel, but never to challenge their authenticity, their relation to dominant cultural and political assumptions.
(See Introduction to Section III.)

The challenging stance, the problem solving one is extraordinary
in literary criticism. Carol Ohmann, for example, takes up the question of class in her examination of the limits of Charlotte Brontë's
feminism. Her conclusion, Ginny Foster would agree, derives from
her own feminist politics, exists beyond any statement Charlotte Brontë
herself would have made.

> It is in its treatment of women that the novel Shirley
> is most nearly radical, most nearly thorough going in

its understanding of the uses of power and the
responses of those who don't have it to those who
do. The novel proceeds relentlessly toward this
conclusion: what women experience they experience as a class, even if they have a clear ₤1,000
a year. They stand outside the corridors and boardrooms of power, outside the testaments of religion,
culture, history. They need history re-written and
a new mythology. They are in want of a sweeping re-
constitution of social, economic, and political
relationships.

Carol Ohmann's paper illustrates two of Ginny Foster's perceptions:
that women are outsiders, and that the outsider's vision, Carol
Ohmann's view of Shirley, is creative by virtue of its minority perspective, its ability to portray connections which an insider would
miss. Similarly, an insider could never have created the warm comfort
of Cynthia Secor's "Alice and Gertrude," or the personal, sad
tone of Judith Newton chiding Joan Didion.

The fourth section, the profile of the Women's Studies Program
at Portland State University, found its way into Closer to the Ground
by a kind of inner necessity. First, we selected papers that seemed
useful, that comprised the degree of specificity characterizing
this year's work, then we discovered that many of those chosen came
from Portland women. The homogeneity of their political perspective,
the cross-references to Portland women, the variety of their subjects, led us to conclude that accepting them all would give us a
rare, objective vision of a community. Though events -- a writing
class, a collective meeting, a political action, may be referred to
only twice or thrice, each woman has experienced the events of the
program even if she doesn't explicate them. These papers construct
a profile or case study, keeping account of organization and governance, funding, accrediting, and the politics of institutional reform,
all updated to a month of the printing deadline, so the steps of
two and a half years are spelled out. Examples of creative work too
are included; undergraduates of teenage and middle age, and graduate
students write with passion, thorough-mindedness, and a firm sense of
connection to the women's movement. The papers, we learned, were
chosen by Portland State women, submitted collectively, and revised
for publication with hours of conversation and care. They carry out
a pledge current from the early days of Portland State Women's Studies:
women should write, get their poems and stories out from between
the matresses, out from under moth-balled sweaters in the bottom
drawer, out from old notebooks and diaries, out from the dark and
light places of the mind, from fantasy, from dream. Portland women
believed from the start Tillie Olsen's charge to women: "Help create
writers, among them yourselves!" Their pride in the accomplishment
is well-deserved and moving.

In the final page of Closer to the Ground, readers will find short
biographical sketches of each contributor. Because the editors conceive
of this book as a substitute for conversations impossible to have, and
a provocation to those that can be, contributors were asked to include
their addresses if they wished correspondence from readers. To a
woman, they said "yes."

I   THE RADICAL PERSPECTIVE ON WOMEN'S STUDIES

INTRODUCTION

We have said above that Ginny Foster's essay provides a framework for the year's work, and for the years to come. It does more
than that. Her opening paragraph spells out the single most important
question that faces us, "whether women's studies will follow the
patriarchal formula which has defined education in the past." It is
not enough to know in our heads that we are socialized and policed by
institutions that are responsive neither to our basic needs nor to
our sense of reality. Rather we must move collectively to "establish
priorities that do not reflect the dominant [masculine] frame of reference." This frame of reference has provided us with mountains of
data, but it has proved useless in translating this data into actions
that can assure us free space -- within our heads and around our bodies.

Most of us, without reading Ginny Foster's essay, understand in
a gut way the crisis facing us in the latter part of this century.
What many of us in literature seem to be groping toward is the manner
in which we can use our very specialized and often esoteric knowledge
and skills to combat the very crude problems of corruption and pollution. Ginny Foster is right when she says that what characterizes
women is our "inability to divorce humanity from [our] daily work or
study." Our reproductive systems and the portion of the world's work
traditionally allotted us have indeed kept us very close to the ground.
And because the majority of us have so little stake in existing intellectual institutions and systems, we are psychically free to
articulate and develop alternatives.

Ginny Foster describes simply and convincingly the task before
us. We must first break out of the dominant frame of reference in
the university, that of specialization and compartmentalization. Our
break is justified because the current dominant mode of behaving, of
knowing, has provided us with neither freedom nor sustenance. The
break will have been accomplished when a new gestalt is established,
when our collective field of vision is unified in a new way. Precisely because we are outsiders, we women are most likely to provide
this new gestalt. Ginny Foster goes a step beyond where many of us
have been when she asserts that human behavior is our necessary subject, and that we must come to understand that all existing disciplines
are but modes of knowing and ordering -- knowing and ordering being
themselves human behaviors. We must study ourselves, she asserts, if
we as a species are to survive.

It is her basic awareness that specialized data begets specialized
data to no end except the establishment of a dynasty, and often of
an academic empire, that leads her to say, "Every time education compartmentalizes off a subject from 'the social sciences' or the study

of human behavior the reification mystifies our experience of knowing."
We in the women's movement know too well that the emperor has no
clothes. What we in literature perhaps can learn from Ginny Foster is
to see literary composition and criticism first and foremost as a
mode of human behavior to be integrated with other modes of human
behavior.

WOMEN AS LIBERATORS

by Ginny Foster

    At this point in the history of education, women are for the
first time in a position to influence institutions of higher learning.
As certificate programs for women's studies are being set up, the
important decisions are not those of content, or of equal rank for
women instructors, or of legitimizing the right of women to study
their own culture, but whether women's studies will follow the patriarchal formula which has defined education in the past.

    Much of what Paulo Freire[1] has written about the adult literacy
process as a possibility of action for freedom seems to be applicable
to women's studies. Freire argues that learning should not be separated from action and that learning need not be induction into the
dominant culture. He points out that the process of learning to read
is usually inextricably entwined with learning the dominant myths of
the culture, not only because the texts refer to experiences far from
the thought-language of the illiterate, but because the material presented further imprisons the new reader in a "culture of silence"
about his own experiences.

> ...Interpreting illiterates as men marginal to
> society, the literacy process reinforces the
> mythification of reality by keeping it opaque
> and by dulling the "empty consciousness" of the
> learner with innumerable alienating words and
> phrases.
>
>   (p. 211)

Women are "marginal to society," imprisoned in a culture of silence,
and their education in universities has been indoctrination in the
myths of the patriarchy, but women's studies offers an opportunity
to re-define education as "cultural action for freedom" -- if we
establish priorities that do not reflect the dominant frame of reference.

    I want to argue that women in universities should become "femmes
de lettres" as opposed to "intellectuelles." Hannah Arendt suggests
the difference:

---

1 "The Adult Literacy Process as Cultural Action for Freedom," Harvard
   Ed. Review, May, 1970.

The distinction between the hommes de lettres and the
intellectuals by no means rests on an obvious difference
in quality; more important in our context is the fundamentally different attitudes these two groups have
shown, ever since the eighteenth century, toward society...
the intellectuals are and always have been part and parcel
of society, to which as a group they even owed their
existence and prominence; all pre-revolutionary governments in eighteenth-century Europe needed and used them
for the building up of a body of specialized knowledge
and procedures indispensable for the growing operation of
their governments on all levels...The men of letters, on
the contrary, resented nothing more than the secrecy of
public affairs; they had started their career by refusing
this sort of governmental service and by withdrawing
from society...They educated themselves and cultivated
their minds in a freely chosen seclusion, thus putting themselves at a calculated distance from the social as well as
the political, from which they were excluded in any case,
in order to look upon both in perspective.

On Revolution, p. 118

These hommes de lettres who "prepared the minds and formulated the
principles of the coming revolution" preserved their separate viewpoint, whereas the intellectuals reflected and furthered the purpose
of the dominant culture.[1] We need women in university study who are
"femmes de lettres" rather than "intellectuelles."

However, given that we are all products of male-dominated schools,
homes, and media -- and that many of the women's writing programs at
the university level are products of male-oriented higher education --
casting off the old values and modes of thinking requires considerable
effort, for our minds keep coming back to the same old categories
when we talk about what we want. Consider, for instance, these
intellectuelles quoted in the American Association of University Women
Journal:

We need to show high school girls they can go to the
universities on the same basis as men, that they have
a chance for an intellectual life within the university
or working life in private industry...Women throughout
society (should) have the same choice about their roles
that men have. That really has to be the focus -- equality.

AAUW Journal, Nov., 1970
(my italics)

---

1 One of the most blatant examples of intellectuals in the service
   of the established society is the book Workingman's Wife: Her Life,

This kind of writing on women's studies is what I re-phrase as "give us our share of the poisoned pie." That women should have an education "on the same basis as men" (which is to say divorced from human needs), that they should have "the same choice about their roles that men have" (which is, to be truthful, none) is equivalent to the man who says that if women were really equal, we should be soldiers -- "ain't it neat to be just like us?" The truth is that education of men and the choice of roles that men have is not the ideal we aspire to. In fact, the structure that teaches men (and some women) to love that poisoned pie is what women's studies **must break** from, if there is to be any hope for education in the university.

Femmes de lettres must begin to think of what women's studies could be, as opposed to the kind of thinking which asks how we can get women's studies into the existing educational system. If we must be illigitimate in terms of the university values, let us.[1] If we must face not having status within a hierarchy, let us deny the hierarchy. They may think us "little darlings playing," but that may be an advantage, for in that way we will not be a threat.[2] But let us be about our business of extricating ourselves from the dominant frame of reference, for reasons of necessity and for reasons of utility.

THE NECESSITY OF A NEW GESTALT

Breaking out of the old myths has both a necessary and a utilitarian function, not only for women but for all of us. A new Gestalt is a matter of necessity because the actions based on the old perceptions of reality are leading us to disaster.[3] What we have seen in the last few years is a growing awareness of the vast discrepancy between myth and reality. The values of power, conquest, and progress may have been suitable for a period in our history but they simply do not work any more. The precepts of the dominant frame of reference are failing us -- witness the falling away of the concept

---

Style, and Personality by Rainwater, Coleman, and Handel (all men, of course) -- "the first intimate marketing portrait of a woman who can make or break America's most widely advertised products," according to the jacket blurb.

1 In an article on Black Studies in the Phi Delta Kappan, Charles Hamilton says "the central question was one of legitimacy."

2 Freire points out the danger "When the popular masses get beyond the stage of fascination with their own emergence, and from demand to demand announce by their action that they are nearing a stage of sufficient organization to be able to break their submissive silence, the power elites violently attempt to arrest the process."

3 Some people think the present heralding of American (and world) doom

of "manifest destiny" as we realize that what we wanted to bring to
other nations is no longer viable even for us. A nation in the throes
of a moral crisis, desperately struggling to find a new way to organize experience no longer, thank God, has the self-confidence to put
its way of life on another people. Those who cling to the old ways
are going mad trying to deny reality, because of the contradictions
they must admit if they cling to the old beliefs.

Perhaps in order to emphasize the need for a new consciousness one
must delineate the breaking up of the old.[1] The following explanation
of the destruction of the myths is perhaps not the only one, but out-
lining the breakdown may perhaps illustrate the necessity of women's
studies proceeding from a new gestalt to find a way of structuring
reality that might liberate us all.

TV AS A MYSTICAL EXPERIENCE

One of the most significant facts about this generation is that
they have spent more of their time in front of the TV set than they
have in school. Some have been face-to-face with pictures of people
more than they have been face-to-face with another person. What is
curious is that although they have been inundated by a media whose
message is capitalism, which embodies every dominant myth of personal
and public life -- from the morning prayer to the "Star Spangled
Banner" at night -- they have not bought the myths. TV is a mystical,
mythical experience -- an effort to structure one's perception of what
is real in accord with the priorities of the dominant culture -- but
it has not worked. Instead, it has been the means by which the discrepancy between those myths and real life has become apparent.

Perhaps I can illustrate this by applying something I learned
very young. When I was little, I could never understand how people
could go to wrestling matches and watch those men being hurt and hurting
each other, while egging on the fighters. Why didn't anyone stop them
from trying to kill each other? The crowd could scream and yell and
drink beer and eat popcorn while they watched. But after I grew
older, I realized that it was all make-believe, that the wrestlers
had practiced holds which only looked as if they hurt, and that they
had a repertoire of agonized expressions. The explanation I came to
was that people watching knew all the time the violence wasn't real.

---

is paranoia, which may be true; but they forget that they have then
the phenomenon of wide-spread paranoia to deal with, which is in
itself a matter of reflection of change.

1 Charles Reich's The Greening of America being of course the most popular
   explanation. The delineation below grew out of a series of discussions with Peggy Plosser after she had read, and referred me to,
   a book by Vine DeLoria, titled We Talk, You Listen.

They couldn't have ever believed the fights were actually happening as I had thought they did, or they would rise in a mass and stop it.

In thinking about humor, I began to recognize that seeing Bud Abbott hit Lou Costello was funny because it wasn't real. If we thought for a minute that it was, we would not be laughing; that is why cartoons can be so brutal and we still laugh. The obvious drawings are so far from real people or animals that we are constantly re-assured that what we see could not possibly be a real person or a real bird being hit; instead we know it is an imaginary Woody Woodpecker.

So TV is also an attempt to structure our reality -- our sense of what is real and what isn't. For a long time we have wondered how people could sit in their living rooms spooning TV dinners into their mouths while watching the news. The only explanation for those who can witness The Atrocity Hour calmly is that they simply must not believe that what they see is true. But there are limits to the human ability to deny reality. No good German frau could have continued about her household tasks, no burgher could have done his work, with-out realizing what was going on -- if he had had to witness the Jews being gassed while he ate his dinner. Those who directly participated were often persuaded by propaganda that the Jews they dealt with were not real, i.e. they were "sub-human." Cp. the label "gook" by which Armed Forces propaganda de-humanizes the North Vietnamese.

Television -- which might have been the means by which we were all accommodated to the horrors of poverty and war by watching them in a structure which equates picture one (the killing of children) on an equal stature with picture two (of the young man picking acne on his face in a soap commercial) -- has instead shocked us so much that many people are denying the structure of reality which is the process of TV.[1]

The message of TV is that the real life -- consuming the products of capitalism -- should continue right on during whatever horrors we are witnessing on the screen. However, the mode of determining what is "real" which TV presents has not worked as a model for all people. In fact, it has backfired and become the mechanism by which we recognize the incredibility of the presentation. TV juxtaposes the starving children of Biafra or Pakistan next to an advertisement for underarm deodorant. We simply cannot assimilate that message. We cannot take seriously a presentation of reality which says that we can know about those starving children and still consider the choice of a deodorant as a meaningful issue in our lives.

---

1 My favorite TV critic, 10-year-old Ted Plosser, has a repertoire of parodies on TV commercial rhymes: "MacDonald's is your kind of place, they feed you rattlesnakes, hamburgers up your nose, French fries between your toes..." He has already discovered that reality can never validate the promise of the commercial.

It is the commercials that we are intended to take seriously.[1]
Sponsors buy the time to present a program only as a vehicle for
selling the myth of consumption. The commercials are what are supposed
to be real to us; it is the ads we are to internalize, to act upon --
and we are supposed to ignore the violence, the contradiction between the happy family and our own, the news of the war. We are to
suppose that the real things in life -- the buying -- can go on in
the face of what we see. The premise is that we will buy the popcorn
at the wrestling matches because we won't take seriously the violence
and destruction we see.

But a lot of people know that what is real on the TV is not the
commercials. It is to our credit that we could not accept this
Weltanschauung, this structuring of our second-hand experience that
TV was almost able to successfully convey. We bought the TV's --
millions of them -- but we did not buy the message of the medium,
even though our rejection of those myths was the equivalent of risking
cultural insanity.

One reason we rejected the planned learning of TV -- that we
learn to accept the myth of "business as usual" -- was that, as in
all learning situations, what the teacher thought we were learning
was not at all what the lesson was. In all learning, according
to the behaviorist model, the goal is to exclude all responses not
legislated by the teacher. But in schools, what people usually learn
is the incidental, unplanned-by-the-teacher learning (such as how
to cheat), which is the real lesson, unbeknownst to the teacher or
the curriculum guide. What we accidentally learned from TV was the
inconsistency and contradictions in our way of life: our declaration
of democratic principles in the face of their obvious violation
(that's what we learned from watching the civil rights struggle on
TV); our declaration of trust in government set next to the obvious
truth that our government lies to us (that's what we learned from
the televised tumult about the Ellsberg papers); our trust in technology and progress set against the facts of pollution, over-population
and the ruin of our environment (that's what we learned from seeing
programs on ecology set next to the ad "Somebody's doing something
about pollution -- Pontiac is")[2]. The young knew it first; they called
it "mind fuck."[3]

---

1 Abbie Hoffman in Revolution for the Hell of It says that the "figure"
   in the TV presentation of the Democratic convention became the
   "ground" against which viewers saw the real "figure" -- the kids
   in the streets.

2 "Jack the Ripper's doing something about murder."

3 Here is an example of "mind fuck" from the March, 1971 American Home
   magazine:

The other day a young man said to me "Life is a movie." I think that at the least what he meant was "I don't know what's real any more." A generation has rejected the official presentation of reality and is asking "Help me sort out what is real." The schools deny the question ("What is real is what we say is real") so the young have tried to find their own ways of sorting out reality.[1]

The idea of access to a "higher" reality runs through many accounts of drug experience, and marijauna smokers quite often discuss whether or not what they experience on dope is what is "really real" as opposed to what is normally called "real" life. Drugs have been one way of denying what one knows, and we are now heading into a great religious revival among young people, another method of denying the contradictions of real life. There are straight young people wearing buttons that say "Not religion, but a relationship with Jesus" as well as the "Jesus Freaks" who preach on the street. The message of the official Christian religion has always been "this life isn't real, but there is an afterlife that is." Both drugs and religion reflect a denial of the official presentation of reality, but are not much help in the search for a new way to categorize experience that might change reality.

Another denial from young people has been the farm-commune solution where an affinity group decides to create their own small world. These groups never have a TV, rarely read a newspaper, and their reading tends to be other-worldly -- mystic or occult. But while they

---

"Gabriel Industries manufactures a product called Exercise Boots. The 'boots' which can be worn by both men and women, are just like regular shoes except they're constructed of cast iron and weigh 5 pounds apiece. .The idea is to use them for leg lifts to strengthen the muscles in your feet, legs, and lower back. What's nice about Exercise Boots is that you can wear them while you're stretched out with a good book or watching TV." Think about that one for a while; the implications and assumptions work over your mind.

1 Mark Kleiman, a high school student, wrote in "High School Reform": "What I remember most about my school is that there is a 10-foot fence around it. In parts, there are three rows of barbed wire strung along the top. What concerns me most about the fence is not that it keeps me in -- but that it keeps the rest of the world out, admitting only those portions of 'reality' which the administration deems safe for us to view. Those responsible for our education have done their utmost to create an artificial community on the high school campus; a community which will demonstrate to us that it is better to "adjust" to an unsuitable society than to change the society into something in which we can live with dignity."

are pulling weeds in the garden, the reality goes right on, and it
is only a matter of time before the mechanized farming industry will
be out determining how many soy-beans can be raised on their fields.

More young people are in therapy or some form of counseling than
ever before (as are adults, of course). When I went to high school
we had one girls' advisor, whom we avoided. Now every school has a
large contingent of counselors in whom students are urged to confide
their problems. Moreover, every teacher is expected to be somewhat
of a counselor; I recently heard an instructor tell teacher trainees
"I just can't separate teaching from counseling," urging the prospective teachers to think of themselves as counselors. The message
of counseling is most often "adjustment"; the problem is in the kid,
not in the structure. Thus we see a frantic effort to adjust young
people to the contradictions of official reality.

Adults who have gotten the message sometimes go to sensitivity
groups -- the main premise of which is "feelings are the only things
that are real." This reliance on internal sensation has a logical
precedent; it happens to be exactly what some traditional philosophers
came to when they began to question "reality." The problem is that
people have to leave their groups and go back into the real world
where they are again faced with an even greater contradiction -- the
contrast between the warm supportive group and their daily lives.
I once heard a woman in a university program say "I'm so sorry not
to be there for the inter-personal relations, but they're having them
in August and I won't be there." She had institutionalized her inter-
personal relations.

And of course there are those adults and young people who go mad.

But all these forms of denial of reality cannot produce a new
center which could hold. The old myths and symbols, the old values
do not work. The solution cannot be found in personal salvation or
through denial of what is, but rather in exploring a new frame of
reference, a new image of what we could be. And we cannot ask the
right questions or even perceive the problems to be solved unless
we bring a new gestalt to our work. Thus it would seem that the present crisis can be solved only by using the resources of those
groups outside the dominant culture. We will not find new values
through using the old -- **power**, conquest, technology, research. We
may find direction through listening to those who have been excluded
from the white male supremacy. Thus our greatest resources for a
new Weltenschauung are members of the minority-groups and women as
a cultural group. But if these groups are absorbed into the patriarchal system of education at the cost of giving up their cultural
identity, their value as change-agents will be lost. For this
reason women say "Not equality, but liberation."

The integration of women into the present university system would be fatal to their ability and potential to create radical changes in our society. If our best thinkers were to spend their time doing the kind of banal research now being done, if our philosophers were to do linguistic analysis on the semantic difference between "chicks" and "girls"[1], if our psychologists were to spend their time measuring "female" traits determined by a male-oriented discipline, if our literature professors were to spend hours analyzing the sentence structure of women authors, if our historians were to spend years detailing our slavery and proving that Mrs. Eli Whitney invented the cotton gin, we will have been sucked into the same mode of study which has already proved itself inadequate to human needs. We don't need studies of our oppression ("ain't it awful?"); we need studies toward a future of freedom, not just for women qua women, but for women qua human beings, which might, in the end, contribute toward saving all of us.

Thus the necessity of recognition of non-dominant gestalts, the crucial need for constant examination of the dominant frame of reference and a continual search for ways to break out of that mode. But there are also utilitarian reasons for women rejecting the "normal" university pattern.

THE UTILITY OF A NEW GESTALT

Perhaps I can best illustrate the utility to be gained by women breaking out of the dominant frame of reference by taking research in social science as an example.

In The Nature of Scientific Revolutions, Thomas Kuhn presents an explanation of scientific discovery which is quite different from the accepted "cumulative theory." Most theories of scientific discovery have rested on the idea that new hypotheses grow out of the accretion of minute detail, which leads to an ultimate and inevitable discovery. Kuhn acknowledges this as the way "normal" science advances -- by the accumulation of bits of atomistic knowledge which are put together within an accepted model or pattern. These "accepted models or patterns" he calls "paradigms." Paradigms are "accepted examples of actual scientific practice -- examples which include law, theory, application, and instrumentation together -- which provide models from which spring particular coherent traditions of scientific research." The established paradigms represent the dominant frame of reference for the particular science and govern the questions asked and the means by which they are answered. For example, the accepted paradigm for astronomy, until Copernicus, was the Ptolemic universe, which was the governing model for all studies in

---

1 An acquaintance of mine (male) once wrote his dissertation on the difference between "hills," "piles," and "mounds."

astronomy, severely limiting what questions could be asked about the universe.

The studies done under an established model Kuhn calls "normal science." But he advances another theory for what he calls "extraordinary" science, by which he means the discovery of revolutionary new paradigms which will, in time -- if proven more useful than the old -- be accepted by the scientific community, which then goes about working out the "puzzles" of normative science.

Kuhn sees discovery coming about when some scientists are not content to solve only the puzzles presented by the accepted paradigm but go on to question the very paradigm itself. Usually this questioning of the restrictions arises from growing awareness of what Kuhn calls "anomaly" -- out of the recognition that "nature has somehow violated the paradigm, defied the expectations that govern normal science." (p. 52). The failure of the paradigm to explain the anomaly gives rise to a "crisis" which will exist until a new paradigm is found and accepted because it accounts for anomalies which are considered acute.

In regard to the social sciences, Kuhn suggests that "it remains an open question what parts of social science have yet acquired such paradigms at all." This suggests that perhaps the paradigms which might prove useful in answering basic questions about human behavior have yet to be discovered; thus the delay in the development of the social sciences. The lack of a coherent framework for study is no surprise to any women interested in psychology or sociology; for what she finds is that the material presented is based on a male definition of human behavior. To take a popular example, Ardrey's and Lorenz' work on "aggression" is taken as an explanation for human behavior when in actuality, it deals with male behavior. Female psychology, as outlined by males, has always taken the view that the female is the mirror image of the male. Even female theorists have reflected the male point of view, the most obvious and pitiful example being Helene Deutsch's explication of women from Freud's frame of reference. Since the work that has been done in the name of human sciences has been about and for and by males, it accounts for only 49 per cent of the population studied. Thus whatever paradigms we might have, severely restrict the phenomenological field under study, limit the questions to be asked, and govern the modes of procedure. In the study of the social sciences, the matter of sex[1] highly influences the scientist-observer in a way that does not so obviously affect the physicist (but may the biologist). Most importantly, useful paradigms cannot be derived from studies done under these

---

1 And cultural identity. Thus the need for recognition of other minority group's unique frame of reference.

restrictions.

Another reason the study of human behavior needs the work of women rests on Kuhn's noting that discoveries of paradigms are usually made by those people who are somewhat removed from normative science:

> Almost always the men who achieve these fundamental
> inventions of a new paradigm have been either
> very young or very new to the field whose para-
> digm they change. (p. 89; see also p. 148 and 165).

Perhaps the "very young or very new to the field" are the dis- coverers of paradigms because they have not been thoroughly grounded in the dominant frame of reference suggested by the established para- digm holding sway in textbooks, lectures, and research. Kuhn does not explore this possibility, but I would suggest that women will be foremost among those who discover the universal paradigms for "normal" social science exactly for the same reason that other dis- coverers were "new to the field" -- because their point of view about human behavior, not being the dominant mode, will lead them to notice anomalies and ask new questions. It is women who will do "extraordinary" science in the social sciences precisely because they come to the subject with a distinctly different gestalt from those now prominent in the study. And it is women who will be able to take these "extraordinary" discoveries as paradigms and continue "nor- mative" science based on them. They will have the point of view re- quired to accept .the new paradigms:

> Therefore, at times of revolution, when the
> normal scientific tradition changes, the
> scientist's perception of his environment
> must be re-educated -- in some familiar sit-
> uations he must learn to see a new gestalt.
> (Kuhn)

We need paradigms in social science (or if we do have some, we need new ones) before we can close the gap in our knowledge and proceed to solve "puzzles"; the new paradigms can be provided only by women who are not products of a masculine-oriented gestalt and study.

Women will ask questions about their subject matter and find procedures never occuring to men. Women might even follow Abraham Maslow's example (in The Psychology of Science)[1] and even question the

---

[1] Incidentally, although Maslow can question the dominant frame of reference, he reveals his own chauvinism in a paragraph regarding the layman's dislike of science: "The girls will often shudder at the thought of marrying a scientist" -- the unconscious assumption is that all scientists are male.

suitability of the meta-paradigm of science as a whole. They might question whether the accepted scientific mode is the appropriate codification of general procedures for study of human behavior. C. Wright Mills has spoken of the predominance of one point of view (usually unwritten but assumed) within all studies: "In every intellectual age, some one style of reflection tends to become a common denominator of cultural life." (The Sociological Imagination, p. 13).

Surely the common denominator of our age has been science; we see the social scientists struggling with their facts and observations and measurements in order to prove that they too are members of the country club. But having membership in that club limits the area of study, particularly in regulating what questions can be asked. As it is now we can only legitimately ask questions in social sciences which can be answered through measurements since that is one of the tenets of science. But women, like the blacks in the country club kitchen, may have a totally different view of what's going on and in asking "unanswerable" questions outside the scientific boundaries, arrive at the paradigms which have yet to be discovered.

In questioning the meta-paradigm of science, women might consider alternative paradigms. For example, the concept of advance and progress in science (which either reflects or has influenced the male point of view in general) might be questioned. We might consider new models for exploration of human behavior; one possibility is that of the arts, where there is no "advance" or "progress" but rather a sense of change without judgment -- Jackson Pollock not being inherently better than Rembrandt just because his style is newer. So we might consider the discoveries we make in human behavior not as the advance of scientific knowledge but rather as one way of looking at human behavior peculiarly appropriate to the time in which it was used, or true to human behavior at the time, for humans have the unique ability to change their behavior (unlike rocks).

In any case, the utility of women's studies to the study of social science lies in the unique point of view women might bring to their work. Thus the criterion for any research done in the name of women's studies might be that the project proceed from what might be called (for want of a less awkward term) the anti-phallocentric point of view. By this I mean that women's studies are most likely to produce significant discoveries when they reflect a questioning of the dominant male frame of reference, not only in studying women but in any work.

THE STUDY OF HUMAN BEHAVIOR

I took the example of the social sciences to illustrate the utility for a new Gestalt as if I could have chosen another subject. That was misleading, for there is only one subject anyone ever studies --

that of human behavior and consciousness, commonly mis-called the "social sciences" and mis-identified as a separate subject within general knowledge.

The university, with its categorization of experience, has mys-tified us all as to what can be known. The only subject we can know is humanity, even though paradoxically that is what we think we know the least about. When we speak of any discipline, we are speaking of human knowledge about human behavior -- when we speak of philosophy, we are talking about what humans have thought; and when we speak of art, we are talking about what humans have created out of imagination; and when we speak of science we are speaking not of the physical universe sans humans, but of the operations man has performed upon the physical world through his consciousness, including the formulating of physical laws which we appear to discover ("dis-cover") as if they had been there all along before humans constituted them through consciousness.[1]

For example, take the science of astronomy, seemingly the furthest removed from the human factor. We cannot know anything about the stars that does not have something to do with a human being, for it is always the human who knows, who makes a hypothesis, who per-forms an experiment, who observes, who writes down the research; the subject is not the star but what humans have done in order to "know" stars and what humans have done or can do with the knowledge of stars. The science of astronomy is actually the history of a certain kind of human behavior; a particular piece of research is a highly per-sonal account of one man's behavior, even though he never writes "I did this," "I saw this," but instead writes sentences which have no agents for the verbs ("it was observed") in an effort to eliminate the human element (that being the hallmark of science).

I do not simply mean that every science must take into account the possibility of error or influence because of the "human factor." I mean literally that nothing "can be known" without someone knowing.[2] Thus anything that is known is part of the study of human behavior -- all that we know about geology is the history of how humans have behaved when they wanted to know about rocks, for instance.

---

1 Husserl (Ideas, p. 85) says "Or should we say, as from another quarter has in fact been said, that we owed the insights of geometry to the 'experiences of our fancy,' drawing them as inductions from experiments on the functioning of fancy?"

2 Husserl's "constituting consciousness" (in Ideas).

Universities have forgotten that knowing is human behavior.
Particularly in science, they have reified the individual subject
matter to having a life of its own sans humanity (even in the "humanities" we see this). The subject of physics may have laws of its
own untouched by humans but these cannot be known to us, for by the
process of becoming known they become part of the arena of human
behavior: "this is how humans have interacted with the physical world
so far." And we can never know what laws of physics could exit
without human knowing, for "physical laws" or any knowledge is what
only the human consciousness can constitute.

Thus the definition of science (or any study) as divorced from
human behavior is impossible -- what is not yet a part of the human
behavior called discovery, what has not been touched by human consciousness, we cannot yet know; and what we do know is part of the
record of human behavior. Every time education compartmentalizes
off a subject from the "social sciences" or the study of human
behavior the reification mystifies our experience of knowing. This
practice also prevents us from making advances in the study of
human behavior because it leads us to think that the social sciences
are a subject apart from others, but instead it is all disciplines.
And of course we can never gather it all together and come up with
paradigms because each discipline clings to its material on human
behavior (which may be called history, or biology, or physics, or
whatever) as a separate domain, to the extent that scholars of
different fields literally cannot speak to each other to share
knowledge. That the specialized vocabularies are a gulf between
cultures is well-known; what hasn't been recognized is that it is
not the sciences whose language should be the lingua franca. For
it is not science to which everything can be reduced -- although
the psychologists and sociologists and historians are mistakenly
trying -- but rather it is to human consciousness that all knowledge
can be related.[1]

---

1 Although Husserl would give science the right to be "dogmatic"
   (i.e., the right not to question its ontological and epistemo-
   logical assumptions) and although he used the method of bracketing
   questions of experience to arrive at the process of "eidetic
   reduction," he does end Ideas with this statement: "A comprehensive solution of the problems of phenomenological shaping which
   shall take equally into consideration the noetic and noematic
   strata of consciousness would be manifestly equivalent to a complete phenomenology of the reason in respect to all its formal and
   material formations, whether non-normal (negatively rational) or
   normal (positively rational). But we are further compelled to admit
   that a phenomenology of the reason so complete as this would coin-
   cide with phenomenology in general, and that in systematically carrying

So, appropriately, there can be no other subject for women's studies than human behavior. Psychology of women is not the scientific study of women (even if done by women); it is part of the history of the growing consciousness of human behavior, of how some human psychologists have looked at a part of human behavior. Thus it is a mistake to automatically adopt the categories of specialization (such as psychology or history) now organizing the university in a mode congruent with the dominant frame of reference -- which is specialization. Our program will better call itself Women's Studies when it describes what has always characterized women -- the inability to divorce humanity from one's daily work or study. We might want to pay particular attention to, for instance, the absence of women in accounts of history (as a peculiarity of the human consciousness up to now) but we must not make the mistake of further specialization, as if women's approach to history might be adding more atomistic bits of knowledge about one specialized area ("The History of Women") to a larger compartmentalized field ("History"). Instead, our truly radical approach, reflecting our unique Gestalt as women, must be to see that every subject we touch comes back to what we know is the only subject anyone can ever study -- human behavior.

Probably the most easily seen and most disastrous example of the violation of that principle of unity was the atom bomb. Scientists made discoveries seemingly divorced from humanity, and lived to see the consequences; Neils Bohr and Einstein realized too late and wrote President Roosevelt an appeal, and other scientists signed the Franck Report of 1945, but to no avail. Materializing now are the fruits of study designed to eliminate the human factor. We have computers and television and planes and napalm and drugs; we know all about how to make these things -- but nothing about their human use and mis-use.

Thus women's studies, in rejecting the now dominant frame of reference of the university -- that of specialization -- might embody the following principles:

1. Women's studies are about human behavior, as are all studies.

2. Human behavior includes all subjects of study -- including the sciences and studies of male behavior, as well as female.

3. All studies are united by a common factor -- the humanity of "knowing" -- and this connection of study and humanity

---

out all the disciplines of consciousness which are demanded under the collective title "constitution of the object" all sundry descriptions of consciousness would need to be included." Thus I see the university as "all sundry descriptions of consciousness."

should be emphasized in women's studies, particularly
in the study of material presented in courses <u>outside</u>
women's studies.

4. To study, experiment, record observations, write a text,
    or lecture on any subject without including its relation
    to human behavior is to be negligent in scholarship.

5. Inter-disciplinary studies and communication among scholars
    is not a convenience or a nicety but a fact of the way
    our knowing is constructed.

If women were to put these principles into action, I am convinced that
their rapid expansion of knowledge about human behavior would be
argument enough (even in the university's own terms) to justify
breaking out of the dominant mode of specialization.

THE ETHICS OF UNIVERSITY PRIORITIES

Thus breaking out of the dominant frame of reference means first
of all not being taken in by the assumptions of the university --
such as the division and specialization of areas. A further consequence of a new consciousness is to question the values of the
University.

The university now has the following priorities: to keep alive
the culture of the past; to further the progress of knowledge through
research, especially in science and technology; and to provide a
credentialing system based on the needs of employers. A recent
priority of universities has been to serve as the intellectual organ
of an apparently mindless government. A further aim of the university, as Ivan Illich points out, is to inculcate the belief that
learning can take place only in institutions and that teachers are
those who have been awarded a place in those institutions.[1]

What the university has forgotten is that priorities reflect
values, and that values are an ethical matter. The current ethic of
the university -- in placing value on needs which are irrelevant at
this time in history -- is immoral.

_____

1 Illich, <u>Deschooling Society</u>. As more and more women and non-white
  males get degrees, the people setting the rules of the game up the
  ante from B.A. to Ph.D. One consequence of going to school and
  getting a B.A. is that you then know you need a Ph.D. That's what
  the institution teaches you.

C.S. Lewis, in The Abolition of Man, speaks of "the power of earlier generations over later ones" and introduces the future as a moral issue:

> Those who write on social matters have not yet learned
> to imitate the physicists by always including Time
> among the dimensions. In order to understand fully
> what Man's power over Nature, and therefore the
> power of some men over other men, really means we
> must picture the race extended in time from the date
> of its emergence to that of its extinction.

For the first time in the history of Ethics we are now seeing the necessity of adding a dimension of time to our consideration.[1] For we realize now that our actions must not be judged in the light of only present good or evil but rather the consequences of our acts projected into the future must be considered. Thus the current ecological concern is a moral, an ethical, matter. What we do now will influence the lives of our descendants -- may determine whether they are allowed to exist or not. The only people who do not have a moral obligation to the future are those who are on the brink of extinction, which condition is the only one which absolves them from consideration of the generations to come. The university ignores this moral imperative.

We have behaved as if we were the last of our species; as if we did not have to consider the Future. We have endowed with value concepts which may have been workable for the present while ignoring the later ramifications (such as the results of our "conquest of Nature"). Thus the university's frame of reference has been the past; the "humanities" has faced the wrong direction. We need a new future-oriented "humanities" which recognizes that priorities of study carry a moral obligation towards not just those people who are living now, but those who might live. In the face of the knowledge that our planet might be destroyed, it is amazing that the universities go their way, teaching the same subjects that have been useful in the past. We study the Theban plays or the history of art or the hind leg of a beetle, when in fact, the beetle we're studying may not exist in twenty-five years -- or for that matter, any of us. Women, if they were to study "famous women authors" or the suffragette movement, would be following the old ethic of higher education. In philosophy, for instance, there can be no other subject to any reasoning human except philosophical consideration of survival and freedom. She who writes on any other subject has not grasped the nature of our peril.

---

1 Science fiction and utopian and anti-utopian novels recognized this first.

This going on "as if" is not limited to the university, of course. The high schools are cheating children of their future every time they place emphasis on non-survival learning.[1] Every teacher should walk into class every day as if on what she did there depended the survival of the human race. For indeed it does. Our publications reflect this same denial of reality. How can "The New York Review of Books" go on publishing esoteric literary studies if it truly believes the implications of what it occasionally prints -- that we are, if not on the brink of destroying our planet, then still even closer to losing our human qualities, of becoming The Cheerful Robot of whom Fromm and C. Wright Mills speak.

Thus the establishment of priorities is not a practical but an ethical matter, and women's studies can be the first to recognize the obligation to include the time dimension in the decision of priorities.

PRIORITIES FOR WOMEN'S STUDIES

Our first task, as always, is to question the priorities of the dominant culture. We might begin by deciding what is absolutely essential, for "priorities" implies a rank order. We must "bracket" their assumptions and begin all over again.[2]

I think first of survival of the species. But just as I wrote that I thought, but there is a choice prior to that. The question is, of course, whether one desires the species to remain without freedom. I am able to conceive that possibility. I think of some descendant of mine walking around like a happy, cheerful robot, unthinking, unquestioning, and I know that I have no moral obligation to the dehumanized human being that might survive. I take the risk of killing him at no second thought. For survival without freedom[3] summons forth

---

1 By this I do not mean classes on "How to Live in the Woods on Nothing."

2 The following priorities are very personal; I list them and outline the process of determination only to suggest a method. Groups of women might arrive at other priorities; what is essential is to avoid any preconceived ideas of what is worth learning.

3 Not just social, but psychological freedom -- so that our desires and motivations are not manipulated against our own interests. See Christian Bay's The Structure of Freedom for a definition of freedom including these concerns.

no moral claim from the future. That leaves me with the priority of freedom, which must then be my prime aim. Survival now I feel sure about for my second value, and the third priority I would put the provision of satisfying basic physical and psychological needs.

These then might be the priorities of women's studies: freedom, survival, and satisfaction of basic needs. These are quite different from the dominant priorities -- perhaps because they include the moral dimension of time. There are those who would cry out about the loss of our past culture. What would happen, they say, if no one kept alive the humanities of the past. Well, they must face the reality that humanities will die when humans die or when they lose their freedom. Perhaps we must go through another Dark Ages when our culture, as defined by great works, must be the province of a select few, like monks. However, it is not likely that any study of freedom would ignore the struggle -- from Prometheus to Invisible Man -- contained in the past records of man. As for those people who rest the case of modern "civilization" on science (an oftimes incriminating record) they need not fear the loss of constructive knowledge for any study of survival would surely draw from science as we know it. And we would not lose, under these priorities, any of the arts which had at their center the definition of freedom of the human spirit.

Once free from the dominant priorities and having set new ones, women might define their own areas of specialization -- perhaps beginning with freedom, survival, and basic needs -- but these would be of necessity inter-disciplinary, united by the concept that all knowing is a matter of the study of the human constituting consciousness. Again, in the study of these subjects, such as freedom, the gestalt of women might prove useful to new discovery.[1]

WOMEN AND PSYCHOLOGICAL FREEDOM

If the writers of the Bill of Rights could have foreseen the technological changes in our world, surely they would not have left out the right to be free from institutional manipulation of motivation against the individual's own interest. Their concern was for social freedom -- which Christian Bay defines as "the relative absence of perceived external restraints on individual behavior." But the greatest danger to freedom is, as women well know, the manipulation of one's mind -- of one's desires, one's motives -- through the control of information. (Probably the best description of the new forms of control is in Herbert Marcuse's One Dimensional Man.) Heretofore, women have assumed the role assigned to them by the

---

1 As all oppressed minority groups are the most likely source of contributions. Thomas Merton, in The Seeds of Destruction, says "I can come up with no better choice than to listen to the Negro, and to what he has to say. I, for one, am absolutely ready to believe that we need him to be free, for our own sake even more than for his own."

dominant male culture, not through external coercion, but rather through unconscious internalization of their role. Any woman who has been bombarded by TV commercials urging her to want to be a sex object, to be young, to desire a wig and false eyelashes, knows the kind of manipulation I am speaking of. We are made to want the tool of our own oppression; we're taught to love the chains that bind us.

Women, because of their experience as the prime victims of unperceived external restraints, are in a position to study and counteract the forces of manipulation that now threaten to control the motivation of all human beings. The least perceived oppression is that of white males by their own institutions. This touches on an important point in women's studies. It is essential that we see ourselves as liberators, not as victims. By our studies and our action, we must free not only ourselves, but human society, including males. Men have won social freedom -- the right to work, to vote, to have education. But it is psychological freedom which is the concern of women.

Men (and women) are now victims of their own institutions. I do not ascribe to a "devil theory" -- I do not think that there is a controlling body of evil men who determine institutional goals and practices. Ratner, men have created institutions which have a life of their own, in which the main purpose is not the stated overt goal -- whether to educate or feed the poor -- but rather to perpetuate the institution itself.

That women recognize the danger of the one, one-dimension institution which dominates our civilization is evident in the many women's groups now appearing. It is not surprising that women are dealing with their "problems" in groups, for groups -- encounter, therapeutic, T-groups -- are endemic to our society. What is new to the form is the structural basis of the women's rap groups, they look not for problems within the person, but rather at the social context of women.

In The Sociological Imagination, C. Wright Mills makes a distinction between what he terms "troubles" and "issues":

> Troubles occur within the character of the individual
> and within the range of his immediate relations with
> others; they have to do with his self and with those
> limited areas of social life of which he is directly
> and personally aware. Accordingly, the statement and
> the resolution of troubles properly lie within the
> individual as a biographical entity and within the
> scope of his immediate milieu -- the social setting
> that is directly open to his personal experience and
> to some extent his willful activity. A trouble is a
> private matter.... Issues have to do with matters that
> transcend these local environments of the individual
> and the range of his inner life. They have to do with
> the organization of many such milieux into the insti-
> tutions of an historical life. An issue is a public

matter....it is the very nature of an issue, unlike
even widespread trouble, that it cannot very well
be defined in terms of the immediate and every day
environments of ordinary men. An issue, in fact,
often involves a crisis in institutional arrangements....

Women's groups are not concerned with the "troubles" of their members, rather they are centered around issues: the institutional
effects of manipulation on women, which has resulted in the private
"troubles," many of which result from resistance to the manipulation.
Thus women's groups are taking a structural approach, one reason why
women's groups so often lead to action-oriented discussion.

Men who perceive the restraints upon their psychological freedom
might come to model groups after women's liberation groups. Women's
struggle to free their minds, to make perceivable the hitherto unperceived restraints on their freedom might prove a model for men.

SURVIVAL

I have discussed survival in the earlier portions of this paper.
Women do not make wars, they do not direct the operations of large
corporations raping the environment. They are essentially organic,
being reminded each month and by each child of their part in a
larger biological process.

SATISFACTION OF BASIC NEEDS

Women also have an orientation toward the satisfaction of basic
needs which is contrary to the dominant mode, and thus could contribute to the study of the fulfillment of basic needs. The old way
was based on a reality of "scarcity"; our technical knowledge in
raising food combined with control of population could provide us
a new reality based on abundance. The scarcity mode has resulted in
the kind of greed that we see in Americans who have their researchers
working out a way to "eat nothing" -- developing a new non-caloric
food -- at the same time that a mother in another country watches her
child die for lack of milk.

I asked a woman I know, who is extremely good at finding ways
of satisfying her family's needs on a limited income, to think about
that concept in relation to women's studies. She replied "What is
there to think about? You figure out what people need and then a
way to get it to them, just as buying food the best way." This is
what every women knows -- she does not ask if her child has earned
his dinner; she feeds those who are hungry in the most efficient
manner possible. There is no political debate possible over who
should have the right to satisfaction of basic needs; one simply does
what has to be done for every one as part of their human rights. If
women could apply their personal principles to study of human problems,

I am convinced that one of their aims in higher education would be
to find ways of providing food, sex, shelter, clothes, health and
education for all. It is to be hoped women would not take the elitist
position that some people have the right (through inheritance, a
major concern of males) to nineteen years of education (through the
Ph.D.) while others do not know how to read and write. I can conceive
of women forsaking erudite studies for the duty of raising the
world literacy level.

And women have long been concerned with the satisfaction of basic
psychological needs; in fact, they have often sacrificed the fulfillment of their own desires in order that their husbands and children
be satisfied (the high cost of this lack of fulfillment is becoming
evident.) The movie "Carnal Knowledge" was viewed by several women
as extremely radical because it let out one of the oldest secrets
of women -- the knowledge that the strength of the male ego often depends on the subordination of the female. A popular book for teenage girls, On Becoming a Women, gives this advice on "How to get--
and Keep--Boys Interested":

> Boys are like anybody else. If you make them feel
> clever, talented, important, they like you for it,
> because it makes them like themselves. This is a
> lesson you can really learn, let's hope, from your
> mother. Watch the way she handles your father. He
> can come home hot, tired and disgruntled, but some-
> how your mother can turn him back into a big, power-
> ful man, king of all he surveys, just by a few warm
> words, a smile, a good meal. She makes home a place
> where your father likes to be.

Although there is a concern for the satisfaction of basic physical
and psychological needs reflected in this passage, there is also a
kind of condescension in the woman's flattering a man as to his
superiority, a catering to what is seen as an ego not strong enough
to stand on its own self esteem. This kind of advice is really saying
"You as a woman, are strong enough to let him think he is superior;
you do not need the ego gratification that he must have by dominating
another." But although this attitude reveals a real concern for
the other person's ego, we can no longer afford the luxury of condescension. Instead, we must transfer this ability to be concerned
with basic physical and ego needs to a search for ways in which this
can be satisfied in reality,[1] in real self-esteem for people of both
sexes, rather than the illusion of superiority for one sex and a
secret smugness on the part of the other.

---

1 Art Pearl suggests "competency, belonging, and usefulness" as
basic needs.

Any number of lists[1] of human needs have been made; but surely we would begin with food, sex, shelter, clothes, health care, and education.[2] We must no longer operate under the zero-sum concept of the dominant culture based on "scarcity;" we are well able to fulfill the physical needs. And most women do not regard the satisfaction of psychological needs as based on zero-sum. What woman ever hestated to have another child because she thought that her love was a limited sum, that loving would deplete her resources?

The other day I was in the Greyhound Bus Depot restroom, standing before a cubicle with a lock which would open only if I inserted a dime, and I felt a rising rage at having to pay to satisfy a basic need. After I entered I saw on the wall the writing "Liberate pay toilets" and I felt a sisterhood with the unknown person who had scrawled those words. I knew two things about that person: that she was a woman and that she had not internalized the dominant myth that people have to earn the right to satisfaction of their basic needs. The world "liberate" identified her as having a commitment to action.

EDUCATION AND PRAXIA

The history of women is the history of action for provision of basic needs. The oldest profession of women is concerned with sexual satisfaction for men -- prostitution. For women to spend their time studying poverty or counting the number of mal-nourished children in Pakistan, and not to take action for fulfillment of these needs (unlike the present conception of reality and needs which sends arms to Pakistan instead of food) would be to imitate the study of men, who divorce their work from their humanity.

Earlier we advanced two principles for women's studies taken from Freire; that learning need not lead to induction into the dominant conciousness, and that learning should lead to action. The problem with being "femmes de lettres" is to maintain our "calculated distance" and still act to effect change. In the study of the satisfaction of basic needs is most clearly to be seen the need for Freire's conection of learning with praxia -- "reflection and then action to change reality."[3]

A. Maslow's "hierarchy of needs" for example.

Women have long carried out these basic functions, despite the lack of recognition and status for their work.

Sartre, in Search for a Method, defines praxia as "organizing project going beyond material conditions towards an objective, and imprinting itself through labor in inorganic matter as a reworking of the practical field and reunification of the means with a view to attaining the end." To Sartre praxis originates in need.

A number of theorists have recognized the link between learning and action, notably James, Whitehead, Dewey, and Counts. A section of Jerome Bruner's On Knowing is titled "The Idea of Action." Even the behaviorists recognize that the demonstration of learning is exhibited in behavior (thus the wide use of demonstrable "behavioral objectives" in education at the present time). A child is said to know how to read when he acts (behaves) in a certain way.

But although the link between learning and action is known, it is almost taken as a given. Adelbert Ames, in his book The Morning Notes of Adelbert Ames, has not taken this connection for granted, but rather explored the process of the relationship. He accounts for the necessity of praxia by taking into consideration the effects of actions on one's perceptions and consciousness. He posits a circular process in which experience structures a Gestalt, Gestalt influences perception, perception influences action, and again new action alters the Gestalt. (This is in contrast to the behaviorist who ignores consciousness as part of the learning process.)

Ames breaks into the synthesis of gestalt, perception, and action by beginning with sensation:

> Although the human organism in its behavior acts
> as a result of stimuli, these stimuli in themselves
> have no meaning. The significances that are related
> to them in consciousness -- and are experienced by
> the organism as sensations -- are derived entirely
> from the organism's prior experience, personal and
> inherited.
>
> (p. 16, his italics)

This prior experience provides significance (meaning) to perception by means of forming a "presumptive world," based on the statistical average of past experience:

> Such presumed specific significances are not of a
> specific significance we experienced in the past,
> but the statistical average of similar specific
> significances we have experienced in the past. That
> is, we bring to the occasion a presumptive world of
> classified significances.....This "presumptive world,"
> far from being based on wishful thinking, exists be-
> cause it provides us with the most reliable prognosis
> for action in carrying out our purposes.
>
> (p. 43)

In Existentialism and Humanism, Sartre states "The doctrine I am presenting you is precisely the opposite of (quietism); since it declares that there is no reality except in action...Man is nothing else but the sum of his actions."

e learn the significance of fire being hot because every time we
ouch it we get burned, and this significance has a predictive
prognostic) value. We arrive at significances based on prior ex-
eriences through the presumptions proving themselves statistically
orrect by way of their "prognostic ability":

> Consider what is meant by the term "prognosis" as
> applied to sensations. A prognosis has to do with
> future events that have not yet occurred. It,
> therefore, cannot be those events themselves. At
> best it can only be something in our minds, a
> sense or concept. That is, the organism is con-
> tinually comparing the prognosis of the contin-
> ually changing new external events with his deter-
> mined form of significances.
>   If they conform, i.e., "work," he is no longer
> interested; but in so far as they do not, he has
> to take stock of the situation.
>
> (p. 7)

f the presumed significance works over a period of time, it becomes
 habit or reflex, or part of our "presumptive world." (We don't
ut our hand in the fire because of the significance learned.)
ignificance and action are related in that the way we test our
resumptions is to act upon them. When we are small, we drink water,
esting the presumption that the significance of water rests on the
ction "you drink it and it slakes your thirst." When the statis-
ical average of experiences concerning water proves the meaning of
he assumption is correct, it then becomes part of our presumptive
orld -- which in turn affects our perception. I see the glass
nd pitcher -- they will be figured in my perceived ground when I
m thirsty -- because my Gestalt, my presumptive world of signi-
icance, has given water that meaning. And in turn what actions I
ake with water to add to my experience will further refine and
e-define the significance of water to me. After I swim in a lake,
 will perceive the lake water not only as "something to drink, but
lso something to swim in." Thus our actions constantly define what
s significant; the significance defines our presumptive world or
estalt; and our Gestalt, in turn, determines what actions will
uggest themselves ("purposeful values") to us based on prior experience.

This union of presumptive world, perception, and action is
hat Ames (after Whitehead) calls a "transaction of living." Without
his union, no transactions could be made, for there would merely
e "functional activity" -- what James labeled as a baby's view of
he universe, a "blooming', buzzin' confusion." Ames outlines the
inimum processes for a "transaction of living" in the following
teps:

1. An organism -- functional activity in

2. an environment consisting of other functional
   activities.
3. The organism's awareness of the significance to it
   of its environment in
4. terms of its valueful purposes.
5. Action by organism in furthering its valueful purposes.
6. The effects of the results of such actions on itself
   and its environment as disclosed by
7. the effectivity of later purposeful action of the
   organism.

(p. 71)

Ames points out that no two people bring the same presumptive world
to the perception of functional activity ("no two persons have the
same perception of a specific object, as a chair or another person").[1]
However, he suggests that some groups share much of the same presumptive world:

> For instance, in our world of visual perception,
> where there has been great similarity in the past
> experiences as well as of identity of purpose
> of all men, the extent, so to speak, of the "common
> world" would presumably be much more inclusive than
> in social perception where the similarity of past
> experience as well as of identity of purpose is
> often limited to small groups.
>
> (p. 46)

Women, who have "similarity of past experience," thus share a common
presumptive world unless they have been co-opted by the dominant
group. This common world of women is what I have been speaking of
in references to the "gestalt" of women. Whether it be by conditioning or through genetic influence, most women bring a Gestalt to
their perception of reality which is far different from men. The
difference lies in the significance they find in their perceptions;
the significances differ because of their prior experience.[2] Women

---

1 Ames, however, distinguishes between the individual unique presumptive world (unique because of the individual's unique prior experiences) and a "Common Form World" shared by all, which includes only
  "general laws concerning perception, such as 'we assume that what
  has happened before will happen again.'" The latter, the Common Form
  World, is what we call "common sense." Very rarely, for instance, do
  people argue about whether a chair is there or not, even though they
  may argue about features of the perception of a chair. Ames sees the
  Common Form World "as the matrix which binds the human race together
  and the basis of the 'we'". (p. 45)

2 Much work needs to be done by women on women's gestalt, their "common
  world."

observe the world differently; they ask different questions; they act _privately_ upon the world in a unique manner. But if they are prevented from bringing their unique Gestalt to the _public_ actions they might take to transform the world, they will still be imprisoned in the "culture of silence" of which Freire speaks, no matter how much education they receive. The presumptive world of a non-dominant group must be tested through action; in turn, the action will, of course, modify their Gestalt.

One of the consequences of the domination of women is that they have been prevented from uniting Gestalt, learning, reflection, and action. Freire says this about illiteracy:

> Illiterates know they are concrete men. They know
> that they do things. What they do not know in the
> culture of silence -- in which they are ambiguous,
> dual beings -- is that men's actions as such are
> transforming, creative and re-creative. Overcome by
> the myths of this culture, including the myth of
> their own "natural inferiority," they do not know
> that _their_ action upon the world is also transforming.
> Prevented from having a "structural perception" of the
> facts involving them, they do not know that they can-
> not "have a voice," i.e., that they cannot exercise
> the right to participate consciously in the socio-
> historical transformation of their society.

Women know that they "do things." What we "do not know in the culture of silence" is that our actions as such could be "transforming, creative and re-creative." The potential of women to transform society will be lost if the education of women is based on the dominant culture, if their action is turned to the service of the present military-industrial-commercial complex, as is men's.

To translate this into the terms of Ames' processes of "transactions of living," it is not enough for women to be recognized by the university as scholars. They must bring their Weltenschauung to "transactions of living" through action to further their "valueful purposes." Only then will the results of such actions on themselves and their environment have effect on the "later purposeful action" of human beings as a whole.[1]

---

1 I hope it is clear that I do not see women's Gestalt as the only answer, but rather as a source of new perception which might contribute to a new mode of thought.

Ames quotes Huxley:

> ....we generate our own values. Some we generate
> consciously; some subconsciously; and some, only
> indirectly, through the structure of the societies
> in which we live. Through a fuller comprehension
> of these mechanisms we shall be able to guide and
> accelerate this process of value creation, which
> is not only essential for our individual lives but
> basic to the achieving of true evolutionary progress
> in the future. (p. 19, Ames)

The prognostic ability of the old perceptions based on the
dominant frame of reference does not work, does not prove itself
valid in the results of action based on its presumptions. We are
witnessing the disintegration of the old mode; we await a new definition of reality. Only women and other minority groups who
have been excluded from the prior experiences which reflected the
dominant mode can contribute to what Ames calls the "emerging un-
expected."

THE MORAL SIGNIFICANCE OF BEING THE MAJORITY

We who have been lepers may have the best opportunity to provide a counter-definition of reality. In The Social Construction of
Reality Peter Berger and Thomas Luckmann delineate the process by
which the reality and self-identity which an individual perceives is
structured by the socialization process he or she undergoes. They
cite the example of the leper as a way that a counter-reality might
be incipient to a counter-definition of the dominant reality.

> For example, lepers and the offspring of lepers may
> be stigmatized in a society. Such stigmatization may
> be limited to those physically afflicted with the
> disease, or it may include others by social defini-
> tion -- say, anyone born in an earthquake. Thus indi-
> viduals may be defined as lepers from birth, and this
> definition may severely affect their primary sociali-
> zation -- say, under the auspices of a crazy old
> woman, who keeps them physically alive beyond the con-
> fines of the community and transmits to them a bare
> minimum of the community's institutional traditions.
> As long as such individuals, even if they number more
> than a handful, do not form a counter-community of
> their own, both their objective and subjective identities
> will be predefined in accordance with the community's
> institutional program for them. They will be lepers,
> and nothing else.
>   The situation begins to change when there is a leper

colony sufficiently large and durable to serve as a
plausibility structure for counter-definitions of
reality -- and of the fate of being a leper. To be
a leper, be it in terms of biological or social assignment, may now be known as the special mark of divine
election. The individuals prevented from fully in-
ternalizing the reality of the community may now be
socialized into the counter-reality of the lepers'
colony; that is, unsuccessful socialization into one
social world may be accompanied by successful socialization into another. At any early stage of such a
process of change the crystallization of counter-reality
and counter-identity may be hidden from the knowledge
of the larger community, which still predefines and on-
goingly identifies these individuals as lepers, and
nothing else. It does not know that, "really," they
are the special sons of the gods. At this point an
individual assigned to the leper category may discover
"hidden depths" within himself. The question "Who
am I?" becomes possible simply because two conflicting
answers are socially available -- the crazy old woman's ("You are a leper") and that of the colony's own
socializing personnel ("You are the son of god"). As
the individual accords a privileged status within his
consciousness to the colony's definitions of reality
and of himself, a rupture occurs between his "visible"
conduct in the larger community and his "invisible"
self-identification as someone quite different.[1] In
other words, a cleavage appears between "appearance"
and "reality: in the individual's self-apprehension.
He no longer is what he is supposed to be. He acts
the leper -- he is a son of god. If we are to push
the example one step further, to the point when this
cleavage becomes known to the non-leprous community,
it is not difficult to see that the community's reality,
too, will be affected by this change. Minimally, it
will no longer be so easy to recognize the identity of
those defined as lepers -- one will no longer be sure
whether an individual so defined identifies himself in

---

1 An example comes to me as I sit at a desk and type this paper in the
   office of _____ High School. As the men administrators of the
   school go by, their definition of reality is that any woman sitting
   at a typewriter is a secretary and thus I am at their service; they
   ask me to take messages and get them things. But my counter-definition of reality and self-identity is validated by my action in
   writing this. There is a "cleavage" between their definition of my
   identity and mine. But it is they who are imprisoned in a role.

the same way or not. Maximally, it will no longer
be an easy matter to recognize anybody's identity --
for if lepers can refuse to be what they are supposed to be, so can others; perhaps, so can oneself.

Women's counter-definition of reality may result in the freeing of men
from the definition of their identity as dominant white males which
prevents men from realizing their own humanity. For if women can
"refuse to be what they are supposed to be, so can others;" perhaps,
so can males. It is only when males as well as females refuse the
roles institutions place upon them, that we can define what being
human could mean. But we must begin by offering a counter-definition
of reality.

However, there is one difference in this analogy between lepers
and women. If the lepers are co-opted by the dominant frame of reference, they are still a minority group. In the case of black
studies, were blacks co-opted into the male culture, assumed their
values and causes, one would feel disappointed but not hopeless. But
the significance of being the majority is a moral one -- if women
are sucked into the same kind of thinking as the dominant Gestalt, it
would be close to our last chance for radical changes leading to survival, for it would mean that the majority of people would be finally
subsumed under the aegis of death and destruction. Better that we
remain in slavery than to become like the masters. Better that we
remain in the preserve of the "culture of silence," than to speak in
the tongues of men.

In the biological metaphors that come so easily to women, it
would be better for women's liberation to abort, than to have it
delivered in the image of the dominant culture.

(I suspect that the writings of women may be much more cooperative
than men's; I owe much to discussions with Linda Roscoe and Peggy
Plosser. Bill McClendon of Reed College Black Studies Center originally gave me academic confirmation of what I knew from Oakland, California -- that blacks should consider themselves liberators, not
victims -- an attitude which I find useful in thinking about women.
Writers having the most influence on the thinking in this paper were
Christian Bay, Herbert Marcuse, Eldrige Cleaver, Doris Lessing, Kate
Millett, Simone de Beauvoir, Germaine Greer, Ivan Illich, Franz Fanon,
and R.D. Laing, in addition to those mentioned in the paper.)

II. THE FEMINIST CLASSROOM

INTRODUCTION

If we began with any assumptions when we selected the essays
which follow, we began with these two: that literature and the literature teacher can very helpfully facilitate the development of feminist consciousness, ·and that feminist pedagogy -- what actually
happens in the classroom -- ought itself to reflect and exemplify
the feminist principles we teach.

In the feminist classroom, then, we ought to be concerned with
more than just the reading. In the feminist classroom, we suspect,
the teacher mitigates her traditional authority, the students are
asked to work collectively, sexual politics are broken down as far as
possible, women are encouraged to overcome traditional passivity,
men to work in a non-sexist manner, all to find personal meaning in
the work at hand. One is not teaching a feminist course, we believe,
if the classroom procedures do not exemplify and test the content
taught.

We learned from the essays reproduced here that the role of the
teacher in the feminist classroom is critical, and that the teacher's
status may be separated from the teacher's function. Collective, non-
sexist, non-hierarchical activity requires the teacher to give up a
number of the privileges of status -- which turn out to be mainly
psychological privileges. The teaching function, on the other hand,
ought not to be discarded, but rather discussed and defined so that
responsibility for the function can be shared among the members of
the group.

A good teacher in a conventional literature classroom provides
authority, expertise, and resources. She legitimizes. She sets
expectations and provides a norm. She monitors and disciplines the
group process, reinforcing useful ideas and ignoring irrelevant comments.
She uses the force of her personality to get some to talk, others to
talk less without resorting either to threats or to therapy. The
problem of the feminist teacher in the literature classroom is to
make sure these functions are distributed in a feminist way.

Phyllis Franklin's classroom is closest to traditional in the
sense that the books she requires are commonly regarded as "good literature" and because she affirms her professional training as useful
to her and her students in dealing with these books. What is untra-
ditional about Phyllis Franklin is her clear focus on the implications
of each book's rhetorical structure for women. Ira Shor's classroom

is closest to radical in the sense that he is using a feminist
analysis of an Anne Sexton poem to provoke his students into an intensive examination of the social institutions (in this case the
institution of marriage) which affect their lives -- with the
ultimate aim of changing those institutions. Melanie Kaye's classroom deals in radical politics like Shor's. Like Shor she assumes
that the class should be shaped by the students and that the books
should be related to the personal lives as well as the politics of
those who are discussing them. What is striking about Melanie Kaye's
classroom -- and seems feminist in the sense described above -- is
the ease with which things happen in it. There is an organic quality
about her classroom as if everyone present trusts it enough to let
it grow its own shape and structure.

Janet Sass presents a model for a self-taught literature course,
one where the professional teacher is nowhere to be found, where
the sequence of books is selected by the women involved, where the
course runs an initially undetermined length of time and ends in an
action project in the community. In some ways this is the ultimate
feminist course described above -- a leaderless group (with the
attendant problems of legitimizing the material under study, dealing
with absence of authority, ego tripping, anger and the like), in a
non-degree setting, where women learn to think together in a way
that is potentially political. Aleta Wallach presents an opposite
kind of model, one for meeting the needs of women students in a
prestige law school. You will find in her essay an account of the
problems which confront all feminists organizing in the traditional
and elite male institutions -- from furnishing the women's lounge
to establishing women's courses as a permanent part of the curriculum,
to an attempt (unsuccessful) to develop part-time study opportunities
for women.

TRADITIONAL LITERARY STUDY -- IN THE SUBJUNCTIVE MOOD

by Phyllis Franklin

These days of Women's Liberation may be the times that try men's
souls, but these are also the times when it feels particularly good
to be a woman. One looks to the future with interest; for women are
beginning, if not to come into their own, at least to undertake in
a concerted way, a search for what that "own" might be. For me, this
sense of exciting prospects is new. I didn't have it eight months
ago when I agreed to teach an experimental course called "Women in
Literature" for the University of Miami. And it didn't happen all
at once. As the semester progressed, I thought frequently, at first
with deep misgivings, and finally with amusement and self-confidence,
of William Vaughn Moody's poem "I Am the Woman." The woman he describes states her challenge in this way:

>I am the Woman, ark of the law and its breaker,
>Who chastened her step and taught her knees to be meek,
>Bridled and bitted her heart and humbled her cheek,
>Parceled her will, and cried, "Take more!" to the taker,
>Shunned what they told her to shun, sought what they bade
>   her seek,
>Locked up her mouth from scornful speaking: now it is
>   open to speak.

No longer chastening steps, or teaching knees to be meek, women
have begun to speak. We are no longer simply holding out cupped
hands to receive attributes from men. Instead, and this for me is
at the heart of Women's Studies, we are trying to assess our heritage -- scientific, economic, social, and cultural -- in an attempt
to discern what we were in that first shining hour in Eden; what
we might have been before man came to see us, made us see ourselves,
paradoxically enough, as both the ark of the law, his law; and the
breaker of that law, again, his law.

This project of self-discovery is not only complex (how does one
go about stripping away centuries of socialization?), but at first
frightening. As I gathered materials, prepared lectures, I felt
myself threatened and depressed, and my students had a similar emotional experience. After all, hostility rarely reassures. The subject seemed complicated, uncertain, and hopeless. In the course of
the semester, however, we lost the sense of hopelessness, though we
could not forget the complexities or uncertainties; for most of us

concluded we were uncertain about the nature of woman, that there were mysteries to solve. And mysteries are frightening.

My particular concern in this paper deals with the question of how those of us engaged in the study of literature can contribute to the development of Women's Studies in both our teaching and research. What are the possibilities? Virginia Woolf totted up in A Room of One's Own: "women and what they are like; or . . . women and the fiction they write; or . . . women and the fiction that is written about them; or . . . all three . . . inextricably mixed together. . . ." And she did not even begin to concern herself about a method, which is at least as important as subject matter.

While I was planning my course, I talked with women who had already taught such courses. They admitted many difficulties. One had used a sociological orientation, and I could see that most of the newly published texts reflected this approach. But it seemed unsatisfactory. For one thing, it wasn't literature, and so evaded me the possibility of finding out truths from literature. And besides I wasn't trained to conduct such a study, though I supposed I could bone up. Another woman told me she had concentrated on literature that presented strong women, so that she could provide her students with good role models. This sounded more attractive. Obviously there was a desperate lack of varied role models for women in our society.

But this too seemed unsatisfactory. What bothered me most was that it meant accepting as valid the literary models provided by our culture. For example, she was teaching Antigone. I found myself wondering whether it would be a good thing for my students to simply accept Antigone as a role model. It's true that she is a brave yong woman who has the strength of her convictions, and so is admirable. But it's also true that she is admirable because she risks and suffers death to fulfill religious and familial obligations, an act of female self-sacrifice not unlike the self-effacement expected of the nineteenth century woman. And surely we have had enough of that. Of course, there is more than self-sacrifice involved in Antigone. There is an abstract problem too, that of duty to one's conscience and duty to one's state, a problem of conflicting loyalties.

Well, why use a woman to exemplify such a problem? Aeschylus in the Oresteia had dealt with a not totally dissimilar dilemma and had used a man. But Sophocles, early in the play, makes the point fairly clear, and we can see why a woman is a clever choice. It is not the way of a woman to disobey, says Ismene, who exemplifies the well-behaved young lady. And just because it is not the way of a woman to disobey, the importance of family tradition and the importance of duty to one's conscience are intensified when even a woman musters up courage to die for her belief. Her daring is more significant than a man's because she is weaker; her challenge more surprising. I concluded that the fact of her sex was structurally significant, and that although she wasn't a bad model, still, studying the play wouldn't particularly clarify the problems women face in our society.

It is interesting, too, that compared with ancient tragic heroes, she is rather passive. To be sure, she makes her initial decision to disregard the edict, but she simply decides to do the deed and take her punishment. Her heroism rests on her willingness to accept an early death, a time-worn literary solution for most female dilemmas. Consider Oedipus -- he doesn't set out to destroy himself. Or Orestes, he doesn't just wait for his fate. Also, while we have passivity before us -- look at the suicides in Sophocles' trilogy: Jocasta and Oedipus, generally speaking, share the same kind of guilt. But Jocasta kills herself, while Oedipus puts out his eyes; unpleasant, but he endures so as to suffer and live and finally to triumph. Similarly, Eurydice is so overcome with grief that she kills herself; while Creon, who has precipitated the situation, like Oedipus, chooses to suffer, and live.

No, I decided, simply using strong female characters as positive role models was not enough. I wanted to understand patterns, try to get beyond, beneath cultural and literary assumptions, and not just accept them. But my particular teaching assignment was such that I could not engage in elaborate studies in single areas. I had been asked to teach a sophomore level course that would be open to all undergraduates. After some agonizing, I put together a reading list and determined an approach for my classroom. Looking back on it now, I see that my decisions reflected three kinds of obligations: to my discipline, to the subject itself, and to my prospective students.

I wanted whatever I did to be academically respectable. I confess to thinking -- well, if the course doesn't do anything much for women or Women's Studies, at least it will be a solid course in literature, just topically oriented. Actually, my Chairman's responses to my reading list revealed that he had the same thing in mind: "They will be doing some good reading," was what he said. I was also interested in the problem of methodology. I thought that once I was safely behind my academic barricade, I could, perhaps, honestly try to discover whether such a course as "Women in Literature" should exist. Was it a legitimate subject? What kinds of things could be discovered? And more important than answers, I decided, were questions. What were the right questions to ask, so that problems could be defined and directions for research marked out?

And I wanted to fulfill as best I could my students' special needs and expectations; and in this area, I felt most presumptuous, most on my own. I knew from talking to some of them before the semester began that they were enrolling because they had questions about

their own identity as women and questions about the ways they might
develop their lives. Because of this, I was afraid to go too far
into the past for reading materials. It seemed to me that before
they could answer their questions they had to have some insight into
the pressures women experience in our society. And so the books I
selected ought to reflect aspects of a woman's life that were still
worth worrying about; that is, they should involve questions related
to life styles. From this point of view, the problems of such figures as Antigone and Joan of Arc seemed less important.

My final reading list consisted of books about women by both
men and women writers of various nations. I asked my students to
read The Romance of Tristan and Iseult, so that we could examine one
source of the love myth in western society; Madame Bovary, so that
we could see the effect of this myth; Little Women, so that we could
examine the very real attractions of a warm and strong family and
consider also the question of sentimentalism; Middlemarch, so that
we could consider women characters drawn by a woman, account for their
evolution, and consider why women had not seemed suitable figures for
tragedy; Anna Karenina, so that we could consider the value of living
within tradition, and the danger, from Tolstoy's point of view, of
fulfilling emotional needs outside marriage; Doll's House, for historical reasons and because it raises the question of male law, male
and female values; Miss Julie, because it clearly reveals the male
as sexual aristocrat and sex as degrading for women, so that sexual
intercourse becomes the cause of the tragedy; Portrait of a Lady,
so that we could consider the concept of the lady and the danger of
denying sexuality; The Awakening, because it is an astonishingly
modern statement of woman's dilemma by a woman who touches the center
of the problem and then, in 1899, doesn't know what to do about it;
Mrs. Dalloway, because it is a woman's portrait of the hostess, the
mother, the virginal wife; and The Bold New Women, because it is new
and worth exploring for its defiant anti-romantic attitude. The
poetry we considered throughout the semester to exemplify one thing
or another, we read as a group in the classroom, and I provided copies.
In addition, I asked them to read either The Second Sex or Sexual
Politics or The Female Eunuch, or Man's World: Woman's Place, recom-
mended in that order.

Also, in response to my students' special needs, I worried about
classroom atmosphere. I knew that all of us would be personally
involved with the subject and with testing our attitudes and arguments on each other, because to a great extent the subject had to be
made. So, personalities would matter, classroom relationships would
have to be different, less formal than in my other classes, I decided,
and (oh dear) my own sense of myself as a woman would matter. Should
I, I wondered, be objective or reveal myself? And on personal or
literary matters? At the beginning I wasn't sure.

But I was certain that the classroom atmosphere had to be comfortable,

that the students should participate. I had chosen the reading list,
and though this might have the taint of autocracy, I felt justified.
But I wanted them to get to know each other as quickly as possible
and to work together. I was with this in mind that I arranged the
first assignment, which required group work. As I made the assignment that first day of class, I reminded them of the general notion
that women could not work well together, and I asked them to examine
their own feelings. Actually, I regarded this as an integral part
of the assignment, and later after the class project was complete,
we talked about the problem of women working together.

This assignment required that, as a group, we develop a picture
of what we called "our straw woman," the modern American woman as
she could be seen in the magazines she reads, magazines written to
appeal to her. I explained that a jointly created description of
this straw woman would provide us with something to react to as the
semester progressed. I also hoped, though I did not say this, that
it would help us more quickly become a group with a common goal. We
discussed the various popular women's magazines, decided which types
to study, and divided into six groups on the basis of expressed interest in the magazines. Each group was charged with analyzing a
magazine, and describing its typical reader. What was she concerned
with, interested in? How bright did the editors think she was? They
were to consider the cover, fiction, non-fiction, advertising, edi-
torials, illustrations, general layout. On the basis of their reports, I put together a profile of this straw woman. This I dup-
licated and handed out by the end of the second week of the semester,
and the class had visible proof of the group effort. The magazines
we considered were Good Housekeeping, MS, New Woman, Cosmopolitan,
Glamour, Playboy, and two confessional magazines. As I considered
their comments, I was led to make the following generalization:

> Our straw woman is sincerely, even terribly worried.
> Heaven only knows how she lives longer than her mate!
> She worries about her body -- is it the right size
> and shape? Does it stink? How should she do her hair?
> What about body odor? What should she wear? Whom
> should she vote for? What kind of furniture, car, food,
> appliances, or stocks should she buy? And what about
> body odor? How should she cook the food, take care
> of the furniture and clothing. What should she do
> about sex (marital or pre-marital or adulterous)? How
> should she feel about the family, marriage, and day
> care centers? And what about body odor? Should she
> make love to one man or more than one man -- seriatim
> or simultaneously? Or should she just let him make
> love to her? Should he chase her or should she chase
> him? Is guilt necessary? Desirable? Who is she?
> What is she? Does she stink? What does she want to be?
> What is she brave enough to be? Is women's lib a threat

or a ray of hope -- or both?
    One thing seems very clear! While the classical
purpose of literature is generally assumed to be
dual -- to teach and delight -- the purpose of popular journalism for American women has only a single
aim: to teach her how to delight others, and to
smell good.

And this was one of the first truths I learned about literature
for women: in general, such literature is, however artistically admirable, designed to be monitory. It was not just the class analysis
that made me aware of this but an interesting complaint lodged by
a male colleague who had borrowed my copy of Doris Lessing's Golden
Notebook. He complained that the book was depressing because there
weren't any admirable male characters he could identify with. And
he was aggrieved because this was clearly a new situation for him.
At first I felt apologetic because I had praised the book; and then I
realized how rare it was for a woman to find an admirable female character to identify with who didn't practice self-sacrifice. There
are lots of stories about more or less wicked or silly women who
are more or less admirable and with whom one can sympathize, but
their stories are warnings: they come to a bad end so often. On the
other hand, there was Mary Poppins, I thought, frantically casting
about, or Alice (maybe), or the nice old lady detective in mystery
stories; and I recalled something a cynical woman had once said to
me -- that the only women people could feel neutral about sexually,
and perhaps therefore the only ones they could write about in a
neutral way, were those who by vocation were exempt from sexual possibility -- nuns and witches, she had said. I added to the list Mary
Poppins, Alice (maybe), and old lady detectives who were clever.

Aside from the first assignment, I stayed close to the traditional. This seemed important because books frequently taught and
frequently written about would be likely to have influenced generations of readers, and therefore would be worth studying. That is, if
we're trying to find out what women are and might have been, it seems
important to look at books that may have helped make us what we are.
Such a book as The Awakening was included for its insights and for
its differences from the more widely read and taught Madame Bovary
and Anna Karenina, but an entire reading list of obscure books
would have defeated my immediate purpose.

My approach to these books was traditional too. It seemed
natural to use my professional training. If I were willing to accept
one or several methods of literary study when I wanted to learn
other things, why shouldn't these methods be helpful now -- if only
I handled them in a more open, hopeful way -- use old methods but
stay in the subjunctive mood. And so I decided that we would study
a book a week, that I would rather briefly review for the class traditional approaches to the book and then we would look at it from our

own perspective -- that of women in 1972. To give them some sense of how we might begin to see things in a new way, I discussed with them approaches to literature found in Katharine Rogers' Troublesome Helpmate and Mary Ellman's Thinking About Women.

Recalling Wayne Booth's list of the various ways one might look at fiction, I rather quickly decided that two of the approaches he reviews would be most fruitful for classroom analysis. First, we should examine the work as an art object, Booth's "autonomous," "well-wrought urn" category. It seemed important to understand what it was in the art work we were responding to, what in the structure and imagery, what quality of language that made us feel as we did about the characters and situations. I hoped that after we had studied the book in this way, we could look at it as a "work of rhetoric," "an imposition by one man on another."[1] And having determined the nature of the book's pattern and its effect upon us, we could then consider the implications of the book's rhetoric for women. What might aesthetically effective books that conveyed values so persuasively have meant to women in the past? What could they mean for us now?

Because of this particular emphasis, I abandoned any serious attempt to deal with biographic questions or even questions concerning the author's conscious or unconscious intentions. The fact that a book or a poem was well known, frequently taught, and therefore, perhaps, influential was fact enough. How or why it got that way were good questions, but I chose not to try to answer them.

This approach proved useful for us, opening up a number of problems. For one thing, we gained some interesting insights into attitudes toward sex. The first book on the reading list was The Romance of Tristan and Iseult, which I had gone back to the Middle Ages for, although many of my colleagues and students thought it a strange choice. From the point of view of methodology, however, it was a good book to start with because Denis de Rougement's study of the Tristan legend showed how an analysis of structure could get beyond a book's charm to a more complete understanding of its rhetoric. For charm the story does have. Even the most hardened anti-romantic in the class found himself responding to and involved with the lovers. Yet the pattern in the book is clearly not what a reasonable reader would expect: two young people very much in love who, instead of avoiding obstacles so that they may freely fulfill their love, accept obstacles, and when none exist, actually create their own. But the pattern does reveal a truth about the book -- that

---

[1] "The Rhetoric of Fiction and the Poetics of Fictions," in Now Don't Try to Reason With Me, Chicago: The University of Chicago Press, 1970, p. 158.

is, that it is just as important for the lovers to be apart as it is for them to be united.

De Rougement has elaborately explored this pattern of unhappy love, love accompanied by the "exquisite anguish" of parting, which he sees as very significant. He says that there is no literary tradition of happy love in Western society and that the very charm of the myth rests on our desire for unhappy love, which in turn he relates to an unconscious death wish.[2] This last I am not sure of. Certainly the legend is effective on a much simpler and more obvious level. That is, it seems directly related to the rhythm of sexual desire -- restraint and increased tension, climactic coming together, and separation -- and all this under the influence of a love potion which excuses, explains, and justifies; so that for a time, while under the spell of the tale, along with the lovers, we willingly abandon moral considerations. And so moved, so caught up in the story, we accept the rhetoric of the legend, which is, that the fulfillment of passionate love under these conditions is rightly bigger than we are and creates its own morality. To yield oneself in a perilous situation, to give all for love, has a very real power to charm us, and we respond for a number of more or less civilized reasons. The legend does ennoble sexual love; it compels our response to the rhythm of sexual desire when rational control gives way to passion; and it reflects the intensity of sexual desire, or perhaps just the intensity of unsanctioned sexual desire.

Well then, what is the significance of this rhetoric for us? A crucial one, I think. Men as well as women are carried away by passion, but women much more than men are defined by the terms of their sexual participation and so passion can have a more devastating effect when they make decisions "under the influence." A consideration of the legend and its tremendous power as a myth to affect us, "usually without our knowing" De Rougement says, can lead, at least, to an intellectual awareness of the aura that surrounds sexual fulfillment in our society. I say "at least" because I suspect that intellectualizations about passion are rarely helpful; but, still, knowledge is supposed to be power. Certainly it is helpful to know that though there are many centuries between Iseult and True Confessions, there is a connection.

Studying the legend in this way does not represent a plea to ignore passion. Rather, it is a plea to know with what part of our bodies we respond to the legend, to know that we may respond positively to the idea of unhappy love, and perhaps, most important of all, to recognize that what we are dealing with is unattainable desire, so that to fulfill it easily, is to destroy it. Events that

2 Trans. Montgomery Belgion, Garden City, New York: Doubleday and Company, Inc., 1940, pp. 1-47.

take place somewhere between "Once upon a time" and "they lived happily ever after" cannot take place in everyday time and stay the same. If we do not understand this, we may be left, as was Emma Bovary, with destructive dissatisfactions. One must decide whether one wants to live always on the brink of ecstatic passion and suffer the consequences, or live with fewer intensities more generally diffused. Knowledge involves recognizing that on the one hand there is Keat's "Heard melodies are sweet, but unheard melodies are sweeter," and on the other hand, there is e.e. cumming's very practical he-man, who says: "A pretty girl who naked is,/is worth a million statues." One must remember that if Tristan had married Iseult, she would be driving a car pool, and he would be taking out the garbage.

A study of August Strindberg's Miss Julie yielded a different insight into sexual matters. As in the Tristan legend, emotional appeal is based on increasing sexual tension between Jean and Miss Julie. This tension results finally in intercourse, and then we are privileged to observe the aftermath. Involved in the erotic tension of the play and influenced by Strindberg's rhetoric, we can hardly help but feel the woman's debasement and the man's pride. Jean, despite his dishonesty and social inferiority, is according to Strindberg, "In the sexual sphere . . . the aristocrat."[3] He is the natural winner; Julie, the natural loser. A sexual encounter cannot diminish him, but not even aristocratic birth can help her. Because she is a woman and because she experiences physical desire, she is doomed either to fall or repress her sexuality. As E.M. Sprinchorn notes: in this play "fate takes the form of erotic passion" and "the tragedy lies ultimately in the act of love itself."[4] Julie's recurrent dream reveals the kind of stress she and so many women have experienced. She dreams of falling from the top of a pillar. She fears the fall, she desires the fall, and she knows that she will have no peace until she falls. But she also knows that once fallen, she will not be able to stop herself from sinking into the dirt. So persuasive is Strindberg's rhetoric that we accept the fact that when lovely woman stoops to folly, the only act that can cover her guilt is death.

Obviously the message here about the nature of sex is quite different from that of the Tristan and Iseult, and it is an important one for women to recognize and talk about. Strindberg's view of the male as sexual aristocrat and his dramatization of woman's fall in sex is illuminating. As far as my class was concerned, one had not only to watch out for the Scylla of idealization, but also to beware

---

3 "The Author's Preface," Miss Julie, trans. E.M. Sprinchorn, San Francisco; Chandler Publishing Company. 1961, p. xx.

4 "Introduction," Miss Julie, ibid., p. xiii.

of the Charybdis of degradation.

We learned other things too. A study of implicit comparisons, for example, led us to see that a sense of women as helpless, animal-like creatures has evolved at least partly because writers either make direct comparisons between women and animals or because in more subtle ways they make us see the fate of women as being like that of animals. Flaubert's very famous scene of the Agricultural show in Madame Bovary sets up this kind of comparison. He describes the "long lines of girls -- servants from farms, wearing blue stockings, low-heeled shoes and silver rings and smelling of the dairy when they came close. They walked holding hands, forming chains the whole length of the meadow, from the row of aspens to the banquet tent. It was time for the judging, and one after another the farmers were filing into a kind of hippodrome marked off by a long rope hung on stakes. Here stood the livestock, noses to the rope, rumps of all shapes and sizes forming a ragged line."[5]

The cinematic possibilities of the scene are good. Few directors would miss the link between the judging of lines of animals inside the hippodrome with the judging of the female animals lined up out-side. Moreover, Flaubert's emphasis in this scene on winning prizes -- farmers for their animals or men winning women -- not only underscores Rodolphe's campaign to win Emma, it also makes us see the relation-ship between men and women in a particular way -- the superior male cleverly winning the less clever female. Using ironic juxtaposition, Flaubert presents Rodolphe's seductive entreaties against a back-ground of voices announcing prizes for the best manures. And the creature who is going to be won by this "manure" is at that very moment held "like a captive dove," while outdoors the peasant wo-men's headdresses look "like fluttering white butterfly wings." Finally, we see Rodolphe, his siege well on the way to success, lead Emma away. In this scene, she wears a green bonnet, and Flaubert also describes the other "masters" leading off the animals: "their horns decked with the green wreaths that were their trophies."[6] Again, few directors filming the scene would miss the intended com-parison between the two kinds of green-hatted creatures, each led away by a master.

---

5   Trans. Francis Steegmuller, New York: The Modern Library, 1957,
    p. 154.

6   Ibid., pp. 168-170.

Tolstoy also makes use of animals in <u>Anna Karenina</u>. D.S. Merezh-
ovsky points out the similarities between Tolstoy's description of
ronsky's horse Frou-Frou and his description of Anna. By making us
ee Frou-Frou as like Anna, by making us see Vronsky treat the horse
s he would a woman he loves, Tolstoy also makes us see the possi-
ility of Anna's death. Frou-Frou dies because Vronsky makes an
unpardonable mistake;" and we watch him kick the fallen horse that
s already in great agony.[7] This we see just before Anna puts her
uture in Vronsky's hands.

The scene is brilliant and conveys several kinds of information.
erezhkovsky says: "In the death of the woman, as in the death of the
nimal, a tragedy has been accomplished -- the eternal violation of
he strong against the weak, the crime of a sensual eros against
nother, spiritual one. . . ."[8] The male critic sees a valid moral
njunction against the exploitation of the weak by the strong. The
elf-conscious feminist reader agrees, but also sees that such a
omparison intensifies for women a sense of weakness and dependence.
urely there is a message here for us, in addition to the one in-
ended by the author: beware of subtle persuasions hidden in juxta-
ositions.

Just as we learned to question the effects of implicit compari-
ons, so did we learn to question the implications of imagery. For
xample, we found William Wordsworth's poem "She Was A Phantom of
elight" a particularly interesting hodgepodge of genuine admiration
or a woman, nineteenth century ideas of women, and older anti-
eminine attitudes, although when first the poem gleamed upon our
ight, it seemed just another nineteenth century glorification of
oman.

In each of the poem's three stanzas, Wordsworth considers diff-
rent aspects of a woman he admires. He is first impressed by her
ppearance; later, he is impressed by her womanly qualities; and
inally, he recognizes her as a being, presumably a human being. This
ast view is the way many of us would like to be seen and so it is
orth starting with. What matters in this stanza is that the woman,
ike other beings, is "A traveler between life and death," and so,
e assume, like other beings must suffer the slings and arrows of
ortune and the <u>angst</u> beings experience who know that one day they
ill not be. In the face of this, she is thoughtful, reasonable,
emperate. She has endurance and foresight and strength and skill.
he is, he says, a perfect woman, and she has been endowed with these
ualities so as to use them.

Eds. Leonard J. Kent and Nina Berberova, New York: The Modern Library,
1965, p. 211.

"Tolstoy's Physical Descriptions," in <u>Anna Karenina</u>, ed. George Gibian,
New York: W.W. Norton and Company, Inc., pp. 802-810.

There is nothing here to offend, nothing here like the misogyny one finds in the literature of the Renaissance, which Katharine Rogers associates with ambivalent attitudes toward love. In this tradition, if women were attractive, it was common to point out that their very attractions were dangerous illusions, that painted exteriors hid weakness, or impurity, or evil. John Marston, for instance, "described women as 'Glowe wormes bright/That soile our soules, and dampe our reasons light,'" and Rogers explains that "The glowworm comparison was popular, since a glowworm, bright and pretty from a distance, is seen in the hand to be an ugly black bug."[9] The dangers and disappointments of these glowing creatures were also explored by John Donne in "Loves Alchymie," where he denies that physical love between a man and a woman can result in an ennobling transformation. A lover may glorify the woman he loves -- "his pregnant pot" Donne calls her -- but he is deluded. The lover gets only a "winter-seeming summer's night" -- a short night that seems long and is therefore dull, and chill instead of warmth. And so Donne concludes, emphasizing the lack of substance in women and love,

> Our ease, our thrift, our honor, and our day,
> Shall we, for this vaine Bubles shadow pay?

With this in mind, it is interesting to look again at Wordsworth's poem, the first stanza this time, in which he praises the woman's appearance. Wordsworth describes her as a phantom, which may simply suggest that she is ethereal. Of course, what the word means is that she lacks substance. Moreover, she is not only a phantom, a being that seems to appear but has no physical presence, but she is also a phantom of delight, which, like Donne's winter-seeming summer's night, suggests unfulfilled promise. And she is an apparition, a "moment's ornament," one whose decorative quality is ephemeral. Here we have the gather ye rosebuds theme, that charming memento mori so frequently addressed to women. (Wasn't it Newsweek that described Women's Studies as the latest "wrinkle" in higher education?) And when we reach the last lines of the stanza, we find that this "image gay" (still not the real thing) has appeared only "To haunt, to startle, and waylay." Now this may simply describe the impression a beautiful woman can make on a man, but being haunted can be both unpleasant and pleasant; being startled is never particularly comfortable; and who wants to be waylaid? Even if it does not involve hostility, it still keeps you from doing whatever it was you set out to do.

Well, how different is Wordsworth's phantom of delight that like the ignis fatuus will startle and waylay, from John Donne's vaine bubles shadow? A major different lies in the fact that the negative elements in Donne's poem are obvious. Donne is disgusted because he finds the "myne of love" empty. Wordsworth accepts a woman's lack of substance as fact, and his compliments echo with reverberations of ancient fears that attraction may not be pleasant. I suppose such

---

9 The Troublesome Helpmate, Seattle: University of Washington Press, 1966, p. 109.

ambiguous compliments are only unfortunate for women who may be led
to think of themselves as haunting creatures and concentrate so on
this that they do in fact become phantoms, without substance as people.

If Wordsworth's first stanza reflects ancient attitudes about
the illusionary qualities of female beauty, the second stanza most
clearly exemplifies nineteenth century assumptions about woman's personality and work. She is a competent housekeeper and accepts as
the extent of her mobility something described as "virgin liberty."
She is sweet, and neither too bright nor too good for her everyday
housekeeping chores; her responses are emotional but not deep; and
her wiles are simple. That is, not being overly bright, her more or
less devious ways are not dangerous, a charge that reflects an old
attitude toward women. Edward de Vere had described man's pursuit of
woman in this way:

> Yet for disport we fawn and flatter both,
> To pass the time when nothing else can please;
> And train them to our lure with subtle oath
> Till, weary of their wiles, ourselves we ease;
> And then we say, when we their fancy try,
> To play with fools, oh, what a fool was I.

There may be a little confusion here as to who is manipulating
whom, but at least there is disgust at the quality of the relationship, though the Earl thinks man superior and woman at fault. But
again, Wordsworth accepts the fact of female wiles, which are not only
not to be feared or disapproved but encouraged because they and she
are so simple.

This poem, then, is much more than a poem of praise. From a
woman's point of view, it exemplifies very nicely centuries of confusion during which men have assigned attributes to women -- but we
have to remember that it is their confusion and not necessarily a
natural result of our nature.

By far the most dangerous and tragic phrase in the poem, however,
is "transient sorrows." Surely a being capable of breathing thoughtful breath, who travels as we all do between life and death, ought
to be capable of more than transient sorrow. Why couldn't Wordsworth
see the contradictions inherent in a creature who was simultaneously
a lovely flimsy who came trailing yards of silk chiffon, a competent
housekeeper who was sweet and silly, and a monolithic Roman matron?
And there is a still more important question for women to ask. Why
was it that the limitation of woman's nature, as it was conceived
in the nineteenth century when she achieved a position somewhere between responsible male adult, child and idiot, was not viewed as
potentially tragic? Why did no artist see her suffering or struggling
in her intermediary position in such a way that she could achieve the

dignity of tragedy? Even a Caliban can get some literary sympathy,
and there is a well-established literary tradition that deals with
men who strive against limitations -- men like Faustus or Ahab.

To be sure, there are women whose struggles involve the violation of sexual mores and who come to a bad end, but that's not what
I mean. George Eliot in the "Prelude" to Middlemarch recognizes
the possibility of unexpressed tragedy in women's lives as she talks
of St. Theresa, whose "passionate, ideal nature demanded an epic
life. . . ." She writes: "Many Theresas have been born who found
for themselves no epic life wherein there was a constant unfolding
of far-resonant action; perhaps only a life of mistakes, the offspring of a certain spiritual grandeur ill-matched with the meanness
of opportunity; perhaps a tragic failure which found no sacred poet
and sank unwept into oblivion." And one expects, after such a beginning that Eliot herself may play the part of sacred poet, that in
Dorothea Brooke, this tragic failure will be exemplified.

This is not the place for a lengthy discussion of why Dorothea's
dilemma falls short of tragedy. But briefly, it is obvious that
marrying your heroine to the man she loves and letting her live
happily ever after provides at least one reason. George Eliot lets
us see that Dorothea is a woman with heroic possibility who settles
for domesticity, but the settling has its satisfactions and so we
do not see her life as wasted. It is interesting, though, that there
is a much stronger sense of loss in Eliot's description of Lydgate's
failure to fulfill his potential. Lydgate, whose career has been
limited by an unfortunate marriage, calls his wife "his basil plant"
and explains that basil flourishes "wonderfully on a murdered man's
brains." Clearly, this "murder" of his brains cannot be compared
with the vague feeling we have that Dorothea might have done something "better"; and the difference in intensity reflects a sharp
difference in attitude toward the quality of disaster when both a
man and a woman fail to utilize their intellectual capacities. Despite her "Prelude," Eliot evades the tragic and accepts the traditional.

But even if she does not dramatize the potential tragedy in a
woman's life, at least Eliot only partially diminishes her heroine:
Dorothea is not sweet or little. It was far more frequent in the
nineteenth century to diminish women so as to gain a sentimental
effect, and I believe that a study of sentimentality will be important
in an understanding of literary attitudes toward women. The tendency to diminish women was so widespread that Bret Harte, writing
about Charles Dickens' children and women, satirized it:

> I see a child, . . . a most unnatural child, a model
> infant. It is prematurely old and philosophic. It
> dies in poverty to slow music. It dies surrounded

by luxury to slow music. . . . Previous to its decease
it makes a will; it repeats the Lord's Prayer, it
kisses the "boofer lady." . . .

"I see a good woman, undersized. I see several
charming women, but they are all undersized. They
are more or less imbecile and idiotic, but always
fascinating and undersized. They wear coquettish
caps and aprons. I observe that femine virtue is
invariably below the medium height, and that it is
always simple and infantine. . . .[10]

Harte, who was himself a clever user of formulas for developing
character, certainly picked up on the technique of gaining sympathy.
For the child, enhance his unchildlike qualities. For the woman,
the adult, enhance her childlike qualities. It is with all the little
Libbies, sweet and small and angelic, with all the Beth March's dying
slowly with amazingly sweet acceptance that we must deal -- and whom
we must analyze. Diminishment is a necessary aspect of sentimentality, and the interesting thing about sentimentality is that it
"is a gross form of emotional reassurance. It tells us that everything is really all right and that suffering, although sad, is only
temporary and not really serious. . . . Wherever it has appeared,
. . . it has relied heavily on the creation and repetition of stock
response materials ('emotional triggers') which are centered around
the emotional values of injustice to the self, manifested as self-
pity, victimization, and martydom."[11] And women, little, sweet
women, are part of the stockpile of emotional triggers.

Because it is emotionally reassuring, sentimentality keeps us
from looking beyond the situation for solutions. Consider a non-
sexual example. The old poem about the poor little newsboy shivering
in tattered clothing in the snow as he tries to sell his newspapers
is a perfect example of a poem so satisfying within itself that we do
not question its resolution. Our sympathies are aroused for the
poor boy, unable to sell his papers. But at last, along comes a
man, well to do, warmly dressed, in a comfortable fur-collared great
coat, perhaps -- there are few details.

> . . . The kind eye glistened
> As the stranger took the sheet,
> And glanced at the stiffened fingers,
> And thought of the icy feet.

---

10   Condensed Novels, Upper Saddle River, New Jersey: Literature House,
     Gregg Press, c. 1871, republished 1969, pp. 98099.

11   Jackson J. Benson, Hemingway . . . The Writer's Art of Self-
     Defense, Minneapolis: University of Minnesota Press, 1969, p. 23 note.

Then dropped in his hand the value
Of his fifty papers sold,
'Ah, Poor little friend,' he faltered,
'Don't you shiver, and ache with cold?'

The boy, with a gulp of gladness,
Sobbed out, as he raised his eye
To the warmth of the face above him --
'I did -- sir -- till you -- passed by!'[12]

The trouble with this ending is its capacity for providing
emotional satisfaction. The immediate problem is solved. There is
an exchange of human warmth and gratitude, and the boy's papers are
sold. But only for today. The price of the fifty papers obviously
means little to the man, who, let us hypothesize, will go home to his
warm fire and sumptuous dinner, while the newsboy, the next evening,
will be back shivering on the corner. Nothing has really changed.
But because of the easy emotional response and the easy emotional
resolution, the deeper, more significant aspects of the situation are
avoided. Instead of thinking, we feel. We feel good about the newsboy; we feel good about Dorothea's marrying Will; we feel good about
poor Beth -- we feel so good that we never look past the poem's
solution to a larger solution which might involve serious questions
about justice or tragedy.

Well, these are the kinds of things we learned, the kinds of
questions we asked, as we examined an art work's aesthetic appeal
and its rhetoric. This procedure was useful, particularly useful
in an undergraduate classroom because it required no special dogmatism,
no certainty as to who the good and bad guys had to be. And it can
be used with any number of different combinations of books that explore various aspects of female experience. Though I was satisfied
with this approach, I also saw, as the semester progressed, that
there were a number of traditional approaches to literature that
offered other possibilities, particularly for research.

Questions about sentimentalism and tragedy, for instance, get
one into the study of genre, which might be productive. Why, for example, do women appear more frequently and in more important roles
in sentimental literature, in comedy, melodrama, and comi-tragedy?
Why do they appear rarely in significant ways in epic or tragedy?
What kinds of genre have attracted women writers? Why? What kinds
have they excelled in? Failed in? Why? What kind of reading attracts,
is designed for, and influences women readers? Have these types changed

12 "The Newsboy," in The Genteel Female, ed. Clifton Joseph Furness,
New York: A.A. Knopf, 1931, pp. 99-100.

n time? Will they continue to change? And perhaps most important
f all -- what have been the conditions of heroism for women?

And there are still other approaches that might be fruitful.
ne could go back to Hippolyte Taine, for instance, and his assumptions
bout literature described in the "Introduction" to History of English
iterature. To him, literature was a transcript of contemporary
anners, a type of a certain kind of mind." It was a "monument," a
"fossil shell" behind which there was a man, whose nature had been
ffected by his race, his surroundings, and his epoch.[13] The object
f literary study was to try to understand the man, the organism that
ad created the monument, the literary shell. He assumed that by
tudying the external aspects of life one could come to an under-
tanding of man's inner nature. Man's products were

> but avenues converging to a centre; you enter them
> simply in order to reach that centre; and that cen-
> tre is the genuine man, I mean that mass of faculties
> and feeling which are produced by the inner man. . . .
> This under-world is a new subject-matter, proper to
> the historian. If his critical education suffice,
> he can lay bare, under every detail of architecture,
> every stroke in a picture, every phrase in a writing,
> the special sensation whence detail, stroke, or
> phrase had issue; he is present at the drama which
> was enacted in the soul of artist or writer; the choice
> of a word, the brevity or length of a sentence, the
> nature of a metaphor, the accent of a verse, the dev-
> elopment of an argument -- everything is a symbol to
> him; while his eyes read the text, his soul and mind
> pursue the continuous development and the ever
> changing succession of the emotions and the conceptions
> out of which the text has sprung: in short, he
> unveils a psychology.[14]

At this point we might make use of his approach. If one can
ead the nature of a man as he is moulded by his nature and instincts
n his writings; if one can read the nature of a nation in its
ccumulated writings, as Taine also believed one could, perhaps one
an undertake a study of the nature of woman in the same way. Could
e not add sex to Taine's race, surroundings, and epoch as a forma-
ive factor that might be isolated and examined?

---

13 Trans. H. Van Laun, New York: Henry Holt and Company, 1886,
    pp. 1-21.

14 "Introduction", ibid., p. 4.

Certainly Taine's assumptions do not violate the beliefs of those modern psychologists and physiologists who remind us that the body makes the mind. And so, the art object, which the mind creates by externalizing aspects of itself (mind, body, and environmental influence) can legitimately be examined so as to determine sexual influences, sexual manifestations -- if we develop our "critical education" sufficiently so that we can read back through the process.

Perhaps long-range studies of the works of women writers of all nations and times which attempt to do this may be helpful. Much thought would have to be given to the project, but we might gain valuable insights, perceive common factors not only in themes and attitudes but in structures, styles, rhythms. Virginia Woolf long ago talked about the difficulties women writers faced, and cited the sentence as a particular problem. She wrote: "To begin with, there is the technical difficulty -- so simple, apparently; in reality, so baffling -- that the very form of the sentence does not fit her. It is a sentence made by men; it is too loose, too heavy, too pompous for a woman's use. Yet in a novel, which covers so wide a stretch of ground, an ordinary and usual type of sentence has to be found to carry the reader on easily and naturally from one end of the book to the other. And this a woman must make for herself, altering and adapting the current sentence until she writes one that takes the natural shape of her thought without crushing or distorting."[15]

Is there, can there be such a thing as a female sentence? Are there structures, styles, rhythms that women find more comfortable, more expressive? And if so, what do they tell us about the nature of woman? This is just one kind of question we might ask. There are many others.

And legends, and myths. Much might be done in this area to re-evaluate ancient messages. Take the stories of Eve and Pandora for instance. In both Hebraic and Greek tradition, the introduction of evil in the world is ascribed to women; and though I imagine that fewer and fewer people take these accounts seriously, I think that we should, because certain common elements in both legends convey a very special message for women. You will recall that both women are ordered by men not to do something -- Eve is not to eat the apple, Pandora is not to open the box. They both disobey, and by their disobedience bring evil upon all of mankind. Although generally we focus on the result of their disobedience with some degree of regret and frustration, it seems far more important to consider the motivation for their disobedience, which is the same in both cases. It is the prospect of knowledge that finally tempts Eve; it is curiosity that leads Pandora to open the box.

---

15 "Women and Fiction," Collected Essays, London: The Hogarth Press, 1966, II, 145.

Curiosity. Interestingly enough, in modern times, human curiosity has not been feared at all, but praised instead. George Sarton in his monumental History of Science says that curiosity is "one of the deepest of human traits, indeed far more ancient than mankind itself," and that it "was perhaps the mainspring of scientific knowledge in the past as it still is today."[16] But curiosity was apparently not so valued in the past, at least not in women. From a man's point of view, the woman who sought knowledge was dangerous, so dangerous that female curiosity was seen as bringing down the worst of disasters. It seems important, therefore, for those of us involved in Women's Studies, to remember that proscriptions against female knowing are both ancient and male.

Not that keeping this in mind will simplify the problem of Women's Studies, which remains both complex and exciting. But it may be comforting to remind ourselves that we are not the first women eager for knowledge and that though men have feared female knowing, we need not fear it -- even if the best way of finding out is not yet perfectly clear. And until we find the best way to solve our problem of methodology, I believe that any valid approach to literary study is at least capable of yielding insights, if our considerations make use of the subjunctive mood -- if we remain open to the possible, the hypothetical, the contingent. We must not be afraid of heuristic studies. That, of course, is what this paper represents.

---

[16] Cambridge: Harvard University Press, 1952, p. 16.

ANNE SEXTON'S "FOR MY LOVER...":
FEMINISM IN THE CLASSROOM

by Ira Shor

I teach in a community college enrolling predominantly white
Italian working class students. My students arrive from high school
with an elaborately constructed ideology. A whole host of opinions
on sexuality, war, racism, welfare, socialism, labor and revolution
has been imposed on them by their daily experience and by the authorities in their lives. Luckily, there is no unanimity in their manners
of thinking, but their dominantly conservative modes of thought indicate
how potent the bourgeois mass media, the conservative parochial and
lower education systems, the patriarchal family, and the male-dominated
job market remain in fashioning their consciousnesses. Radical education designed to foster counter-consciousness has to be as comprehensive
as the forces outside college, to match the depth of off-campus mind-
making. In my classes, a consideration of women's liberation has been
integral to piecing together education for personal and social change.

Life for my students is not exactly a struggle, but the terms of
life are still ones of toughness. For the working class, life is a
hassle with clear rules, but a hassle justified by the reality of
American prosperity. Scrambling with the hassles of Army, government,
teacher, boss, wife, kids and cops, my students are tough and competitive and looking for a small economic niche which will guarantee them
security. For the men, this means a liberal arts transfer or a business or technology curriculum leading to a school or counseling or
draftsman or managerial or accounting post, or to a skilled trade.
If college fails, the men have the police, fire and sanitation departments of the city, or the post office, or bank jobs, or, with some
pull, a trade-union apprenticeship, or with no pull anywhere, the Army.

For the women, the limited present focuses their attention on a
limited future. The same business or technology curriculum leads to
lower aspirations to be legal or medical secretaries, computer clerks,
or nurses, combined into the bourgeois life-formula: marriage, kids,
the man earning the real bread. No other forms of life have been
validated or even suggested to them. The only models from which they
can fashion their own lives are the ones they see other people doing
around them. When radical feminism or radical teachers enter a student's life, the hermetic encirclement of consciousness ceases. The

evolution of a student's life then has a chance to escape the predictable bourgeois continuum of nuclear family, career and debts. A confrontation with feminism facilitates a student's revaluation of that process, and provokes alternative modes of male-female life.

Politically and philosophically, by the age of eighteen, minds of male and female workers have been formed as far as bourgeois society cares to form them. Men have learned to be the aggressive principle which women have learned to defer to. An almost religious feeling about the eternity of the status quo and a fatality about the uselessness of rebellion run deep. Both women and men think of politics as something to do in a ballot box every two years. They think socialism synonymous with totalitarianism, and terrorism with revolution. They do not see a prob lematic or systematic politics in sex, marriage or labor. Some students romanticize how good their labor or their marriage might be, but, especially with labor, delusions are few. (One of my classes could imagine only two jobs which were fun -- international pilot or international salesman. Given the alienated state of labor in our society they are probably right. More significant was the state of their imagination: they could not, on the first day of class, imagine a situation in which ordinary labor could be socially useful and personally satisfying.)

Our college was not established to shake their imagination, sexuality, or their ideology. It was designed to give working class students a mechanical or clerical or technical expertise useful to business and to governmental bureaucracies. Some radical teachers, predominantly in liberal arts, choose to challenge imposed ideology, but the institution justified itself to the system by easing students into jobs which they perform unquestioningly. In exchange, the jobs give our students the money to eat and to use for fun in a variety of places far from the scenes of work, school, family and marriage. Exotic vacation is the penultimate and longed-for model of the good life. My students correctly judge work, school, family and marriage as scenes of no or compromised pleasure. They do not think the alienation of enjoyment from daily life is remediable, but see it as a frozen duality in society. They don't celebrate America with flags and firecrackers, but face it with fatality.

On elite campuses in the years of the Vietnam escalation, college proved itself to be an important arena for unfreezing consciousness and history. The situation at a community college is more difficult, for obvious reasons -- the students are here for only two years, they still live in the patriarchal family, and commute lengthy distances, their attention and energy are drained by long hours on part-time jobs. Further, a purely intellectual or theoretical attack on politics and sexuality is hampered by our students' suspicion of education and intellectualism. Twelve years of pre-college school has managed to instill deep dislike for mental work. Our students read little, and disregard High Culture.

TV, movies, pop magazines, radio, rock music and concerts have dominated the culture presented to them. Their major energy focuses
on visceral things (sex, dancing, fast cars, sports) or on the great
American pastime, consumerism. To provoke their radical intelligence
means to combat the ideology trying to neutralize their minds. To
expose the consequences of their ideology, or even to make it apparent
that systematic ideology exists in their minds, takes some ingenuity
in an English course, as well as the conviction that the form no less
than the content of a course is in question. The very atmosphere of
a classroom is an irresistible invitation more often than not for students to put their energies to sleep. In school, they train for the
discipline and boredom of their future jobs, and begin dreaming of the
only tangible liberation -- money and a Florida vacation.

Partial people can become whole by understanding what situations
have robbed them of their power. Achieving this knowledge, students and
teachers wind up designing education as consciousness-raising groups.
To reconstruct consciousness, a classroom has to be casual, unthreatening
and personal. The material in question has to evolve into and through
students' own experience or else it will never evoke their energy or
transform their ideology. Students must create during class debate as
much as is brought to them at the outset, so that they do not feel over-
whelmed by texts, reading lists and **artifacts** presented to them. Education for them (and for us) has been an enormous and mysterious body of
knowledge outside our needs and our experience. This classroom gestalt
has to be broken as a stark announcement that the immediate inside and
outside of a student's life are necessary starting points for class discussion. The contradiction we have to deal with is something like this --
the immediate circumstances of a student's life contain the situations
which have limited her or his consciousness but are also the situations
through which liberation can occur, via a searching reassessment of that
past. Quite simply, an English class in my college has to talk to students about who they are and where they've been, or else the discussion
will be too distant, too detached, too much about the teacher's thing for
real personal changes to occur. In this setting, English education does
not place standard usage or great literature above student biography,
but uses language as a means for provoking a student's conscious sense
of self. That seems to be a starting point for transforming needs and
expectations.

A long consideration of women's liberation can be one class project
organic to the transformation of consciousness. In my classes, men and
women struggle with and against each other, and, so far, the men have
failed to dominate. (A number of community college teachers here have
noted that female students are superior intellectually to their male
counterparts. They are more mature, serious and thoughtful. Men as
successful as our women enroll at four year and elite colleges, pushed

ahead by family and society, unlike their female equals and betters who often have to fight to get into community college.) Men and women discuss the issues together, not separately, which has its liabilities, because only the most aggressive women argue. Women should have the experience of talking among themselves without male interference, but the desire to have a separate women's group presupposes a level of consciousness not existing in most of my female students. When the debate first begins, no feminists are identifiable in class, while a lot of hostility to the women's movement is apparent, in both men and women. The bourgeois media has done its work in discrediting the movement as hysterical, sick and extremist. Crediting women's issues is not only a class project involving personal transformation, but is also an event which strengthens an insurgent democratic movement which may liberate us all.

My students are generally suspicious of movements. The most articulate complaint is fear of losing one's individuality. So many institutions (family, school, police, church, employers) control their lives that they assert their uniqueness by refusing participation in movements. This resistance to extra-parliamentary politics is also part of their failure to believe that things get changed that way. Students have observed that in our society you have to make it on your own. The failure of any movement to penetrate their lives, to change the competitive and atomized circumstances of their lives, justifies their low opinion of radical politics. The women's movement, in this respect, is subjected to the same disregard and contempt as the anti-war movement.

But it also receives attitudes organic to its being a women's movement. The dominant class sentiment has always been anti-women's liberation as discussion begins, even though a number of women, by their disposition to oppose male dominance, are unacknowledged feminists. Even the unacknowledged feminists believe in the hysterical image of the movement fed to them by the media. Further, they are insulted by notions that they need liberation, and are threatened by feminist proposals that they can be more than they are. A number of black women feel the movement is a middle-class white female trip, and talk about the first item on their agenda of black liberation: liberating the black man. The older and married women in class chuckle about how a woman knows how to get anything she wants from a man, and it's only a few young, natural militants who complain at using their bodies to get what should be theirs in the first place. While neat irony and serious limits punctuate a male teacher's attempt to introduce female students to the women's movement, there is a further problem in focusing the question in terms of male liberation also. Lastly, in valuing a national movement, our discussion has to be personal and immediate at the same time that it is ideological and collective.

A lot of interesting work on these questions evolved out of a long class project we did from a poem by Anne Sexton, "For My Lover, Returning to His Wife."   The poem goes like this:

FOR MY LOVER, RETURNING TO HIS WIFE

She is all there.
She was melted carefully down for you
and cast up from your childhood,
cast up from your one hundred favorite aggies.

She has always been there, my darling.
She is, in fact exquisite.
Fireworks in the dull middle of February,
and as real as cast-iron pot.

Let's face it, I have been momentary.
A luxury. A bright red sloop in the harbor.
My hair rising like smoke from the car window.
Littleneck clams out of season.

She is more than that. She is your have to have,
has grown your practical your tropical growth.
This is not an experiment. She is all harmony.
She sees to oars and oarlocks for the dinghy,

has placed wild flowers at the window at breakfast,
sat by the potter's wheel at midday,
set forth three children under the moon,
three cherubs drawn by Michelangelo,

done this with her legs spread out
in the terrible months in the chapel.
If you glance up, the children are there
like delicate balloons resting on the ceiling.

She has also carried each one down the hall
after supper, their heads privately bent,
two legs protesting, person to person,
her face flushed with a song and their little sleep.

I give you back your heart.
I give you permission--

For the fuse inside her, throbbing
angrily in the dirt, for the bitch in her
and the burying of her wound--
for the burying of her small red wound alive--

For the pale flickering flare under her ribs,
for the drunken sailor who waits in her left pulse,
for the mother's knee, for the stockings,
for the garter belt, for the call--
the curious call
when you will burrow in arms and breasts
and tug at the orange ribbons in her hair
and answer the call, the curious call.

She is so naked and singular.
She is the sum of yourself and your dream.
Climb her like a monument, step after step.
She is solid.

As for me, I am a watercolor.
I wash off.

                    --Anne Sexton

It began the semster's discussion of women's liberation and grew into
an event which exposed how literature worked as well as how a feminist
world-view revalued the world we all had been looking at.

    Casual discussion of the poem's diction is one useful place to begin.
The form of the poem evolves its content through a number of devices,
and diction is one of them. Image inventories helped us characterize
the two women involved:

Wife	Lover
marble, cast-iron pot	red sloop
fireworks in dull February	smoke
wild flowers at the window	Littleneck clams
monument	watercolor
flickering flare	

The language immediately gave us a distinct sense of the two women.
One's life is heavy, metallic, dark and only touched with color. The
other's life is bright, gay, romantic. That the love triangle focuses
on a specifically woman's problem is indicated by the absence of male
characterization. Only one line describes the husband, and it discusses
how his family life has made him heavy and slothful with commitments:
"She ... has grown you practical your tropical growth."

    This woman's poem about the origins and effects of a love triangle
has more elaborate structural meaning. The analysis we did in class of
structure as well as diction, never became abstractly formalistic. All
gestures of form served to demonstrate content. The triangle itself
served as the controlling formal principle. If we draw a triangle we

could place at each point a character from the poem:

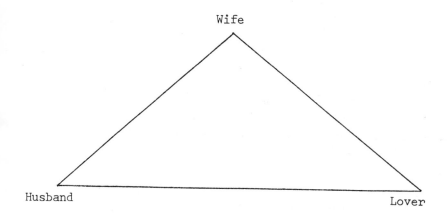

I handed out blank sheets with this triangle on it, to the class. I
then asked what relationship could describe the side of each triangle
connecting two people. Here's what next came up -

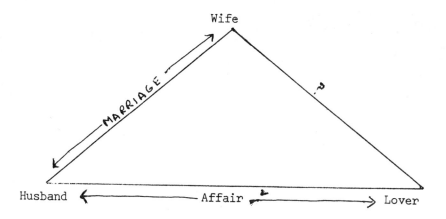

It became apparent that the only person in the triangle with two relationships was also the only man. Our discussion lingered on the fact
that the two women were each involved in only one side of the triangle,
and that the man had access to both worlds while the women were locked
into one. Following the fact that only a questionmark defined the
women's relationship to each other and that only one relationship
linked each woman to the situation, I asked the class to give me more
titles for each point in the triangle. Here's what came out:

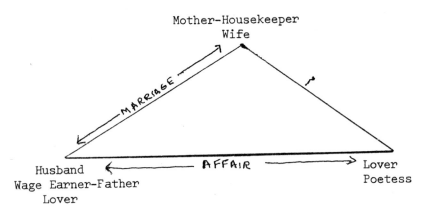

Again, the man had something more than the women, four roles and two sexual worlds to the one world and three or two roles of the women. To make the nature of the worlds more apparent, I then asked the class to place on each side of the triangle the words appropriate to each relationship. What then emerged was like this:

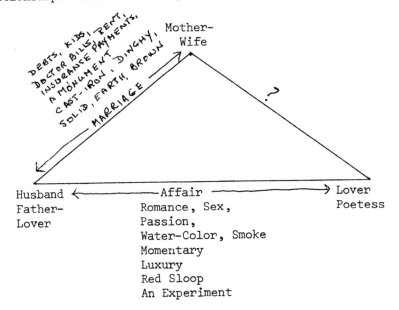

Some of the descriptive words came right out of the poem to contrast marriage from the affair, while other words derived from the students' own articulation of what family life and what romance really are. We discussed how marriage with its commitments made romance unlikely, while romance with its luxurious lack of debts and domicile, made longevity unlikely.

It was becoming apparent that the man was having the best of both worlds. There was a security and a harmony to married life talked about in the poem which was at the husband's disposal. And there was a passion and vitality to romance which was his also. In marriage, the husband had to pay the bills, but the drudgery of domestic life was his wife's job. We discovered that the great preoccupation of children, which chains the mother to the house, is at the poem's physical center and receives more lines (19-28) than any other piece of the narrative. In the romance, away from wife, house, kids and debts, the husband had his passion, but to the female lover, without a home, fell the bitter loneliness which made the poem so poignantly beautiful. The man had separate times and spaces for all his needs; the women had only single dimensions open to them.

The man was not only having the best of both worlds, but he was the principle causing the questionmark on the women's side of the triangle. The husband was dividing the women against each other because his regime installed one as mother-wife and the other as lover, two domains made exclusive to each other, but a separation satisfactory to male sexuality. The questionmark on the female side struck me as an illuminating fact of society, and I thought of asking the class to invent a relationship between the two women. We attempted this in two ways: we wrote letters from mistress to wife and wife to mistress, and we taped impromptu dialogues between female students playing the two women. This part of the project was the least successful because it was the least tangible. On my mind was an idea of women transcending the divisions imposed on them by males and coming together. Politically it was a paradigm of the women's movement. Sexually, it was lesbianism or bisexuality. No female students managed these transcendences. The women's attitudes to each other in the letters and dialogues were dominated by anger, bitterness and sarcasm, with no solidarity or sympathy. As a male teacher I felt the limits of how much I could provoke. A female model was needed in class to raise the next level of questions.

I then backtracked and asked the class to invent encounters between the husband and wife, and the husband and mistress. Within the accepted institutions of marriage, heterosexuality and promiscuity, the students felt familiar enough to design convincing encounters on tape and through letters. In this part of the project the husbands were always very guilty, meek and apologetic, while the wives were tough, hurt, and angry. The women invariably took back their men, but on their own terms, usually involving increased housework for the man and more outside free time for the woman. The females in class insistently redesigned the kind of marriage they saw on the husband-wife side of the triangle. And whenever the man complained that the wife had not been sexual enough in their marriage, the women defended themselves in terms of the unacknowledged and unpaid rigors of house and child care. Among the most emotional events was when all the women laughed and applauded whenever a wife, on the tapes we played back in class, gave her returning husband a hell of a time for leaving her. The women's responses to the men proved to be far more probing than the men's responses to the women. Male students playing the husbands could only say they were sorry for being "infatuated" by "the other woman." None of them suggested that monogamy was incompatible with human sexuality, especially with the aggressive male sexuality our society imposes on men. They did not give an institutional defense of their impulses.

Up to this point, our analysis of the poem was able to expose how the wife buried her passions, talents and ambitions to serve husband, house and kids, and how the mistress had a romantic freedom at the cost of her loneliness and insecurity. Students had been vigorously writing, speaking, acting and arguing on issues they felt strongly about.

I then raised the question of having both sides of the duality, of unfreezing the alienation of passion from security, of women being all they can be and still enjoying romance. Few thought this was possible. Some women romanticized their future marriages as capable of both freedom and stability. Older women in our class demystified this illusion, in a very direct and fruitful exchange between different aged females. I had been uncomfortable with the dichotomy posed by the poem and found no transcendence in the narrative of its beautifully articulated dilemma. The class couldn't imagine one either. With a friend who is a radical feminist I taped a dialogue between the husband and the mistress where we discussed the institutional dimension of the dilemma, the replacement of monogamy-promiscuity with communal marriage. The class listened to the tape and thought the proposal was abstract and unconvincing. As I listened to that tape again, I too kept feeling an unreality to the dialogue. A number of couples I know now are considering the issue of open marriage and accept its theoretical correctness, but the resolution of this impulse has yet to become an historical fact which convinces us of its practical possibility.

Did the poem tell us anything about men's liberation? We tended to agree that the husband had had other affairs before and that he would have another affair again. Few believed that monogamy would satisfy the man's sexuality even though most of the men in class were unmarried, and could not speak from direct experience. What was more on their minds than the romance with the poetess, were the consequences of marriage. They saw their marriage side of the triangle -- all the bills and debts were theirs alone to make good. The wife was imprisoned at home, and the husband at-large in the world, but the price of the husband's freedom was his entrapment by the competitive job system, by career, boss and creditor. The wife could avoid these, but she had to invest all her emotions in children who would grow up and away from her, in a house that always needed cleaning, in a husband whose sexual needs could not be satisfied by her body alone. On balance, we agreed that the man still had the better deal. To escalate the consequences of male privilege, I quoted statistics on how men die early from high blood pressure, ulcers and heart attacks. This prophecy sunk in only momentarily, because young people have a certain feeling of physical invulnerability.

On the whole, our long attention to this beautifully crafted poem did more for the women than for the men. The men with their sense of privilege seem more willing to play society's bourgeois game than the women with their individual sense of exploitation. For the balance of the semester there remained an articulate women's voice in class which the men never matched. Towards the end of the term, a committee of women evolved to study women's liberation and over two class hours they made a very detailed, researched and positive report on the history and current status of feminism. Two men started an anti-women's liberation committee and made a report as well. The women in class rose in a body, tore down each of their arguments and nearly hooted them out of the room.

DIVING INTO THE WRECK:
THE WOMAN WRITER IN THE TWENTIETH CENTURY

by Melanie Kaye

> the thing I came for:
> the wreck and not the story of
> the wreck...*

It is a relief to be writing this essay at a time when I no longer
have to justify the existence of women's studies, but can instead share
what I learned about how a women's class works, what its possibilities
are, from teaching such a course. I write not only from experience
sifted through the haze of memory, but from running journal comments of
mine and of my students, from tapes of our classes, student evaluations,
and long conversations.** In a sense, this essay constitutes our collective evaluation of our course on the woman writer in the twentieth
century.

I

Your class is great, but it needs a leader to watch
over it.... I don't think the books we've read were given
their justice.

The class discussions, particularly towards the end,
were very good. Surprisingly good, I thought.... Towards
the beginning of the class, I was worried that it wouldn't
work -- that we were too directionless, and any possibility
that you could salvage the class was lost because you were
taking too weak a role.... I'm so used to being lectured at
that I don't think as much as I know I should.... The non-
teacher teacher role you took in the class was very effective.

The discussions were generally stimulating and fruitful,
although I felt personality conflicts which were never completely worked through.... The class was something we all
cared about and were very involved in.

I found the group discussions upsetting and rarely
fruitful. The smaller group meetings, in contrast, were

* From Adrienne Rich, "Diving Into the Wreck."
** I want to thank Lauren Coodley, Sandra Flitterman, Dianne Levitin,
and Ruth Wilson, class members and friends, for their suggestions; and
to acknowledge my debt, intellectual and other, to Nancy Hoffman.
Hoffman's articles, "A Class of Our Own" (Female Studies IV) and
"Women's Poetry: The Meaning and Our Lives" (College English, Oct. 72)
have been both helpful and inspiring to me.

wonderful, for in those we treated each other as humans deserving of courtesy. Large discussions were usually dominated by a few people. The most valuable experience of the class was in how it started me seeing things in a new light, and increased my awareness.

These are excerpts from some of the open-ended evaluations I requested at term end. At first, I was bewildered by the variety of responses: were they talking about the same class? But recalling the essays they had written at the beginning of the quarter, explaining why they wanted the class, what they hoped to accomplish in it, I realized what should have been obvious: women took the class for different reasons (from "I'm an English major and everywhere I look I see men: male writers, male heroes, male professors. I want to know where I fit in," to "I'm curious about why women writers are inferior to men."), had different expectations, and therefore acted and reacted in widely differing ways. Some students wanted more direction from me, wanted the class to be an academic literature class dealing with a specified subject which, in this case, happened to be literature by women. Most, I think, agreed with me in principle that the class should be shaped by the students, that the books should be discussed in terms of our lives and our politics, that we should use these books to find out about ourselves and other women, to shape for ourselves a world vision in which we would be "subjects", not "others". I happen to believe that the point of formal literary analysis is to figure out what is being said so that one can evaluate it and use it; some of the more political or less literary women were impatient with this first step.

Part of our difficulty came from the composition of the class. I wanted a heterogeneous group, not easy to attain at an elite university. I selected a cross-section of upper and lower class-women, majors and non-majors, and left space for some auditors, a couple of married women with children, a couple of women like myself who had been married. I wanted women with different experiences to bring to the class; about one-quarter of the women were feminists, perhaps one-half had had no previous contact with any aspect of the women's movement.*

* In response to the question I am asked any time I talk about the course: "What about men students?": A few men wanted to enroll in the class. I preferred to restrict the class to women, for reasons which Nancy Hoffman has elaborated (in "A Class of Our Own") and because I wanted a small class and didn't want to displace women by men. So I arranged a compromise with the few interested men. They enrolled in the class, read the books, and met with each other, apart from the class. I met with them a few times during the term, so that they had, basically, an independent studies course. They kept journals on their reading, thinking, and discussions, as did the women. I had felt a bit shaky about the separate but equal solution initially, but the journals and our meetings convinced me that such a compromise provides a valuable experience for the men without infringing upon the women.

What happened is something I've seen happen in consciousness-raising groups, something I've read about in feminist publications. The radical women tended to see the class as <u>their</u> class; they were the most articulate and confident; and our first few group discussions were largely dominated by these women sharing amongst themselves feminist truths. I believe in these truths, and certainly didn't want to put down women who were finally getting a chance to bring their most important beliefs into the classroom. And I thought the less aware women would learn from the more involved (I think they probably did). But those who had not yet been exposed to feminism felt intimidated; a "more radical than thou" atmosphere quickly permeated the class; the radical women, feeling their oats, were by and large insensitive to the discomfort of their sisters; in short, a new caste of "men" was developing in the class, and the remaining "women" sat passively, accepting their subjugation. One student writes: "In the large discussions, I got so frustrated sometimes, that I stopped listening."

I don't think this problem was ever entirely solved. The women who have "expertise" should somehow be made to feel responsible for those who don't, should be concerned with explaining rather than proselytizing, and, frankly, I don't know how to make this happen in a first-term class. However, several women from this term's class will work in the women's classes next year as discussion leaders and co-planners. Sensitized to the problem of intimidation, and with a teacher's sense of responsibility to her students, these women will, I think, help set a different tone during the first awkward weeks.*

But structures and processes evolved which <u>did</u> help the class to work. I made a list of suggested supplementary readings on feminist theory (appended at end) from the anthologies <u>Sisterhood is Powerful</u> and <u>The Black Woman</u>. This should be done on the first day of class, so that women who come into the class cold can get some sense of what feminism is about, learn the vocabulary, have a chance to ponder the issues in private before mind-blowing concepts are thrown at them.

We structured the class so that once a week, we all met together (referred to above as the "large discussions"); during our other weekly meeting, we broke into small rap groups. The more vocal women preferred the larger meetings, but it was in the small groups that the quieter women got to talk and listen, got to feel comfortable ("although," as Jamie wrote, "the books themselves were not always discussed."). I had to hold myself back sometimes from pushing literary analysis on students whose minds went from the books to their own lives; and I know some of the women were frustrated by the lack of "justice" done particularly to the books we read early in the term, while we were still finding a way to talk about books and life together.

* At date of publication, this is happening -- 3 women from last spring's class are working as discussion leaders and, as expected, the stratification of the spring class has not shown itself.

For the large group meetings, a few of the students prepared class presentations, drawing upon other works, critical sources in the few cases where these existed, and their own questions and insights about the books. Sometimes these worked, sometimes they were uninspiring or simply dull. I know I learned far more as a teacher than I ever did in my nine years as a university student, so I think the experience of preparing a class is invaluable for the students who are doing it, but is it fair to the others? Is it fair to the books? Here, the key factor seems to me to be time: if the teacher and students can prepare well in advance, meet together and plan the class, these student preparations do work. I did not take charge of the sometimes floundering discussions, in an effort to salvage them which tends to translate as "you are in charge as long as you run the class as I do." The result was that in this class, unlike any other I've either taught or participated in, the students' sense of commitment and sense of responsibility equalled the teacher's. By mid-term, we no longer needed formal presentations as a starting-point. Women brought books, articles, poems, came to class talking, and stayed late to continue. Class discussions took on the quality of intense conversation.

In addition to a substantial reading list (appended at end), each student was required to keep a journal and to do a project. The journal was to consist of three strands: notes, thoughts, and responses to the reading; reaction to and evaluation of each class meeting; and whatever one would normally write in a journal. I was motivated to make this assignment by Lessing's The Golden Notebook: an attempt to put together in one place some of the fragments of a normal student's life. I did not ask to read the journals, but the women brought them to class, and when we met in small groups, might read from them. The students who wrote responses to the books were able to contribute most to discussions and to profit most from them (again, my evidence is the evaluations). And those who kept tabs on the class, as I was doing, were better equipped to deal with some of the problems I have already described. Nearly everyone was enthusiastic about the more private uses of the journal; the students stressed its value both for improving their writing and examining their lives.

The projects were astonishing. I offered advice when requested, but left the choice of subject and genre open; and I can best urge other teachers to encourage such space in their own classes by describing some of the results: a taped interview on sexual attitudes and roles with male and female residents of a student cooperative; a comparison of Esther in The Bell Jar with Maria in Play It as It Lays; an autobiography culled from ten years of diaries; an analysis of the roles of the oppressor and the oppressed as seen in literature; a mixed media autobiography, composed of creative vignettes, photographs, and poetry; a paper on the psychology of women, drawing upon the literature we read and upon observations of the class; a slide and tape rendering of Solanis' SCUM MANIFESTO; a superb piece of biographical criticism on Dorothy Parker.

And the best film I've seen on women, created from scratch by seven of the students, using paintings, photographs, and poetry, music,

excerpts from literature, and a series of questions, organized the-
matically to progress from images of oppression to images of strength.
Beginning with a shot of Botticelli's Venus on the half-shell, moving
up her legs, as a man might eye a woman, with Janis Joplin singing "Take
another little piece of my heart." Later, the camera scanning a paint-
ing by the Surrealist Delvaux which depicts women rooted to the ground,
their lower torsos metamorphosing into trees, as a woman says:

> We are all one. We are all sisters. We are bound by the
> same constraints. If some of us are more successful than
> others, it is only because we are less crippled. Not
> because we are superior. Not because we are different.

Ending with photographs of Georgia O'Keefe, and Buffy Sainte Marie singing "It's My Way." We intend to make prints of this film and hope to
show it to other women's classes, to high school audiences, to women's
clubs. Valerie wrote, "Despite the amount of time it took to produce,
and the disputes, we, a group of seven women, created from nothing a
statement about our feelings and questions we have. What is beautiful
is that we can share it with others...."

Those who elected to write literary essays did not write the kinds
of papers I had written for my literature classes or listened to in
seminars, papers useful only to the writer. They did not avoid the
techniques of formal literary analysis (as Vicki wrote, "that would
give the impression that the work couldn't withstand a formal analysis"),
but they also dealt with the lives of women: their own lives, the lives
of the writers, the lives of the characters; and they confronted the
political realities shaping these lives.

Another facet of our class, and one which generated many of the
projects, was the extra meetings. Reading Maya Angelou's moving autobiography, I Know Why the Caged Bird Sings, I conceived the idea of
asking all of us to write an autobiographical episode, and we met evenings
in small groups to read them to each other. For many of us, it was the
first attempt at non-academic writing in a long time, and certainly the
first time we'd presented something so close to ourselves to a group of
classmates. Several things happened: we were all amazed to hear so
much good writing. Comments ran not "that's good" but "what was it like?
how did you feel? what happened?" Instead of criticizing, we tried to
understand each other, and the warmth and communication showed up in
class. Women began to work on their own creative writing, and a writing
workshop sprang up. Some women decided to write autobiographies or
stories for their projects. We know many more male writers than female,
and while part of the explanation lies in discriminatory standards of
judgment (what Mary Ellman has called "phallic criticism"), we have to
acknowledge that more men write and publish than women. With women
writers as models, with structures like the autobiography meetings (a
relatively unfrightening beginning) and the writing workshop, those of
our students who used to write -- and how many students of literature
used to write -- can be encouraged to try again.

Other extra meetings just happened. From reading The Golden Note-book came a meeting on sexuality. From The Bell Jar and I Never Promised You a Rose Garden came a potluck dinner with a woman psychologist to discuss with us "women and madness." From the encroaching end of the term came an extra meeting on poetry. Lauren discovered the Women's Media Workshop in San Francisco and brought a series of tapes for yet another extra meeting. Some of us went to see a dramatization of Nin's diary, and talked afterwards with the actresses. I instigated some of these meetings, others were set up by students. I think that had I presented my students with a series of dazzling literary analyses, these extra meetings would not have happened. Organization is always a problem in an open structure such as our class was, but my relinquishing power released energy in the students. Some women came to class and went home. Many more participated in the extra activities, which were valuable in themselves and for the sense of cohesion which carried over into the class.

II

> has Nature shown
> her household books to you, daughter-in-law,
> that her sons never saw?*

The structures I have mentioned above facilitated our hearing each other. I will concentrate below on some of the classes that did work, and on the questions that were fruitful.

Janet Lewis' novel, The Wife of Martin Guerre, drawn from the annals of sixteenth century France, gave us an historical perspective on woman's status; and as we examined each facet of woman's oppression then, we were forced to ask about the other works we read, about our own lives: how different is it now?

We look through Bertrande's eyes at her father-in-law and see how women depended on masculine authority, how the whole cosmos was ordered for her by the patriarchal presence:

> He ruled, as the contemporary records say, using the
> verb which belongs to royalty, and the young girl seated
> beside him, in feeling this, felt also the great peace which
> his authority created for his household. It was the first of
> many evenings in which his presence should testify for her
> that the beasts were safe, that the grain was safe, that
> neither the wolves, whose voices could be heard on winter
> nights, nor marauding bands of mercenaries such as the cur-
> rent hearsay from the larger valleys sometimes reported,
> could do anything to harm the hearth beside which this man
> was seated. Because of him the farm was safe, and therefore
> Artigues, and therefore Languedoc, and therefore France, and
> therefore the whole world was safe and as it should be." (p. 23)

* From Adrienne Rich, "Snapshots of a Daughter-in-Law."

"How safe," someone asks, "do we feel without a man?"

In Bertrande, we find the archetypal figure of Penelope, the woman waiting, whom we recognize in The Golden Notebook ("the stupid standing at the window waiting for a man whom she knew, quite well, would never come to her again." p. 227), in Toni Brown's song, "Red Wine at Noon":

The man that I married, he travels in Europe
And he brings me back presents from over the sea.
He meets with officials and shakes hands with strangers
Then comes home to visit with me....
...I'll be here when the evening comes,
And where have you been so long?"*

and, with pain, in our own lives. We are frightened by the way in which Bertrande experiences history, as something she hears about from travellers, over which she has no control, which concerns her only insofar as it affects the man for whom she waits. Beauvoir's concepts, transcendence and immanence, are starkly exemplified, and someone asks, "how many of our mothers wait at home while our fathers deal with the larger world?"

Sandy remarks that the historical authenticity of the story forces us to take it more seriously, and someone raises the more general question: Why are women writers so attached to truth, to autobiography or near-autobiography (Angelou, Nin, Lessing, Sexton, Plath, Green)? Why is the gap between art and life so horrifying to Lessing?

We look at the novel's end, at the wife of Martin Guerre who "walk[s] through a great emptiness...knowing herself at last free, in her bitter, solitary justice, of both passions and of both men," (p. 108) and ask, what is this burned-out freedom she achieves? Can we be free and remain in touch with our sexuality? Can we love if we have no identity of our own, if our very name is "the wife of....?" Or Mrs. John Smith?

Lauren rewrites a section of Shirley Williams' story, "Tell Martha Not to Moan," changing the pungent and poetic black dialect of the narrative to the language of Cosmopolitan magazine, and reads it to us. We talk about the loss of impact, the nature of Black language(s). We ask, do women have their own language? and the questions we come back to throughout the term and never satisfactorily answer: what is different about literature by women? what do we mean by "women's language," what Woolf calls a "woman's sentence?" How does the experience of the black woman differ from that of the white woman? The one black woman in the class expresses some anger at us for talking about Martha's experience as though Martha represents all black women. What of the black middle-class woman like myself? she asks. Someone talks about the archetypal figures in the story, the black mother, the black bitch, and again Ruth hallenges us: archetype sounds to her suspiciously close to stereotype.

* from "The Joy of Cooking" (first album).

Someone raises the question of audience: is the story geared to
black or white readers? I mention that Martha's lover, Time, twice
parrots Iago's assertion of his ethic: "Put money in my purse;" "I am not
what I am." How important is it that we catch the allusion? What does
it mean for the black musician who says "black is beautiful" to echo the
white Machiavellian who betrays and entraps the magnificent Moor? Has
whitey gotten into Time? Is Martha to be pitied for her naive belief
that Time will come back (does time ever come back?), or envied for the
strength it gives her?

In a discussion of Anaïs Nin's second diary, the women who liked
Nin were attacked by those who preferred Lessing because they saw the
choice as a political -- or apolitical -- choice. "Nin thinks you make
the revolution inside your head. She's elitist. She's always looking
for justification from men." I talk of Nin's sometimes devastating
honesty, her perceptions about women, the sense I get from her of what to
avoid, the dangers of being a man-centered woman, and Cathy reads the
remarkable passage in the second diary on mirrors, ending:

> Every girl of fifteen has put the same question to a
> mirror: "Am I beautiful?" The face is masklike. It does
> not smile. It does not want to charm the mirror or deceive
> the mirror, or flirt with it and gain a false answer. The
> girl is in a trance. She does not want to frighten the re-
> flection away herself. Someone has said she is very pale.
> She approaches the mirror and stands very still like a
> statue. Immobile. Waxy. She never makes a gesture. Sur-
> prised. Somnambulistic? She only moves to become someone
> else, impersonating Sarah Bernhardt, Mélisande, La Dame aux
> Camélias, Madame Bovary, Thaïs. She is never Anaïs Nin who
> goes to school, and grows vegetables and flowers in her back-
> yard. She is immobile, haunting, like a figure moving in a
> dream. She is discomposed before the mirror into a hundred
> personages, recomposed into paleness and immobility. Silence.
> She is watching for an expression which will betray the spirit.
> You can never catch the face alive, laughing, or loving. At
> sixteen she is looking at the mirror with her hair up for the
> first time. There is always the question. The mirror is not
> going to answer it. She will have to look for the answer in
> the eyes and faces of the boys who dance with her, men later,
> and above all the painters. (p. 182)

We talk of the connection between women and mirrors, our need of them; the
symbol of women, the sign of Venus that we have adopted for our movement:
♀, the looking glass; and the opening lines of Marilyn Hoff's song, "I
Can Live Alone:"

> Nothing hides behind the mirror
>   but a nail driven deep in the wall
> and the face of a featureless terror,
>   if ever the mirror should fall....

From other women I have learned that the Nin-Lessing dichotomy seems to be endemic to a women's literature class. Our students need models of new women, and if Molly and Anna seem only a step above Nin, and Lessing herself provides no answers but madness and art that must lie, still, she does depict the texture of lives that come close to ours, she does grapple with political questions. Some of our students are angered by Nin, by writers who trace a path that leads to the eyes of a man, or to immersion in Mother Earth, to separation from the less gifted, less lucky women. Lauren suggests that we are disturbed by Nin because we are still attracted by the paths we have only very recently learned to shun.

At our last class of the term, on A Room of One's Own, we tried to evaluate Woolf's contention that fine art must come from the "incandescent mind," a mind untroubled by anger, a mind without points to strike home; and in terms of this contention, to measure the works we had read during the term. Is Woolf saying that art should not embody political thought? Did she write A Room of One's Own to keep her novels free from feminist rage?

Sir Philip Sidney is often mocked for himself mocking the mingling of kings and clowns, hornpipes and funerals, in English tragedy, but would he have condemned such a mixture had he lived to see Shakespeare? Would Woolf have condemned political art had she lived to read Lessing? What should be the relationship between art and politics? Must the artist, in our own time, be antagonistic to the values of her society, and does such antagonism doom us to second-rate art? Do we need to re-define "great art?" (An emphatic "yes!") Can we afford the luxury of what has been traditionally defined as great art? Should our artists, should we, set ourselves apart from the turmoil with which we are sur-rounded in an attempt to render our minds incandescent?

III

Betty Friedan wrote of the problem that has no name. In our class, we asked mostly questions that have no answers. This was upsetting and frustrating, because our questions are not arbitrary intellectual exercises. We need the answers.

But as I write this essay, mid-August, our class is still meeting; not for credit, not for grades, but because we are still trying to create those answers. The students who will be working with next year's classes will not only make the classes function better, but will form a base from which a woman's studies program can be launched. We are talking of sending out groups of women into the community, to high schools, women's clubs, to show our film, to present programs on women and lit-erature. We are meeting with other women who are teaching women's classes to figure out ways of sharing resources, of learning from each other's disciplines. Funding a women's studies department seems to me not very crucial at this stage. We live in an imperfect world and money is useful; but I think a core group of students, committed to establishing women's studies and permitted a base to operate from, makes a better beginning than an administratively-controlled department.

I can best conclude this essay in the mood in which our class was largely conducted: the interrogative. At our most recent meeting, after discussing Joan Didion's Play It as It Lays, another journey into a kind of madness foreign to most of us, and making plans to read Christina Stead's masterpiece, The Man Who Loved Children, a brilliant but painful examination of the nuclear family, Vicki asked "aren't there any uppers?" Woolf comes as close to any of our writers to finding sense in the whole business of living, but her own end makes us suspicious or frightened of its value. We have read, talked about, meditated upon the sources of our oppression, our collective madness, and the outrageously high price we must pay for our "sanity." What now?

Adrienne Rich writes of our search for the sunken treasure of our selves, our descent into our undiscovered past, carrying "a book of myths/ in which/ our names do not appear."* In our class, we read together books in which our names do appear, and what we read will, like it or not, affect our lives. We who are privileged to teach women's classes must leave space in our classrooms for our students to deal openly with these changes. And we must provide a place for them (and for ourselves) to continue growing, more women's classes to explore our potential for change, and structures for sharing these changes with the community of women.

* Again, from "Diving Into the Wreck."

Syllabus for Comparative Literature 40C,
"The Woman Writer in the Twentieth Century" (10 weeks) Spring '72

Simone de Beauvoir, The Second Sex.
Janet Lewis, The Wife of Martin Guerre.
Maya Angelou, I Know Why the Caged Bird Sings.
Shirley Williams, "Tell Martha Not To Moan," in The Black Woman,
    ed. Toni Cade.
Nikki Giovanni and Gwendolyn Brooks, poems.
Anais Nin, Diary, vol. II. (Several students suggested, and I agree, that
    we should have begun with the first volume.)
Doris Lessing, The Golden Notebook.
Hannah Green, I Never Promised You a Rose Garden. (This seemed to me
    the most dispensible book we read; many of the students had read it
    before, found the style not particularly admirable, and the tone a
    little simple-minded as compared to Plath.)
Sylvia Plath, The Bell Jar.
Plath, poems from Colossus and Ariel.
Anne Sexton, poems from Love Poems and Live or Die.
Virginia Woolf, Mrs. Dalloway and A Room of One's Own. (Some of the
    students thought it would be better to begin the course with A Room
    of One's Own.)

**A semester course would have included the following books which have
    spilled over into the summer:

Joan Didion, Play It As It Lays.
Christina Stead, The Man Who Loved Children.
Djuna Barnes, Nightwood.
Marge Piercy, poems from Breaking Camp and Hard Loving.
Joanna Griffin, poems (alas, unpublished).
Denise Levertov, poems from The Sorrow Dance and Learning the Alphabet.
Adrienne Rich, poems from Snapshots for a Daughter-in-Law, Leaflets,
    The Will to Change.

Supplementary Reading:

In The Black Woman:
Beale, "Double Jeopardy: To Be Black and Female," pp. 90-100.
Clark, "Motherhood," pp. 73-79.
In Sisterhood is Powerful:
Piercy, "The Grand Coolie Damn," pp. 421-437.
Moss, "It Hurts to be Alive and Obsolete: The Aging Woman," pp. 170-174.
Jones, "The Dynamics of Marriage and Motherhood," pp. 46-61.
Weisstein, "Kinder, Küche, Kirche" as Scientific Law: Psychology Constructs
    the Female," pp. 205-220.
"Know Your Enemy: A Sampling of Sexist Quotes," pp. 31-36.
Joreen, "The 51% Minority Group: A Statistical Essay," pp. 37-45.
Damon, "The Least of These: The Minority Whose Screams Haven't Yet Been
    Heard," pp. 297-306.
Shelley, "Notes of a Radical Lesbian," pp. 306-310.
Piercy, "The Song of the Fucked Duck," pp. 502-504.

A LITERATURE COURSE OF OUR OWN: WOMEN'S STUDIES WITHOUT WALLS

by Janet Sass

Our course differs from many "woman and literature" courses in traditional and free universities, for we read only women writers and teach ourselves. In addition to introducing us to women writers, our course is consciousness raising; teaches us how to work together; and increases our self-confidence and critical ability. Many of us needed women friends and the course fulfilled that need.

Now we want to share our experiences with other women. We propose that you participate in a similar woman-writer oriented, self-taught course within a university or high school, or in the community.

Our course (there are nine of us[1]) began in Fall 1971, co-sponsored by two Washington, D.C., women's groups. It was originally designed as a non-credit seminar with the traditional teacher, students and syllabi. But due to the teacher's disorganization, we "students" soon realized that the class would fold -- or we would have to make decisions regarding subject matter and structure. It was at this point that our literature course really began.

WHY READ ONLY WOMEN?

Our teacher had chosen Sinclair Lewis' Main Street as the first reading; but the students, after four hours of discussion, decided that Lewis had given Carol Kennicott a raw deal. Contrary to the book jacket blurb, Main Street better describes the failure of the Progressive Movement in the early 20th century than it does the problems of an emancipated woman in small-town USA. And if Carol fails to work

---

1 We come from blue-collar and middle and upper-middle class backgrounds. We are married, single and gay. One of us is black, the rest white, ranging in age from 22 to 65. One woman has a Ph.D. in literature; many of us have had some graduate training; all of us have B.A.'s. Some of us are members of other women's groups. At this point in our lives, we are housewives, mothers, dropout graduate students, professionals, artists and part-time typists.
   In addition, we had two important things in common. We were all readers who believed in the power of literature. It went beyond our everyday experiences and defined the realm of human possibility. Reading was a way to learn about ourselves and to grow. Secondly,

out her ambivalence regarding women's roles and her personal goals,
it may be because Lewis wants her to fail -- not because she has
to fail given the limits of his book.

Reading Lewis made us question other men writers: "Was it really
possible that all these so-called literary greats had bypassed --
or at best distorted -- the female half of human experience?" asks
Marie, one of our group's members. "Was it possible that we had read
men for years and never noticed this peculiarity? Was it possible
that we had never read Mary Ann Evans, Doris Lessing, Sylvia Plath,
Simone de Beauvoir, Virginia Woolf and Gertrude Stein, to name only
a few, and never cared before whether we did or not?"

As with other similar revelations of the past few years, our
immediate response was resentment and anger: we'd been duped and
cheated again. But we eventually realized that this sort of revelation
was what personal and group growth was all about. A sense of discovery crept over us. Like Doris Lessing's Martha Quest, we began
to wonder:

Would we find any women who could describe women's culture and
consciousness; any women who had managed to survive the blinding of
conditioning and convention; any women who could offer some insight
into the forces that had shaped our lives and ways to overcome those
forces?

And we did. It was exciting, electrifying. American Literature
201 was never like this. We read Mary Ann Evans (Middlemarch); Doris
Lessing (A Proper Marriage); Simone de Beauvoir (The Second Sex,
Prime of Life); Jane Addams (Twenty Years at Hull-House); Maya Angelou
(I Know Why the Caged Bird Sings); Sylvia Plath (The Bell Jar, Ariel);
and Margaret Mead (Male and Female). (But reading Sinclair Lewis
wasn't a total waste of time. Lewis didn't completely ignore women's
experiences and consciousness and Main Street sensitized us to questions we needed to think about as we read women.)

Since we had nearly always read men writers in high school and
college (for example, less than 7% of the novels used by the University of Maryland's English Department are by women), reading women
was a positive educational experience. It introduced us to women
writers and increased our appreciation of them. We learned that women were not second-rate authors, contrary to our conditioning.

We began to see women as active as opposed to passive individuals. Many women's books center on a woman trying to make the best
of a bad situation or, against all odds, trying to overcome limiting
circumstances. Although there were suicides and failures, we found

---

we all felt a need, no matter how incoherently expressed, to interact with other women.

these attempts by women to gain control over their lives courageous and epic-like. Barbara says it well: "I have acquired a new understanding of the complexity of women's lives and their struggles. Realizing the complexity helps eliminate sterotypical thinking about women."

Reading women also made us more aware of the positive aspects of female culture, such as women's strong concern with relationships and attention to detail. We haven't been much concerned with the traditional tools of literary analysis -- plot, characterization, imagery -- but have posed the following questions in an attempt to define "a feminist view of literature."

What is unique about the female writer's point of view? What does this book tell us about women of a certain age, class or historical period? Does this writer portray women in relation to men or as distinct individuals? Could a man have written this book? How does literature socialize women? What is the difference between a feminist rebellion and a middle-class rebellion? What does this book say about my life?

Despite nearly seven months of painful examinations and incoherent ramblings, we haven't yet defined "a feminist viewpoint" to our satisfaction. We look forward to help from other women in this project.

CONSCIOUSNESS RAISING SIMILARITIES

Since we are individually concerned with understanding ourselves as women, a literature course can be consciousness raising -- as well as educational in the academic sense. For example, formal education had compartmentalized us. We now sensed a gap between what we were taught in school and the reality of our present lives. Discussion of women writers' books, because they described experiences common to us as women -- pregnancy, child care, housework, marriage, loss of virginity -- brought together our intellect and our feelings; made "book learning" relevant.

Sara says, "For two and a half years, I had been drifing from the first complacency of late marriage and first child down and down into the confusion of integrating these two myth-laden experiences with the rest of my life. No amount of rationalizing the joy of being at home with free time had ever worked. . . .

"I read madly. I laughed wildly, with joy and pain until my husband asked what was so funny; and when I read him the passages, he said he couldn't see what was so funny. But, what was funny was that Mary Ann Evans had been there all along, and I'd been unaware of her. Now the phrases which had shot over the head of the little-experienced college girl I had been shot right into my head and heart."

Suzi, who joined the course very late in the year and missed
much of the experience, says of herself: "She had missed most of it,
but a little had been wonderful. She needed these people who cared
about books, and women, and the men and children and illusions in
their lives. And from this group, and this feminist viewpoint, she
might have learned how she could begin to discipline her freedom, her
reading, her fear and distrust of all the things the world expected
of her: the JOB, the Mortgage, the Wonderful, Glorious, Fringe Benefits,
the Social Security and running out the door to catch the bus 365
days a year and the role playing to bosses and fellow employees and
potential husbands. . . ."

Francelia experienced isolation as the group's only Black member, but came to define her relationship to the Women's Movement
partly through participating in the course. "Black women (and men)
have GOT to be part of the movement. They must put far, far, behind
them the fear, distrust and hatred of white women and forget the
interracial sex problem; and fling themselves wholeheartedly into
the battle for equal pay, freedom of reproduction, egalitarian family
styles and political power."

As you can see, our course is similar to consciousness raising
in that it helps us deal with our personal and political lives. Yet
it differs from CR in that we are not exploring our problems and
feelings directly but through literature, using the ideas and experiences of both group members and women writers as resources. In
other words, we discuss our personal reactions to a book -- why it
"touches" us -- but rarely our personal problems at length. Barbara
might say in a discussion, "I sympathize with Martha Quest. I too
could never get myself to like baby spinach thrown at me." But instead of talking about Barbara's attitudes toward infant care, we
discussed Lessing's analysis of the way marriage limits a woman's
alternatives. Or Janet might say, "Reading de Beauvoir was a nightmare. I had expected her to be a role model for my life but instead
found her elitist." Rather than talking about Janet's need for a
role model, we discussed the assumptions and values underlying The
Second Sex.

Unlike CR, our course does not demand emotional intimacy between
group members. A literature course (or any feminist course) is a
safe beginning for those women who need to interact with other women, but are not yet able to reveal their feelings or personal problems -- or deal with other women's personal problems -- in CR.

IMPORTANCE OF STRUCTURE

It seems to us that many women studies programs, which invest
enormous energy into defining subject matter, ignore the importance
of classroom structure. Textbooks and lectures are not the only
sources of learning in the classroom; values are also transmitted

through the structure of the learning environment. We think a collective (or self-taught) classroom environment is particularly good for women.

In the traditional classroom, the teacher -- whether male or female -- is often an authority figure. This authority figure reinforces the woman student's passivity, lack of confidence and dependence on leaders. She turns to the teacher for knowledge, rather than developing critical skills and self-confidence in expressing her opinions.

The traditional classroom is also competitive and devisive with its emphasis on grades. Students and teacher often play one-upmanship games and try to impress each other with their knowledge; women are often intimidated by men students and those people with articulateness. These factors limit real communication. Competition may be useful in certain situations, but learning depends on meaningful exchanges, not ego games. The traditional classroom doesn't teach people how to work together for common goals; it doesn't delineate when competition is appropriate behavior and when cooperation is. It divides feelings from intellect.

Our classroom environment is very different from that described above. There are no authority figures and we try to maximize cooperation between members. We encourage people to care genuinely about each other and each others' ideas. We encourage reflection on personal experiences when that reflection is relevant to the point being disucssed. We try to work together as a group. It's a give-and-take interaction between women rather than the lecture/test approach.

This structure evolved very slowly and very gradually over the weeks, in response to our needs. Decisions were reached only after a problem of organization arose and we talked until we reached consensus. Many of us had difficulty working and learning in a non-hierarchical setting. Products of this society, we could only function when authority was clearly delineated. We could take orders or give orders, but couldn't work in an egalitarian setting or discipline ourselves to assume responsibility.

Our first group decision was that each woman would choose a book for the class to read and would "lead" that particular meeting. She would interrupt chit-chat at the beginning of the class to open discussion; she would provide pertinent background information; she could center the discussion on questions that interested her; she would explain why she chose that particular author. In a sense, she played the role of the "teacher" or "expert," but with one important difference -- each woman was an "expert."

We came to believe that each woman in the group, because of her experiences as a woman, could contribute to a discussion of feminist literature; each woman had something to contribute to the group. As a result of this attitude, educational and class categories broke down. We deferred less and less to the class Ph.D.

As we discussed books among ourselves, tried to define "a feminist view of literature" and planned the structure, we became more confident of our opinions and less willing to automatically accept those viewpoints of "authorities," such as establishment literary critics. Our respect for ourselves and each other increased.

Penny says, "Our course is not part of the lonely, isolating, competitive, grade-stressing academic scene that had freaked me out in graduate school. This is my first course in which the class is supportive enough for me to express as freely as I can my ideas, often half-baked, as they come to me."

Just as the course was supportive intellectually, it was supportive emotionally. No one had to say (and no one did), "Janet, don't feel so insecure. You're not inadequate or stupid." The structure in itself made her feel secure, adequate and bright.

Other group decisions: We decided to sit in a circle, for good communication is enhanced by eye-to-eye contact. We tried to develop listening skills: hearing what is expressed, what is implied, and the importance of what is left out. (Women often have so little self-confidence because no one really listens to them or attempts to draw them out.) We decided it was important to convene the course outside of someone's home, with its implications of coffee and cookies. Meeting in a women's professional building was good psychologically. It gave us a sense of seriousness. This was especially important to those women who questioned the legitimacy of women's concerns versus child care or other commitments.

We realize that educational reformers in high schools and universities are limited by administrators, classroom size and the demand for grades. The kind of structure described here isn't completely applicable in a rigid school system. But teachers can let their students participate in setting goals, defining standards and grading. They can be nondogmatic and let their students make their own discoveries. They can allow students to discuss their personal feelings without eliminating such discussion as silly or worthless. They can cut down on lectures and encourage discussions and group projects.

PROBLEMS....

Of course, we continue to have group dynamic problems: How to get some women to interrupt less and listen more; how to be supportive of women you don't like; how to deal with the unintended stupidities

of some class members regarding ideas, life-styles or sexual prefer-
ences of others; how to deal with women who set up roadblocks to
group closeness or good discussion. (For an outline of problem areas,
see Cynthia's questions at the end of the article.)

For example, disciplining is supposed to be a communal affar.
In theory, any woman can tell another, "You're interrupting." "You're
on a tangent." "You're ego-tripping." In practice, this is difficult
to accomplish. Too often women are afraid of offending another,
without realizing it's possible to be critical without being cruel.
Then we've been conditioned to smile and be sweet -- even when doubled
with anger. (How do we overcome all our inhibitions against expressing
anger?) As you can see, we've been able to define our problems with
great success, but it's been a struggle to solve them.

So far, we've found it's necessary to try constantly to be tolerant, open, and understanding. Disagreements are inevitable in any
group, but disagreements in an atmosphere of openness can prevent
anger from fragmenting the group into hostility or confusion. In an
atmosphere of openness, a confrontation can clear the air and strengthen
the group. It's destructive to repress anger in order to avoid a
scene, being stigmatized "emotional," or to avoid revealing true feelings
to the group. Repressed anger eventually surfaces later, disguised,
and much more difficult to cope with.

There's an unfortunate tendency in some groups to insist that
personality conflicts are unimportant, that it is a waste of time to
deal with them when there are "larger" problems of goals, theories,
projects, We disagree. It's nearly impossible to deal with those
"larger" problems when the group is fragmented by personality differences.

But despite these problems and the struggle to solve them, the
course continues to be a positive experience for us -- for all the
reasons mentioned above; introducing us to women writers; consciousness raising; and providing intellectual and emotional support. One
of the most important aspects of our course has been its painful
attempt to work out a structure which encourages responsibility in all
members and discourages leaders. In the long run, one of the major
achievements of feminism may be its attempt to organize people in
ways which maximize personal fulfillment and growth and minimize
friction and stagnation. It's a way of organizing which is applicable
to every institution and relationship in our society.

In the meantime, we hope that you will participate in a similar
woman-writer oriented, self-taught course within the university or
high school or in the community. We hope your discoveries will be
as rewarding as ours.

MAJOR PROBLEM AREAS

Authority:

1. How does one come to accept one's own experience as having authority?
2. Why are we more likely to attack each other than a male teacher?
3. How does one lay down the habit of "authority" if that habit is part of one's defenses and self-definition?
4. If one does not have advanced academic degrees, how does one get over being awed by them?
5. How does one gain confidence in one's own opinion if one is not in the habit of being listened to?
6. Do we really take seriously intellectual work done by women?

Legitimacy of the Study of Literature:

1. If one has little time to read, why read literature when biography, history or political theory is available?
2. Do we really take literary figures as models?
3. Is literature really an institution that socializes us?
4. Is the cathartic experience of reading good fiction ultimately conducive to political passivity?
5. Do women writers function ultimately and insidiously as role models for political passivity?

Self-discipline and Mutual Discipline in Discussion:

1. How to get some women to talk and others to talk less without ultimately resorting to either group therapy or to consciousness raising?
2. How to break bad group habits once they have become entrenched? (This was a particular problem for us. We began in a conventional way and worked gropingly toward consensus on our collective model.)
3. How to be supportive of strangers whom you don't like?
4. How to formulate clearly new questions in the process of answering old ones?

Emotion (Obviously it was the negative emotions that gave us most of our problems):

1. Anger at the world, at men, at each other constantly threatened to disrupt us as the course progressed: how can one tie into the energy released by honest anger without being paralyzed by it?
2. Fear of intimacy: how can we encourage sharing of private and sometimes threatening experience with women whom we have not yet reason to trust?

3. If one is not used to relating positively to other women, or feeling love and affection toward them, how can this experience be maximized without its being threatening?
4. How does one deal humanely with a class member who is clearly going off the deep end, but who is not in therapy or consciousness raising?
5. How do the minority women in the class, the black, the elderly, the lesbian, deal with the intentional or unintentional stupidities of the rest of the class?
6. How does the class deal with members who are hurt or fearful or angry and who therefore either withdraw or lash out?
7. In short, how do the individuals come to trust the class and how does the class come to support the individuals?

Consciousness Raising:

1. What are the distinctive goals and procedures of feminist consciousness raising?
2. Which of these can be incorporated into a literature course without demanding of its members intimacy and willingness to endure confrontations?
3. How does one define a feminist consciousness?
4. What if the development of feminist consciousness is not a shared goal of all class members?

WOMEN'S STUDIES IN THE LAW SCHOOL

by Aleta Wallach

It seems to me that any collection of articles about women's studies programs should contain something about developments in the law school, for there advances are being made of a rather heroic sort. As an educational institution, the law school traditionally has been and to a large extent still is a more singularly male enclave than the typical coeducational liberal arts institution. Until recently the only women visible in the law school were nonacademic staff personnel, and perhaps an occasional woman law student. Because of this the law school presents a more formidable resistance to feminist change than the college or university which has been educating both women and men for at least several decades. I do not mean to imply that in these latter institutions the mere presence of women students has necessarily influenced feminist consciousness or curriculum, but I do think that the barriers to developing them are less psychologically debilitating and insurmountable when the fact of being a woman student is not in itself a strange or alienated condition.

It is because the law school seems to be like a men's club, an institution generically exclusive of women, that the changes women have wrought there are remarkable, and should be made known to women in other academic fields and to those outside of academia altogether. But I also want to relate these changes to you in the context of my own law school experience at UCLA, for there in three years time I witnessed a spectacular transformation, one for which certain men in the law school deserve no small credit. This history should be most encouraging to women who are attempting to initiate feminist studies and consciousness in the bastions of male professionalism -- law school, medical school, business school and most graduate schools.

When I entered UCLA law school in the fall of 1969 I felt as though I had stepped into one of the male clubs described by Marc Fasteau in the second issue of MS. magazine[1], whose very identity was defined by its maleness. It was not that my class was the first

---

For a recent article on men's clubs, see generally Marc Fasteau, "Men: Clubbishness," Ms., vol. I, no. 2, pp. 32-33, Aug., 1972.

one to admit women in more than token numbers, for at least a couple
of antecedent classes admitted more women than one could count on
ten fingers, and it was said that women at that time constituted
ten percent of the student body. Although it never seemed to me as
if there were that many women around, insufficient numerosity did not
appear to be the primary problem.

Rather, women students were ignored and not taken seriously. The
law school was unconcerned with the facts that women graduates could
not get jobs in law firms and that wherever they did find employment
they often received lower salaries than men. The discriminators
were never denied use of law school facilities to recruit male students. Moreover, the general ambiance was insulting. Women as a
class were ridiculed and put down in lectures where male teachers
used sexist jokes and hypotheticals[2] to gain laughs and popularity
from male students who always seemed to come raucously and licentiously
alive at such moments. In this male club professors achieved status
by demonstrating a dexterous and clever sexist wit, instances of which
occurred despite the fact that women were present in the classroom.
Accordingly, women's status was debased. There was a total lack of
feminist consciousness or even basic courtesy for that matter, and
no one objected to the fact that women were insulted daily.

At this time, the fall of 1969, there was one woman on the law
faculty, no women's course existed, law relevant to women was deleted
from course curricula even when it was an organic part of a body of
legal doctrine, and women themselves were not yet getting themselves
together. When I graduated in the spring of 1972 the UCLA Law Women's Association was an officially recognized group, the Women and
the Law course had been offered twice and was a permanent part of
the curriculum as was a Women and the Law seminar, three new women
faculty members were hired for the academic year 1972-1973, and we
had one woman studying law part time, an occurrence which was totally
against the grain of a prestigious, full-time law school. Most significantly, sexism in the classroom was replaced, for the most part,
by restraint if not sensitivity, and thus women ceased as frequently
to suffer verbal indignity and aggression.

I think that this change, which brought relief to many women,
was not so much the result of the arrival among students of a gen-
eralized feminist consciousness which now declined to accord status
to such professorial behavior as it was, rather surprisingly, just
the opposite. Our fellow students were as willing and ready to laugh

---

2 Unfortunately, "to give color" the standard derogatory female stereotypes were used as stock characters in hypotheticals (the standard
   technique of legal education). These women were always auxiliary
   players to male central characters: the helpless widow, the dependent

at the drop of a sexist put-down as they were before, and they demonstrated this propensity on the now rare occasions which afforded
them appropriate opportunity. The difference was that many law professors were unwilling to continue to use women in this manner as soon
as they gained self-awareness and feminist consciousness, which was
the direct result of our active endeavors in that regard, of the
presence of a strong feminist force. I feel that this was our
greatest legacy to future members of the law school community, and
it could not have come about without the concommitant remarkable good
will of many of the male professors at UCLA. It is certain that
without their good faith and in some cases affirmative support, we
would not have been successful in our attempt to institute the long
overdue changes in the law school which were prerequisites to creating
for women the psychologically warm environment absolutely essential
to optimal study of law and intellectual growth. These in turn required great physical and mental involvement in the school itself.[3]

The Women's Association

Initially the most challenging problem we faced was organizing
ourselves into a body which would be an omnipresent entity and continue through time regardless of which individual women happened to
be in the law school at a particular interval. We never really did
get more than just a nominal group together. The programs we undertook were carried out primarily by a few women who did all of the work.
Group mindedness and communal effort never evolved. One reason for
this may have been the generally low level of feminist consciousness
among the women themselves who were just not willing to sink a large
part of their lives or commitment into organizing the law school,
although they gladly benefitted from any improvements which were
achieved. Self-promotion in terms of status, prestige and achievement
in old-style law careers attract many women law students as well as
men. The net result was that those women who had social consciousness
before entering law school were the ones who most quickly became

---

wife, the deceptive bitch, the innocent virgin, the irrational or
hysterical female, the silly consumer who is easily conned by
slick male exploiters, the rape victim who wanted to be raped, or
any stupid loathesome creature.

Some women chose to remain as distant as possible and come to school
only when absolutely necessary. Those of us who involved ourselves
did so because we knew that staying away was surrendering our
power without a struggle, and that change could not come about without our involvement in the organs of the law school -- its committees,
student bar association, law review, moot court, etc.

committed to developing feminist consciousness in the law school; the size of our group was not noticeably increased by newly awakened women.

The issue raised by this experience is the huge problem of professional elitism and opportunism among liberation groups. We as a women's organization never dealt with it at all. Restraints on our time prevented us from both developing an internally cohesive collective and effecting objective changes in the law school. Moreover, because the visible personal benefits appear to many to accrue only from the latter, few wanted to waste time on the former. And yet it seems that support for our efforts would have been stronger and our power greater if we had first spent time building the internal unity and strength of our group before we turned our attention to external matters. But the reality of the situation was that we were all transient in the law school context, and to spend a year or two getting it together as sisters would have obviated attaining any external changes. Moreover, very few of us were full-time feminists; most of us were full-time law students in both the literal and figurative sense, and had at most a passing or detached interest in "women's liberation."

As a loosely formed women's group, then, we turned our attention to specific projects concerning the physical facility and the women's course.

The Lounge

The law school had a women's lounge which was dim and dirty, crammed with old worn out ugly plastic furniture. The women who were most outraged by this condition, undertook with vigor to make this a major issue and to organize women to make appropriate protests and to improve the situation. The lounge was painted and carpeted, although furniture was never obtained. As this was the first big effort, it gained the active support and effort of many women students. However, the enthusiasm was short lived and continued participation in women's projects did not materialize. One explanation might be that this was the issue that most women could relate to since they used the lounge and lavatory daily; thus they were willing to work on a project which could benefit them directly and immediately. Also, the blighted physical premise was the most visible evidence of women's inferior status, and therefore engendered the strongest emotional response.

Meanwhile, others were working on the development of a Women and the Law course to add to the curriculum.

The Women's Course

In my second year several of us worked full time on putting together materials for a women's course which would cover those areas of law pertinent to women which had been omitted from regular classes.[4] We received strong support from certain professors who were ready to assist in any way possible (although plenty were laughing at us), and one very good friend sponsored the class through the faculty approval stage. He played the role of advisor in an essentially student taught course. Not only was the course approved on an experimental basis (the usual procedure for new courses) but we were encouraged to assume responsibility. Some professors even perceived us as making a valuable contribution to the law school. Thus having received accreditation, after an extended internal debate on the issue of men in the class[5] we enrolled both men and women for three credits in spring 1971 and collectively concentrated on criminal, family, welfare and labor law as they affect women.

We were rather parochial in our methodology and followed the lecture system, accented with a few field trips to such places as Sybil Brand Institute for Women, and the California Institute for Women at Frontera. In many ways the pilot venture was a marvellous success, and the students enrolled in it were delighted. We tried to operate as a learning and teaching collective, and we were small enough in numbers (about 15) to become well acquainted with each other and to have a good internal criticism class at the end. This session was by far the most important one because people had good ideas on how to improve the course next time. And we recognized for the first time that one's evaluation is framed with reference to one's initial expectations. Thus it is important to identify at the outset why persons are in the course, so as to shape the content in terms of their purposes and intentions. Inevitably, of course, we ran into the fundamental and irreconcilable opposition of those who thought that the women's course should be for women only and pure consciousness raising, and those who wanted to learn the black letter law, with many shades in between. But we did manage to satisfy a majority of the students.

The following year the demand for the course had increased and we got it approved as a regular offering and also got the faculty to approve a seminar under the same rubric, which allowed maximum flexibility in the future when a teacher would be hired to teach the course. For the second year, however, the women who had been most closely associated in its development taught the course again, this time under the sponsorship of another faculty member, who, with his wife, was

---

A detailed history of the creation of the Women and the Law course and its first year of existence can be read in Wallach, "The Genesis of a 'Women and the Law' Course: The Dawn of Consciousness at UCLA School of Law," 24, J. of Legal Ed., 309 (1972).

For a description of the debate, see id. at 315.

experienced in group communication. Since many men and women were
enrolled this time and we were not all well acquainted with one
another, we began the first session with consciousness raising and
role playing, led by the professor's wife. They worked as a team
and were great, and everyone felt that this was the best class of all.
We planned to do it again two quarters later at the end of the class
to see where people had changed and come to but we never did, mainly
because no one took the initiative to arrange it.

This time the class was less formal and we had more discussion
and argument on feminist issues such as child care, rape, prostitution
and the family. We tried to show films at every other class: e.g.,
The Woman's Film, Growing Up Female, You Don't Have to Buy War Mrs.
Smith. On the days when films were scheduled we put up notices all
over the law school, and drew people into our class experience. The
existence of the course in the law school created a general awareness
that women were taking themselves seriously, and soon others began to
also, and we had frequent visitors.

We usually met in the faculty lounge and sat around the room so
that we could see each other. We even had feminist theatre performed
by the students in charge of the "Our Bodies Our Selves" section of
the course which covered contraception, abortion, and menstruation.
They showed the menstruation film Very Personally Yours, which is
shown to girls in grade school, and they dressed up as nurses and
school administrators, and distributed literature to us, the sixth
graders. Another time they read feminist poetry and acted out Myrna
Lamb's abortion play.

These various techniques made the class experience rich. Each
group of student-teachers had a different teaching methodology. They
varied in the degree of legalistic orientation, but they were all very
talented teachers. Certain men became very committed to the class
and made outstanding contributions. Because of the looseness in
structure we were often able to relate oppression of women to other
forms of oppression in our society. We talked a lot about housework,
the discriminatory tax structure, child birth and child care responsibility, and, of course, the nuclear family. Inevitably, the course
gradually turned into consciousness raising for men, rather than for
women, and men dominated and converted the situation into the one
that best suited them, as men so often seem to do if they are allowed
in. The men were fascinated and wanted to learn from the women. But
they were defensive, constantly unable to accept criticism of themselves as individual or group oppressors, and claiming that they,
too, were victims.

Some women stopped coming to class because they could no longer
tolerate the anger and frustration rising inside of them. At the
final evaluation session one woman exclaimed that she was sick of

teaching men about what it is like to be a woman. This was a waste of her time and she was angry that once again women were helping men solve their problem rather than being free to work with women on their common problems and to develop their own ideology and consciousness. It is not surprising then that the men really liked the class and learned a tremendous amount. Some thought that it was the most stimulating one they took in law school, and that new horizons and depths were opened to them and they were grateful. On the other hand, some women were unable to get out of it what they wanted and needed, and in this respect it was not truly a women's class controlled by women. One woman felt at the end of the course that women are always going to be inferior no matter what, and this truth was revealed to her during the course, and was deeply depressing.

But I think we recognized that education takes place in many ways, and that although we might have failed to educate ourselves in the way we would have preferred we were able profoundly to educate others, especially some of the men in the class, and thus raise the general level of collective education on feminist issues. To be sure, rationalizing our experience in this way bears overtones of justifying women's business as being of secondary importance -- to revolutionary and antiwar values at one moment, to the abolition movement at another, and now to men's or collective education. But still I think that there is some validity to the view that an intrinsic part of the women's movement is to raise the consciousness of those around us with respect to how their own behavior and attitudes oppress us as women on a daily basis. There were men in our class who will never again commit those sexist transgressions of which they became aware. Wherever they are now, they are responsible for their further enlightenment. But it can be hypothesized that they would not be on the road to their own salvation had we not come together as we did at this particular moment in time. Obviously I have deeply ambivalent feelings about what happened in the women's class and I cannot say I am certain that the values we did achieve redeem those which we did not. But there are limits on what can be done in a state supported professional school ostensibly committed to non-exclusive egalitarianism. It would not have been permissible, prudent, nor, in my personal opinion, desirable to keep men out.

Textbooks

A major problem both years was the total absence of legal casebooks on women and the law. Although several are currently in preparation, none of them was in any state of readiness for us. Many thought this was a disguised benefit, because we would have to use works by and about women as our basic texts: e.g. Our Bodies Our Selves; Sisterhood is Powerful; Notes from the Second Year; Women, a Journal of Liberation; Century of Struggle. But heavy reliance on feminist works disturbed those who mainly wanted to learn black letter law and tool-up on legal skills. Others, however, were pleased with these materials because they felt that foundation in feminist analysis was prerequisite to any legal analysis pertaining to women.

In any event we were, hampered by the unavailability of a case-book, and it was a constant bureaucratic problem to arrange for duplication and distribution of cases and other legal materials. The law school did its best to cooperate and was extremely generous to the women's class in monetary allowance for duplication and film fees, even in an extremely tight budget year.

All the while we were developing our own syllabus, which eventually became about 300 pages of articles and cases organized under the following table of contents:

I   The Suffrage Movement: Legal Change and Feminism

II   Constitutional Status

III Family and Welfare Law

     A. Illegitimacy
     B. Marriage
     C. Same-sex Marriage
     D. Legal Relations of the Family
     E. Divorce and Child Custody
     F. Community Property
     G. Welfare and Family Law
     H. Child Care

IV   Control of Our Bodies

     A. Abortion
     B. Female Sexuality
     C. Woman-defined Woman (female homosexuality)
     D. Birth Control
     E. Artificial Insemination
     F. Sterilization

V   Criminal Law

     A. Prostitution
     B. Rape
     C. Statutory Rape
     D. Women in Prison
     E. Parole
     F. Juvenile Women

VI   Labor and Employment

     A. Economic Background
     B. Equal Pay Act of 1963

C. Executive Order 11246
D. State Protective Legislation
E. Title VII of the 1964 Civil Rights Act
F. Women and the Unions
G. The Work We Ignore: Prostitution, Housework, Welfare
H. Other Countries: Soviet Union and Sweden
I. Unemployment Benefits

VII Media: Images and Legal Strategies

The law school arranged for this important sourcebook to be printed at the university printing office and sold through the bookstore. It was our basic material used the second year the course was offered, and it is in the truest sense the history of our class and thought. We thus discovered that teaching a women's study course first of all involved creating our own textual material, and that creating women's studies courses inevitably casts us into the role of being our own historians.

The Part-Time Program

It became immediately apparent to us that the major barrier to women's entrance into the law school (or any professional school) was the lack of a part-time study program for those women who have full-time child care and homemaking responsibilities. Such woman are certainly at a competitive disadvantage with their male counterparts who can be full-time law students while their women service them, their clothes, homes and children.

The most significant and far-reaching of the waves we made in the law school was the issue of the part-time program. Curiously enough the faculty, for the most part, was quick to recognize that true equality required that a part-time program be avilable for women who, otherwise qualified, could not attend because of domestic and child care responsibilities. Since recruitment of women students was a high priority, the establishment of a part-time program was taken seriously by some, and in the fall of 1971 one "exceptional" woman who had already been accepted as a full-time student petitioned to attend part time and was supported by the women's association. Her petition was granted and a faculty subcommittee was then appointed to consult with women students and to develop the parameters of a part-time program to be submitted to the whole faculty in time for 1972-1973 admissions.

We did manage to get a part-time proposal before the faculty but this is where everything fell apart and we were forced to recognize the part-time program as the most difficult and complex problem to be faced by women and law faculties in the future. Basically, the problem could be characterized as one of conflict of interest. True, many professors agreed that a part-time program was of vital importance to women and equal accessibility to law school was dependent upon it. Yet at the same time it was out of the realm of possibility that the law school would voluntarily demote itself to a part-time law school. Within the pecking order of institutions for the study of law, part-time and night schools (the ones which best accommodate working class persons) are of the lowest status, whereas full-time law schools enjoy the aristocratic reputation characteristic of educational institutions which are elite and exclusive. There is thus a basic contradiction between the desire to open up the law school to those traditionally excluded from it and the desire of elite professors to protect their own status and privilege, which is tied to the status of the institution with which they are associated. This fundamental class structure of our educational system must be recognized and dealt with as it directly relates to the accessibility of "first rate" education to women and other deprived persons.

The law school, then, was willing to do something, but not to become a part-time institution where persons once accepted could attend part time at their option. It would, however, entertain a part-time program of a limited number of slots to be filled by persons satisfying elegibility criteria for the part-time program. Of course, it was impossible to agree on those criteria, because many could not find rational and justifiable standards by which to limit the class of eligible persons. Surely if women with children were to be included so too should men with children, or men working full-time, and blacks and chicanos. The final result was inability to agree on the class of potential part-time students; the spectre of a part-time institution lurked at the bottom of the tired and worn slippery slope. No other woman was admitted on a part-time basis, and the part-time program itself is dead. Women must think hard about how to deal with this kind of problem for it is certain that the perpetuation of such institutional methods of discrimination affects equal educational opportunity.

Conclusion

The UCLA experience is relevant to attempts to develop women's studies in any institutional educational setting. It seems to me that the obstacles are similar in law schools, English departments, or health sciences: overcoming resistance, converting resources to the use of women's studies courses, creating course materials, focusing academic attention on the needs of women (e.g., artistic, health, legal) and devoting research resources to specific subjects affecting women (e.g., discovering women poets, development of birth control for men, litigation of test cases in areas of legalized sex discrimination). The sum total of all these efforts is the development of feminist consciousness in the school environment, and necessarily among women too.

After my own three year experience I have come to regard women's studies as a consciousness and not only as a particular classroom end in itself. I found that feminist education was more than offering a class on some women's subjects. Education occurred around us, outside the class, in the institution proper, as a re-action to our mere organized existence. The women at UCLA educated the law school through the process of organizing and obtaining a Women and the Law course and through existing as an on-going force which urged every feminist argument at every opportunity, as much as through the specific content of the course itself. And the women themselves were educated in the politics, strategy and class nature of institutionalized discrimination, knowledge of which women are often woefully ignorant. It is gained through the struggle to create feminist consciousness wherever one may be.

Although we did not achieve all that we attempted to do, UCLA law school had undergone a profound transformation when I left. Always an enlightened group of scholars, it was quick to respond to the presence and some of the needs of its women. With a desire to recruit as many qualified women as it can, and four women law pro-fessors, it is the vanguard law school in the nation right now. Its recruitment efforts, however, will primarily benefit those women who have not made mistakes, who are not buried under the domestic heap, or those who can afford to hire others to assume their own responsi-bilities. Although at times the persons who regarded us as thorny irritants might not have agreed, in retrospect I am proud because while some of us went to law school to "get our equal educational oppor-tunity," in my heart I know that we gave back to that school deep and lasting values, our spirits and part of our lives.

III FEMINIST CRITICISM

INTRODUCTION

Even given the framework laid out in "Women as Liberators," it
is still too early for us to state definitively the parameters of
feminist criticism. Its two major functions, however, are already
clear.

First, feminist criticism must sensitize us to the fact that
literature is an institution, which like other institutions has its
own history, its own rules, and its own practices; that literature is
a masculine institution, developed and perpetuated by men; and, finally
that it is a socializing institution that shapes both women and men.
Literature provides us with role models; we have only to think of
Isabelle Archer, Lady Brett Ashley, or Molly Bloom. It provides us
with patterns of expected behavior; we have only to think of the
thousands of novels that end for the woman in marriage, or more recently in insanity or suicide, and the countless novels of manners that
teach a woman just what it is she can and can't do. It provides us
with fantasies and plots that teach us to organize thus our own experience. Feminist criticism, then, is concerned to examine the representation of women in literature, the motives and behaviors assigned
to them, their function in the plot, the images and symbols associated with them, and the descriptive and judgmental biases of the
narrative point of view. Here the feminist critic is showing how
stereotypes function in a literary work, as in other forms of institutionalized behavior.

Beyond this analysis of stereotypes, there are literary repu-
tations to consider. These are established by publishers, critics,
and teachers, who are for the most part men, or an occasional woman
who more often than not has absorbed or affected the masculine point
of view and masculine habits of thought so necessary if she is to
pursue successfully her professional career. Such persons determine
what is to be published, kept in print, and established in the university curriculum. Their decisions, past and present, must, of course,
be carefully examined and challenged where necessary, for these
decisions reflect the masculine gestalt we are seeking to replace.

In general, the masculine bias thus revealed in literature and
in literary criticism must first be widely recognized for the gestalt
that it is and then must be purposefully corrected by the creation
and celebration of feminine works. If in time a truly androgynous
sensibility emerges, it is likely to do so only as the feminist sensibility is fully explored and appreciated.

The use of these terms -- feminine, masculine, and androgynous --

point up the second, less familiar and fundamentally more challenging function of feminist criticism. Feminist criticism raises implicitly that fundamental question to which we are just beginning to address ourselves -- need women and men have distinctly different consciousnesses? The answer is obviously yes insofar as we are socialized human beings -- two genders separated experientially from birth, given different attitudes and self-images. But whether the differences in our reproductive organs are accompanied by natural differences in temperament and consciousness is a question to ask, if not yet to answer. Perhaps in the near future the life sciences and psychology will yield useful data. Judith Bardwick's work with infants, for example, is suggestive. It would seem clear that if feminist criticism is going to address itself successfully to questions of consciousness, of gestalt, feminist critics are going to have to develop a multi-disciplinary perspective that will permit us to use comfortably the findings of biology, psychology, sociology, and anthropology, in short, the findings of all the disciplines that address themselves to human behavior.

As traditional critics, we have been trained to recognize the necessary tension that exists between generic demands and the individualized creative impulse of the artist. What we as feminist critics need to point up and explore is the fact that traditional genres represent in codified or fossilized form -- depending on your point of view -- the fantasies of male writers and the curves of emotional experience that satisfy these fantasies. It is not at all clear that women have the same fantasies as men or that given a literature written completely or almost completely by women that the same genres would have emerged.

Neither Freudian nor Jungian literary critics, moreover, have taken into account what should be one of the most obvious conclusions to be drawn from their respective theoretical systems -- namely that whereas women and men have fundamentally different psyches, they must accordingly have fundamentally different literary experiences, whether as artists or as readers. A male and a female student, unless rigidly trained, simply do not read Virginia Woolf in the same way, or Joseph Conrad. Likewise, George Eliot and William Wordsworth both read Milton with great care, but the ultimate use to which they put his work can probably be shown to be dependent on their own feminine and masculine natures.

Once we accept the existence of radically different consciousnesses in women and men, at least women and men socialized as we in recorded history have been socialized, the questions to be raised by feminist criticism become staggering. We must literally redo all the criticism that has been done, or that failing -- and there is no particularly compelling reason why we should want to bother to redo most of it -- we must strike out and develop a theory of literary history, of literary genre, and of literary technique that does justice to the feminine consciousness and feminine culture.

But in reality it is too early to speak of feminist criticism, as
if an acknowledged body, of theory and practice exists. Rather it is
timely to speak of a feminist perspective as Carol Ohmann does here.
The essays that follow were selected for their feminist perspectives
and so as to show some of the uses to which feminist critics are
currently putting their knowledge of literature. Good literary criticism, whatever its ideological coloration, happens when the sensibility of the critic actively engages the sensibility of the writer.
They establish a dialogue such as Nancy Porter records. In her dialogue
with Doris Lessing she is actively trying to clarify her own past and
her present politics. Similarly, Cynthia Secor has sought out Alice
B. Toklas and Gertrude Stein so that she can better understand how
women can in the future retain the rich domesticity that characterizes
feminine culture while yet developing fully the feminine intellect.
With the sympathy of a sister traveller, Carol Ohmann engages
Charlotte Brontë in an effort to understand both how and why she
stopped short of a radical feminist critique of society. Judith Davis
has learned from a woman long dead when to withdraw from debate about
feminism in favor of one's own work. And Alleen Nilsen is happily
settled in bed with dictionary in hand, figuring out what common
language really is, while Josephine Donovan asks if that language
is made to form distinctively male and female sentences. Each of
these essays is indeed very close to the ground. Most of these women
seem to be satisfying for themselves a basic need, most seem engaged
in integrating their professional skills with personal needs. Typical
of the immediacy of these encounters is that of Judith Newton struggling
with her love of Joan Didion and her anger at Didion's recent criticism
of women's movement.

SEXISM IN ENGLISH: A FEMINIST VIEW

by Alleen Pace Nilsen

Does culture shape language? Or does language shape culture?
This is as difficult a question as the old puzzler of which came
first, the chicken or the egg, because there's no clear separation
between language and culture.

A well accepted linguistic principle is that as culture
changes so will the language. The reverse of this -- as a language
changes so will the culture -- is not so readily accepted. This
is why some linguists smile (or even scoff) at feminist attempts
to replace Mrs. and Miss with Ms. and to find replacements for
those all inclusive words which specify masculinity, e.g.
chairman, mankind, brotherhood, freshman, etc.

Perhaps they are amused for the same reason that it is the doctor at a cocktail party who laughs the loudest at the joke about
the man who couldn't afford an operation so he offered the doctor
a little something to touch up the x-ray. A person working constantly with language is likely to be more aware of how really deep-
seated sexism is in our communication system.

Last winter I took a standard desk dictionary and gave it a
place of honor on my night table. Every night that I didn't have
anything more interesting to do, I read myself to sleep making a
card for each entry that seemed to tell something about male and
female. By spring I had a rather dog-eared dictionary, but I also
had a collection of note cards filling two shoe boxes. The cards
tell some rather interesting things about American English.

First, in our culture it is a woman's body which is considered
important while it is a man's mind or his activities which are
valued. A woman is sexy. A man is successful.

I made a card for all the words which came into modern English
from somebody's name. I have a two-and one-half inch stack of cards
which are men's names now used as everyday words. The women's
stack is less than a half inch high and most of them came from
Greek mythology. Fairly recent words coming from the names of
famous American men include pasteurization, lynch, sousaphone, sideburns, pullman, ricketts, shick test, winchester rifle, franklin
stove, teddy bear, and boysenberry. The only really common words

coming from the names of American women are bloomers (after Amelia
Jenks Bloomer) and Mae West jacket. Both of these words are related in some way to a woman's physical anatomy, while the male
words (except for sideburns after General Burnsides) have nothing
to do with the namesake's body.

This reminded me of an earlier observation that my husband and
I made about geographical names. A few years ago we became interested in what we called "Topless Topography" when we learned that
the Grand Tetons used to be simply called The Tetons by French
explorers and The Teats by American frontiersmen. We wrote letters
to several map makers and found the following listings: Nippletop
and Little Nipple Top near Mt. Marcy in the Adirondacks, Nipple
Mountain in Archuleta County, Colorado, Nipple Peak in Coke County,
Texas, Nipple Butte in Pennington, South Dakota, Squaw Peak in
Placer County, California (and many other places), Maiden's Peak and
Squaw Tit (they're the same mountain) in the Cascade Range in Ore-
gon, Jane Russell Peaks near Stark, New Hampshire, and Mary's
Nipple near Salt Lake City, Utah.

We might compare these names to Jackson Hole, Wyoming, or
Pikes Peak, Colorado. I'm sure we would get all kinds of protests
from the Jackson and Pike descendents if we tried to say that these
topographical features were named because they in some way resembled
the bodies of Jackson and Pike, respectively.

This pre-occupation with women's breasts is neither new nor
strictly American. I was amused to read the derivation of the word
Amazon. According to Greek folk etymology, the a means without as
in atypical or amoral while mazon comes from mazos meaning breast.
According to the legend, these women cut off one breast so that
they could better shoot their bows. Perhaps the feeling was that the
women had to trade in part of their femininity in exchange for
their active or masculine role.

There are certain pairs of words which illustrate the way in
which sexual connotations are given to feminine words while the
masculine words retain a serious business-like aura. For example,
being a call-boy is perfectly respectable. It simply refers to a
person who calls actors when it is time for them to go on stage,
but being a call-girl is being a prostitute.

Also we might compare sir and madam. Sir is a term of respect
while Madam has acquired the meaning of a brothel manager. The
same thing has happened to the formerly cognate terms, master and
mistress. Because of its acquired sexual connotations, mistress
is now carefully avoided in certain contexts. For example, the Boy
Scouts have scoutmasters but certainly not scoutmistresses. And in

a dog show the female owner of a dog is never referred to as the dog's mistress, but rather as the dog's master.

Master appears in such terms as master plan, concert master, school master, mixmaster, master charge, master craftsman, etc. But mistress appears in very few compounds. This is the way it is with dozens of words which have male and female counterparts. I found two hundred such terms, e.g. usher-usherette, heir-heiress, hero-heroine, etc. In nearly all cases it is the masculine word which is the base with a feminine suffix being added for the alternate version. The masculine word also travels into compounds while the feminine word is a dead end, e.g. from king-queen comes kingdom but not queendom, from sportsman-sportslady comes sportsmanship but not sportsladyship, etc. There is one -- and only one -- semantic area in which the masculine word is not the base or more powerful word. This is in the area dealing with sex and marriage. Here it is the feminine word which is dominant. Prostitute is the base word with male prostitute being the derived term. Bride appears in bridal shower, bridal gown, bridal attendant, bridesmaid, and even in bridegroom, while groom in the sense of bridegroom does not appear in any compounds, not even to name the groom's attendants or his pre-nuptial party.

At the end of a marriage, this same emphasis is on the female. If it ends in divorce, the woman gets the title of divorcée while the man is usually described with a statement such as "He's divorced." When the marriage ends in death, the woman is a widow and the -er suffix which seems to connote masculine (probably because it is an agentive or actor type suffix) is added to make widower. Widower doesn't appear in any compounds (except for grass widower, which is another companion term), but widow appears in several compounds and in addition has some acquired meanings such as the extra hand dealt to the table in certain card games and an undesirable left-over line of type in printing.

If I were an anthropological linguist making observations about a strange and primitive tribe, I would duly note on my tape recorder that I had found linguistic evidence to show that in the area of sex and marriage the female appears to be more important than the male, but in all other areas of the culture, it seems that the reverse is true.

But since I am not an anthropological linguist, I will simply go on to my second observation which is that women are expected to play a passive role while men play an active one.

One indication of women's passive role is the fact that they are often identified as something to eat. What's more passive than a plate of food? Last spring I saw an announcement advertising the

Indiana University English Department picnic. It read "Good Food!
Delicious Women!" The publicity committee was probably jumped on
by local feminists, but it's nothing new to look on women as
"delectable morsels." Even women compliment each other with "You
look good enough to eat," or "You have a peaches and cream complexion."
Modern slang constantly comes up with new terms, but some of the
old stand-bys for women are: a cute tomato, a dish, a peach, a
sharp cookie, cheese cake, honey, sugar and sweetie-pie. A man may
occasionally be addressed as honey or described as a hunk of meat,
but certainly men are not laid out on a buffet and labelled as women
are.

Women's passivity is also shown in the comparisons made to
plants. For example, to deflower a woman is to take away her virginity. A girl can be described as a clinging vine, a shrinking
violet, or a wall flower. On the other hand, men are too active to
be thought of as plants. The only time we make the comparison is
when insulting a man we say he is like a woman by calling him a pansy.

We also see the active-passive contrast in the animal terms
used with males and females. Men are referred to as studs, bucks,
and wolves, and they go tom-catting around. These are all aggressive
roles, but women have such pet names as kitten, bunny, beaver, bird,
chick, lamb, and fox. The idea of being a pet seems much more closely
related to females than to males. For instance, little girls grow
up wearing pigtails and pony tails and they dress in halters and
dog collars.

The active-passive contrast is also seen in the proper names
given to boy babies and girl babies. Girls are much more likely to
be given names like Ivy, Rose, Ruby, Jewel, Pearl, Flora, Joy, etc.
while boys are given names describing active roles such as Martin
(war-like), Leo (lion), William (protector), Ernest (resolute fighter),
etc.

Another way that women play a passive role is that they are
defined in relationship to someone else. This is what feminists are
protesting when they ask to be identified as Ms. rather than as
Mrs. or Miss. It is a constant source of irritation to women's
organization that when they turn in items to newspapers under their
own names, i.e. Susan Glascoe, Jeanette Jones, etc. the editors
consistently rewrite the item so that the names read Mrs. John Glascoe,
Mrs. Robert E. Jones, etc.

In the dictionary I found what appears to be an attitude on
the part of editors that it is almost indecent to let a respectable
woman's name march unaccompanied across the pages of a dictionary.
A woman's name must somehow be escorted by a male's name regardless
of whether or not the male contributed to the woman's reason for
being in the dictionary, or in his own right, was as famous as the

woman. For example, Charlotte Brontë is identified as Mrs. Arthur
B. Nicholls, Amelia Earhart is identified as Mrs. George Palmer
Putnam, Helen Hayes is identified as Mrs. Charles Macarthur, Zona
Gale is identified as Mrs. William Llwelyn Breese, and Jenny Lind is
identified as Mme. Otto Goldschmidt.

Although most of the women are identified as Mrs. _____
or as the wife of _____, other women are listed with brothers,
fathers, or lovers. Cornelia Otis Skinner is identified as the
daughter of Otis, Marriet Beecher Stowe is identified as the sister
of Henry Ward Beecher, Edith Sitwell is identified as the sister of
Osbert and Sacheverell, Nell Gwyn is identified as the mistress of
Charles II, and Madam Pompadour is identified as the Mistress of
Louis XV.

The women who did get into the dictionary without the benefit
of a masculine escort are a group sort of on the fringes of respectability. They are the rebels and the crusaders: temperance
leaders Frances Elizabeth Caroline Willard and Carry Nation, women's
rights leaders Carrie Chapman Catt and Elizabeth Cady Stanton,
birth control educator Margaret Sanger, religious leader Mary Baker
Eddy, and slaves Harriet Tubman and Phillis Wheatley.

I would estimate that far more than fifty percent of the women
listed in the dictionary were identified as someone's wife. But
of all the men -- and there are probably ten times as many men as
women -- only one was identified as "the husband of..." This was
the unusual case of Frederic Joliot who took the last name of
Joliot-Curie and was identified as "husband of Irene." Apparently
Irene, the daughter of Pierre and Marie Curie, did not want to give
up her maiden name when she married and so the couple took the
hyphenated last name.

There are several pairs of words which also illustrate the
more powerful role of the male and the relational role of the
female. For example a count is a high political officer with a
countess being simply the wife of a count. The same is true for
a duke and a duchess and a king and a queen. The fact that a
king is usually more powerful than a queen might be the reason
that Queen Elizabeth's husband is given the title of Prince rather
than King. Since king is a stronger word than queen, it is reserved for a true heir to the throne because if it were given to
someone coming into the royal family by marriage, then the subjects
might forget where the true power lies. With the weaker word of
queen, this would not be a problem so a woman marrying a ruling
monarch is given the title without question.

My third observation is that there are many positive connotations connected with the concept of masculine while there are
either trivial or negative connotations connected with the corresponding

feminine concept.

Conditioning toward the superiority of the masculine role
starts very early in life. Child psychologists point out that the
only area in which a girl has more freedom than a boy is in experi-
menting with an appropriate sex role. She is much freer to be a
tomboy than is her brother to be a sissy. The proper names given
to children reflect this same attitude. It's perfectly alright for
a girl to have a boy's name, but not the other way around. As girls
are given more and more of the boys' names, parents shy away from
using boy names that might be mistaken for girl names, so the number of available masculine names is constantly shrinking. Fifty
years ago Hazel, Beverley, Marion, Frances, and Shirley were all perfectly acceptable boys' names. Today few parents give these names
to baby boys and adult men who are stuck with them self-consciously
go by their initials or by abbreviated forms such as Haze or Shirl.
But parents of little girls keep crowding the masculine set and
currently popular girls' names include Jo, Kelly, Teri, Cris, Pat,
Shawn, Toni, and Sam.

When the mother of one of these little girls tells her to be
a lady, she means for her to sit with her knees together. But when
the father of a little boy tells him to be a man, he means for him
to be noble, strong, and virtuous. The whole concept of manliness
has such positive connotations that it is a compliment to call a
male a he-man, a manly man, or a virile man (virile comes from the
Indo-European vir, meaning man). In each of these three terms, we
are implying that someone is doubly good because he is doubly a man.

Compare chef with cook, tailor with seamstress, and poet with
poetess. In each case, the masculine form carries with it an added
degree of excellence. In comparing the masculine governor with
the feminine governess and the masculine major with the feminine
majorette, the added feature is power.

The difference between positive male and negative female connotations can be seen in several pairs of words which differ
denotatively only in the matter of sex. For instance compare
bachelor with the terms spinster and old maid. Bachelor has such
positive connotations that modern girls have tried to borrow the
feeling in the term bachelor-girl. Bachelor appears in glamorous
terms such as bachelor pad, bachelor party and bachelor button.
But old maid has such strong negative feelings that it has been
adopted into other areas, taking with it the feeling of unde-
sirability. It has the metaphorical meaning of shrivelled and
unwanted kernels of pop corn and it's the name of the last unwanted
card in a popular game for children.

Patron and matron (Middle English for father and mother) are
another set where women have tried to borrow the positive masculine
connotations, this time through the word patroness, which literally

means "female father." Such a peculiar term came about because
of the high prestige attached to the word patron in such phrases
as "a patron of the arts" or "a patron saint". Matron is more apt
to be used in talking about a woman who is in charge of a jail or
a public restroom.

Even lord and lady have different levels of connotation. Our
Lord is used as a title for deity, while the corresponding Our Lady
is a relational title for Mary, the moral mother of Jesus. Landlord
has more dignity than landlady probably because the landlord is more
likely to be thought of as the owner while the landlady is the person
who collects the rent and enforces the rules. Lady is used in many
insignificant places where the corresponding lord would never be used,
for example, ladies room, ladies sizes, ladies aid society, lady bug, etc.

This overuse of lady might be compared to the overuse of queen
which is rapidly losing its prestige as compared to king. Hundreds
of beauty queens are crowned each year and nearly every community in
the United States has its Dairy Queen or its Freezer Queen, etc.
Male homosexuals have adopted the term to identify the "feminine"
partner. And advertisers who are constantly on the look out for
euphemisms to make unpleasant sounding products saleable have recently dealt what might be a death blow to the prestige of the word
queen. They have begun to use it as an indication of size. For
example, queen-size panty hose are panty hose for fat women. The
meaning comes through a comparison with king-size, meaning big. However, there's a subtle difference in that our culture considers
it desirable for males to be big because size is an indication of
power, but we prefer that females be small and petite. So using
king-size as a term to indicate bigness partially enhances the prestige
of king, but using queen-size to indicate bigness brings unpleasant
associations to the word queen.

Another set that might be compared are brave and squaw. The
word brave carries with it the connotations of youth, vigor, and
courage, while squaw implies almost opposite characteristics.
With the set wizard and witch, the main difference is that wizard
implies skill and wisdom combined with magic, while witch implies
evil intentions combined with magic. Part of the unattractiveness
of both squaw and witch is that they suggest old age, which in
women is particularly undesirable. When I lived in Afghanistan
(1967-1969), I was horrified to hear a proverb stating that when
you see an old man you should sit down and take a lesson, but when
you see an old woman you should throw a stone. I was equally
startled when I went to compare the connotations of our two phrases
grandfatherly advice and old wives tales. Certainly it isn't
expressed with the same force as in the Afghan proverb, but the
implication is similar.

In some of the animal terms used for women the extreme un-
desirability of female old age is also seen. For instance consider
the unattractiveness of old nag as compared to filly, of old crow
or old bat as compared to bird, and of being catty as compared
to being kittenish. The chicken metaphor tells the whole story of
a girl's life. In her youth she is a chick, then she marries and
begins feeling cooped up, so she goes to hen parties where she
cackles with her friends. Then she has her brood and begins to hen-
peck her husband. Finally she turns into an old biddy.

JOAN DIDION, 1972

by Judith Newton

"Sometime in the night she had moved into
a realm of miseries peculiar to women,...."
Play It As It Lays[1]

Joan Didion is finally writing about the Women's Movement,
and she is writing badly. (New York Times Book Review, July 30.)
She is usually a fine writer, and to those of us who have admired
her for the deftness and subtlety of her observation, for the clean
grace of her prose, this essay on the Women's Movement is an appalling
departure from what we have come to expect.

This sudden collapse of Didion's stylistic control suggests how
out of measure her response to the Women's Movement is. Didion does
not analyze the Movement in her essay. She merely reacts to it,
and she reacts defensively -- more defensively than even the most
hostile critics of her latest novel, Play It As It Lays. Didion's
reviewers, in fact, appear to have taught her, momentarily, how not to
review. Some of the most distorted assessments of her latest novel
were by women, women who were plenty mad at Didion for what they saw
as a betrayal of our sex. Their charge was that Didion had made her
heroine too vulnerable, too full of feeling, too adolescent, too
demanding of men. Didion's heroine was an insult to all women, they
implied. The reviewers were insulted, and they seemed rather threatened
too. Their reactions to Didion's heroine were finally so self-pro-
tective that their reviews did little justice to the complexity or
the reality of Didion's vision.

It is painful -- and maddening -- to watch Didion move into
the same realm of misery, that realm peculiar to women whose uneasi-
ness about their own vulnerability provokes distorted visions and defensive judgments of other women who have chosen to admit that, yes,
they are vulnerable and who have set about confronting that vulnerability, asking where it all began. It is painful because Didion
was once given to that kind of confrontation, and now, two years after
Play It As It Lays, she is denying what she saw. We find her, in the

---

1 Joan Didion, Play It As It Lays (New York: Farrar, Straus & Giroux,
   1970), p. 62.

pose of her own defensive critics, attacking the Movement for making women seem too vulnerable, too full of feeling, too adolescent, too romantic, too demanding of men. In Didion's new terms Movement women are "everyone's victim but [our] own," "scared of adult sexual life," "too fragile for the streets," "perpetual adolescents," insistent on "romance," "too sensitive for the difficulties and ambiguities of adult life."[2]

As a feminist I find these distortions outrageous, but there is something else that concerns me, something more disturbing than my anger. In her ill-conceived attack on the Movement I am witnessing the collapse of a quality which I have always admired in Didion -- her effort to see what is most troubling in herself and her culture, her insistence on surviving by confronting what is there, inside and out. What we have in her latest essay is not confrontation but escape. Her construction of the Movement is so rigid, so extreme, so without complexity, nerve, or maturity that she does not have to bother with rejecting it -- she can write about it in the past tense as if it no longer existed. How could anything that ridiculous have survived, she seems to ask. How could it have had any bearing on her if it had? She is safe, and establishing her safety is what that essay is finally about.

This is not the stance of the woman who wrote "On Keeping a Notebook,"[3] "a problem of making connections,"[4] or Play It As It Lays. The woman who wrote "On Keeping a Notebook" insists on facing the people she is or has been lest they "turn up unannounced" at "4 a.m. of a bad night"[5] and one of the persons she has been is too "fragile," "too tender," "too sensitive for the difficulties and ambiguities of adult life."[6] The twenty-three-year-old Didion was

---

2 Joan Didion, "The Women's Movement," The New York Times Book Review, July 30, 1972, pp. 2, 14.

3 Joan Didion, "On Keeping a Notebook," Slouching Toward Bethlehem, Delta (New York: Dell Publishing Co., Inc., 1968), pp. 131-141.

4 Joan Didion, "a problem of making connections," Life Magazine, December 5, 1969, p. 34.

5 "Notebook," STB, p. 139.

6 "The Women's Movement," NYTBR, p. 14.

always a good deal of trouble and I suspect she will
reappear when I least want to see her, skirts too
long, shy to the point of aggravation, always the
injured party, full of recriminations and little hurts
and stories I do not want to hear again, at once
saddening me and angering me with her vulnerability
and ignorance, an apparition all the more insistent
for being·so long banished.

(STB, p. 140)

This is 1966. In 1969 Didion is still confronting her "vulnerability." In fact, she is being pretty aggressive about setting
it all down on the pages of Life Magazine. She is on the verge of
divorce, is "alert only to the stuff of bad dreams," is holding on
to an "essentially romantic ethic," and she does not pass this off
as profoundly cultural. She is not "society in microcosm" but a
"34-year-old woman with long straight hair and an old bikini bathing
suit and bad nerves...." Why tell us this?

I tell you this. . . because I want you to know,
during the time that I will be writing for this
page, precisely who I am and where I am and what is
on my mind. I want you to understand what you are
getting ....

("Connections," p. 34)

I like her aggression. She's not ashamed to talk about herself, to
fill the page with it, though women in this culture are supposed
to feel embarrassed at just that "subjectivity." She's not ashamed
to talk about her suffering and to talk about it as if it were of
interest. (Women are allowed to suffer but not to insist that it
is of interest to anybody.) Although she is not yet "making connections" between her "bad nerves" and the sexist nature of her culture, she is facing the existance of her nerves, and that is important.

In Play It As It Lays Didion finally does make connections between the sexism of a culture economically and socially dominated by
men and the various forms of helplessness and vulnerability which
women are forced into and then clutch at with both hands. Maria,
of course, is not everywoman, for not every woman enters adult life
that ready for exploitation. Maria has had "bad nerves" from an
early age: picturing herself at ten, she must already keep the be-
traying figure of her father "out of it" (Play, p. 80). But what
happens to Maria in the novel does happen to women in life, and her
complicity is a severe version of the complicity we are taught to have
in regard to our own abortions -- mental, emotional, and physical.

Feminists sometimes complain that Didion exaggerates, that things
are not that bad, and yes, it seems to me the book is radically limited

in imagination. It allows for so little alliance between women, so few modes of dealing with sexist games. But no artist, after all, is under contract to write about positive role-models. She writes what she sees. And what I find in the severity of that book is another instance of Didion's determination to confront the worst. The novel always strikes me as an exploration of disasters which Didion may or may not feel are potential in herself and in her life. The primary disaster is that of being a woman in a sexist culture, a woman with a version of Didion's bad nerves and vulnerability but without her toughness, her insistence on coming to terms with herself and her world. Maria, unlike Didion, persistently refuses to see how things add up, how they apply. Knowing how things apply has, until now, seemed to me the impulse behind almost all of Didion's writing.

I say "almost all" because Didion has occasionally brought to her writing a version of the self-defensiveness which is so dominant in her review of the Women's Movement. In Slouching Toward Bethlehem, for example, Didion does occasionally chastise what she sees as excessive vulnerability, feeling, or tenderness with an asperity that is controlled but which leaves her just this side of being overtly patronizing. In her essay on Joan Baez, "Where the Kissing Never Stops," the balance is especially precarious. As the title might suggest, the essay suffers from a case of overkill. There are a few too many references to what has already been established.

> Above all, [Baez] is the girl who "feels things,"
> who has hung on to the freshness and pain of
> adolescence, the girl ever wounded, ever young.
> Now, at an age when the wounds begin to heal
> whether one wants them to or not, Joan Baez rarely
> leaves the Carmel valley.
>
> (STB, p. 48)

One is reminded throughout the essay of that wounded twenty-three-year-old whom Didion is still trying to banish.

This tendency to purge the self by attacking external and unacknowledged self-reflections has its corollary in the way Didion portrays female relations in Play It As It Lays. With the careful exception of mothers and daughters, or mother and daughter figures, all women in the book are either frightened or hostile when they see themselves in each other: "Sometimes Maria was depressed by how much she and Felicia had in common." (Play, p. 66) Just before her abortion and at other times when Maria moves into the "realm of miseries peculiar to women," the only women she can call on are her dead mother and her retarded daughter, Kate. Unless there is the overriding strength of a mother-daughter relationship, the fact that women are like each other is exactly what keeps them apart.

This limited view of the potential for female relations is particularly striking because the novel presents alliance between females as the most positive mode of dealing with male domination. The alliance, however, is exclusively between mother and daughter. Francine Wyeth, for example, thinks briefly of uniting with Maria in a venture which might secure them economic, therefore social, therefore psychic independence from the man in control, Maria's father: "Maria and I can always open a hash house. When we get sick of you all." (Play, p. 210) The one woman who achieves economic, social, and psychological independence is also putting woman's work into the labor market. She is running a cafe in a desert town. It's bleak, but as she tells Maria, "You can't call this a bad place. . . . I've lived in worse." (Play, p. 188) So has Maria. This woman acts as a mother figure to Maria by taking her home with her and giving her some indirect advice: "Have you ever made a decision?" (Play, p. 199) Her own decision is to do without the man who betrayed her. Ultimately, however, mothers and daughters also fail or are about to fail each other. Francine runs her car off the road; Maria gets herself into a sanitarium; and the woman on the desert can't offer Maria enough. Hostile or not, women just can't get it together.

In her essay on the Movement, Didion maintains that stance, not with sympathy or a sense of loss, but with an almost vengeful vigor. In her own person, moreover, she turns upon Movement women the same kind of hostility and dread which the lost women in Play It As It Lays turn upon each other -- upon their selves as reflected in each other. She imitates too the tendency of her female characters to deny, except to mothers or daughters, that there even is "a realm of miseries peculiar to women." Insofar as the "miseries" exist, they are dismissed as "trivial." ("Women's Movement," p. 2)

Now this is what strikes me as the greatest departure. Didion was once very aware of that "realm of miseries," and in Play It As It Lays she will not allow us to dismiss them as "trivial" or worse, as the products of a masochistic self-indulgence. Maria is a very complicit victim, but Didion demands a sympathy for her that is intended to keep us from scorning her, from simply demanding why Maria doesn't "get herself another gynecologist." ("Women's Movement," p. 2) Nor will Didion let us dismiss Maria for feeling "terror and revulsion" when an unemployed actor observes her with dutiful "sexual appreciation" (Play, p. 23). I would suggest that the actor's unwanted attentions are no harder to take than those of construction workers. Yet Didion ridicules women who feel the very "terror and revulsion" which we are meant to take seriously in Maria. ("Women's Movement, p. 14) In Play It As It Lays Didion also elicits a certain empathy for the mute and mundane sufferings of ordinary women, women who appear as cameos in the novels: the imagined "wife" with her "scented douches" and "secret sexual grievances," the beautiful, wheedling girl with the pelvic abcess, the lonely women in supermarkets buying groceries for one, the woman who is "mentally ill." (Play, pp. 81, 121,

122, 101) Maria, in fact, reaches an epiphany about the nothingness of her life while she watches a woman in a muu muu cross the street to a supermarket: "Maria watched the woman, for it seemed to her then that she was watching the dead still center of the world . . . ." (Play, p. 67) Didion strongly implies that these women are complicit in their suffering, but she still insists that their suffering is real. In her essay on the Movement, however, Didion is writing as if she had never encountered those miseries -- in life or in fiction, even her own.

Didion, then, appears to have misplaced that remarkable blend of critical and sympathetic perception which she brings to the very complicit victims of Play It As It Lays -- one wonders why. Perhaps in backing off from empathy she is backing off from some of the pessimism implicit in her fictional explorations. In Play It As It Lays there is a stark sense that escape is the only mode of dealing with male games -- no one fights successfully from within. Escape, moreover, is either into death, as for B.Z. and Francine, or into some bare survival almost stripped of mental or emotional life -- see the woman in the desert and Maria at the end of the novel. Perhaps, like her characters, Didion reached some dead end of her own in writing that novel, some decision about the futility of fighting from within and the futility of escape, some judgment about the permanent alienation of women. If so, it is not strange that she should seek survival in denial, denial of what she has seen about being a woman. Nor is it surprising that she should seek to detach herself from her vulnerability and from her sense of the common miseries by falling back upon that indirect purgation of the self which marks her essay on Joan Baez.

Those of us who have admired Didion as a writer and those of us who have touched base with our own dead ends, however momentarily, can sympathize with the impulse. But Didion is capable of so much more than that. She is too fine an observer to persist in mistaking flight from self as resolution of conflict, too exercised in confrontation to deny what she has already seen. I trust she will return to confrontation, to making things apply, to real explorations. For if we are to lose the sensibility which marks Slouching Toward Bethelehem and Play It As It Lays -- that unflinching recognition of the worst, that blend of criticism and sympathy which she brings to the experience of being a woman -- then we are to lose something of value to all of us.

CHRISTINE DE PISAN AND CHAUVINIST DIPLOMACY

by Judith M. Davis

Sophisticated as they may be in their own discipline, male intellectuals are rarely distinguished for their enlightened attitudes toward women. Any female who has watched the wheels of the gods grind slowly through an Affirmative Action program, or who has tried to convince an administrator that women are not too emotional to serve on important committees, knows the resistance of academics to feminine encroachment on masculine prerogatives.

To combat this resistance, educated women have developed a kind of chauvinist diplomacy which combines subtle infiltration and argument with varying degrees of militant attack. Chauvinist diplomacy demands a great deal of patience and a high tolerance for frustration; its practitioners work slowly and carefully within a system controlled by males who react with diplomatic counterploys of condescension and procrastination. Nevertheless, many women believe that such diplomacy is necessary to attain their goals; their chances for success are greater if they bargain with properly academic restraint, pressing reasonably and logically for recognition of their efforts.

The art of chauvinist diplomacy is over five hundred years old; if it had been truly successful, today we would not need Women's Caucuses in politics, Women's Studies in universities, and Women's Workshops in professional organizations. I submit that in our present efforts to gain recognition and equality we are using techniques that were tried and found wanting in the fifteenth century; at that time Christine de Pisan was practicing chauvinist diplomacy in a feminist cause that appears to have had much in common with our own. A study of one episode in this remarkable woman's fight to counteract male prejudice may produce some insights into women's struggles in the twentieth century.

Christine de Pisan "was not only a woman writer making her mark in an almost exclusively masculine society, but also a completely professional author."[1] Born in Italy about 1364, she and

1 Janet M. Ferrier, French Prose Writers of the Fourteenth and Fifteenth Centuries (London: Pergamon Press, 1966), p. 98.

her family moved to France in 1368 when her father was appointed court doctor and astrologer to Charles V. Married at fifteen to Etienne de Castel, secretary to the king, she lived a contented and pampered court life until the death of her husband in 1389. The shock of widowhood was severe: bereft of the husband whom she adored, she faced alone the formidable task of providing for her three children and widowed mother. At the age of twenty-five she was suddenly transformed, as she tells us, "into a man."[2] Confronted with a man's obligations, she returned to the studies begun with her father and deliberately began to develop the skills which would transform her into a "man of letters." Through judicious cultivation of her talents and her protectors, she succeeded completely.

Christine was a well established courtly poet when she took up her first feminist cause: Jean de Meun's witty denigration of women in his Roman de la Rose. The first recorded quarrel in French literary history[3] centered on the defamation of feminine character which pervades the entire second half of the Roman; and it was Christine who struck the first blow with a sarcastic reference to Jean de Meun in her Epistre au dieu d'Amours (1399). She devoted seven lines to "the drawn-out process, the difficulties, the learned efforts . . . the struggles . . . to deceive -- that's all -- one maiden . . . "[4] Almost immediately she was reprimanded, for the Roman de la Rose had enjoyed an unparalleled success since its completion about 1278;[5] its author had been acknowledged a master of erudition and subtlety. After a series of discussions with Jean de Montreuil and Jean Gerson, two eminent and scholarly clerics, Christine received a letter from Montreuil in defense of his "master" de Meun,[6] and sent him a detailed reply. Her correspondence with Montreuil and others reveals the techniques of chauvinist diplomacy, and -- more importantly -- reveals their shortcomings.

2 Mutacion de la Fortune, Book I, Chapter I. Cited by Marie-Josephe Pinet, Christine de Pisan: Etude biographique et litteraire (Paris: Champion, 1927), p. 306.

3 Guillaume de Lorris et Jean de Meun, Le Roman de la Rose, ed. Felix Lecoy, I (Paris: Champion, 1965), p. xxix.

4 Cited by Pinet, p. 67.

5 Lecoy, p. viii.

6 The letter has been lost, according to Charles Frederick Ward, The Epistles of the Romance of the Rose and Other Documents in the Debate (Chicago: University of Chicago Press, 1911), p. 7.

She began her missive to Montreuil (written in 1401) with
a lengthy salutation designed to flatter him and to prevent
any assumption that she did not know her place:

> To your reverence, honor and esteem, Prévost
> de Lisle, most cherished lord and master wise
> in manner, devotee of science, learned in cler-
> ical arts, expert in rhetoric, from Christine
> de Pisan. [I ask your indulgence toward] an
> ignorant and flighty woman; in your wisdom do
> no despise the slight import of my reasoning,
> I beg you, in consideration of my femine
> frailty . . . [7]

The conventions observed, she continued (with well-placed references to her "lack of expertise") to her attack on the Roman de la
Rose: "I wish to state, proclaim and maintain openly that (save
your Grace) wrongly and for no good reason [you] praise so highly
this work which could better be called an idle diversion than
a worth-while book . . . " (p. 17).

It must be noted that Christine could be so positive in her
attack because she had enlisted the sympathies of Gerson, who as
Chancellor of the University of Paris wielded considerable influence in the intellectual and spiritual controversies of the day.
She therefore objected to the Roman first of all on the basis of
its obscene language.[8] She argued her point as subtly as a
Parisian Master of Theology: since Jean de Meun depicts Reason
allegorically as the daughter of God, her manner of speaking
should be holy and truthful; but Reason speaks with unholy frankness
about immoral behavior; therefore, Reason is not a true daughter
of God but a persona of Jean de Meun; therefore, both Reason
and Jean de Meun repudiate their heavenly Father. Christine's argument from orthodoxy was designed not only to appeal to the moral
rectitude of clerics like Gerson but to cloud the theological
reputation of Jean de Meun enough to render suspect his pious
pronouncements on women's depravity. After implying that Jean de
Meun was a heretic, and assuring herself thereby of additional
support from Gerson, Christine was free to address herself directly
to the point: de Meun's rampant misogyny. "Good Lord God!" she

7 Ward, p. 17. Unless otherwise noted, all references to correspondence in the debate are taken from Ward's edition. The translations are my own.

8 Jean de Meun was a master of rnetoric in finding allegorical expressions for genitalia; however, he could be frank when he chose,
and the word "balls" appears with such frequency that one can only
wonder at his obvious obsession.

said. "What revolting dishonesty!. . . What [moral] deformity is attributed to women!" Not only does de Meun's character Jealousy speak in the antifeminine accents of St. Jerome, but the author himself adds "lies which can only make women's condition worse," testifying that women are subject to "every perversity" (p. 20). Christine found it strange and contradictory that de Meun devoted so much time to the pursuit of creatures whom, he says, men ought to flee "as venomous serpents" (p. 22). To the old accusation that women importune men and lead them into iniquity, Christine answered pointedly that men can always refuse to be lured (p. 23); she suggested that the author and his fellow clerics spent their time with prostitutes and from them inferred that all women are whores (pp. 24-25). Furthermore, de Meun said nothing new when he described the age-old chase of male after female; therefore, he cannot be defended by those who proclaim the novelty of his assertions (pp. 25-26).

Christine emphasized that she was refuting Jean de Meun not because she was a woman, but because she was a person dedicated to truth (p. 25). She was also objective in her literary criticism:

> I do not condemn the Roman de la Rose entirely;
> it certainly contains good passages and points
> well made, which is precisely why it is a
> dangerous book: the authentic and the spurious
> are mixed in such a fashion that it is diffi-
> cult to distinguish between them. His [de Meun's]
> technique subtly plants errors in the midst of
> truth. And just as his priest Genius says,
> "Flee women, flee the evil serpent concealed in
> the grass," so I reply, "Flee, flee the malice
> hidden under a mantle of virtue."
>
> (pp. 26-27)

She finished her letter with a ringing defense of herself and her sisters:

> And lest people consider it foolish, arrogant,
> or presumptuous for one woman to dare attack
> and criticize such a subtle author, depriving
> him of the praise [considered] due his work, let
> them [also] consider the fact that one man dared
> to undertake the defamation and condemnation
> of all women, without exception.
>
> (p. 28)

After this letter, Montreuil evidently found it expedient to enlist the support of other men; the next document in the debate came from one Gontier Col, secretary to the king, who wrote to Christine in September, 1401, asking her for a copy of her communication

with Montreuil. The tone of the document is typically condes-
cending; Gontier obliquely threatened Christine with organized
opposition:

> I have heard from several notable clerics that
> your other studies and virtuous works are much
> to be praised; as I understand it . . . you
> have just written an invective against my tea-
> cher and late fatherly master Jean de Meun, a
> true Catholic, Master and Doctor of his time
> in sacred theology, an accomplished and ex-
> cellent philosopher . . . whose glory and re-
> nown lives and will live in times to come . . .
>
> (p. 29)

With his request for her correspondence, Gontier sent her a
"little treasury" of critiques upholding the scholarly reputation
of de Meun, in the hopes that it would "correct" her views. It
is significant that he addressed Christine as "tu" (the pronoun
reserved for intimates, children and animals) although it is
evident that he did not know her at all;[9] much less was he on
familiar enough terms with her to use the intimate pronoun in
writing to her.

Later that month, after Christine's prompt dispatch of her
letter, Gontier replied to her criticisms in the tone of a kindly
confessor who undertakes the rehabilitation of an ignorant sinner.
The tone is not unfamiliar: "I exhort, advise and pray you to
correct and make reparation for [the] evident error, foolishness
and agitation engendered by presumption or pride in a woman who
becomes too passionate about matters like this . . . " (p. 31).
To soften the blow of his egotism (and perhaps because he had heard
from others that she was offended), he added a conciliatory note
about his use of the "tu" form in addressing her, claiming that
was the manner in which he always wrote to friends. Gontier was
no mean practitioner of chauvinist diplomacy himself. His
attitude reveals a medieval and paternalistic mind-set found in
many a Master and Doctor of the twentieth century.

Christine was not deceived by his unctuous rudeness. Her
reply to him implied that his writing revealed his bias; she
cited as evidence his "two insulting letters" and his invitation
to "repent" as if he were extending her the "pardon due the
publican" of biblical fame. She told him flatly that he needn't
resort to threats, a tactic commonly attributed to cowards, and
assured him that she would defend her assertions before all,
submitting them to the judgment of all theologians and people of
"honest and praiseworthy life" (pp. 32-33).

9 Pinet, p. 71.

So she did. She enlisted the aid of Guillaume de Tignonville,
Prévost of Paris; she sent copies of her correspondence with
Montreuil and Gontier to the Queen of France; she enlisted in her
support the rhetoric of Jean Gerson, the Bossuet of the fifteenth
century; and she continued to answer the antifeminist accusations
of her rhetoric-wielding opponents with far more logic than
they deserved. Their arguments were riddled with the logical
fallacy of the argumentum ad feminam: "You resemble the pelican,
killing yourself with your own beak," wrote Gontier's brother Pierre
Col in an angry letter of 1402, implying that Christine would ruin
herself by daring to argue with her intellectual superiors. He
attacked further:

> O most foolish presumption! O thoughtless
> opinion tumbling too soon and without reflection
> from the mouth of a woman, who condemns a man of
> such high learning, such fervent study . . .
> When you have read [the Roman de la Rose] a hun-
> dred times, if you [then] understand most of it,
> you will never employ your time or reason better
> [than in appreciating it] . . . You are not as
> perceptive or as gracious as Gerson . . . I
> suppose it is because [de Meun] has spoken the
> truth that you want to bite him. But I suggest
> you keep your mouth shut.   (p. 65)

Jean de Montreuil wrote his friends about the quarrel, venting
his spleen against Christine whom he compared to the prostitute
who dared to criticize the learned Theophrastus.[10] He did not
insult her directly, but preferred to defend his colleagues'
arguments by insinuating that Christine was demented or depraved.

     Christine displayed remarkable restraint in refuting the
more objective arguments of Pierre and Gontier Col, carefully citing
each point they raised and speaking directly to that point. Her
last letter to Pierre Col followed the scholarly philosophical
form of objection and response:

> You say that even if [Jean de Meun] has spoken
> evil of women and has defamed the feminine sex,
> he is only repeating what other authors have said.
> RESPONSE. I know very well that he is not the
> first to have spoken against women; the point is
> that he amplifies the defamatory episodes when he
> records them.
>   (p. 106)

10 Pinet, p. 81.

At this time (October 1402) the debate had lasted more than a year; Christine began to sense the futility of chauvinist diplomacy. Her opponents ostensibly respected her intelligence but derided her reasoning; they belittled her criticisms and reacted furiously to her logical defense of them; and when they failed to move her mind, they attacked her reputation. In her last letter (cited above), Christine withdrew from the debate. "As for me, I do not plan to write any more [about the Roman de la Rose] no matter who writes to me, for I haven't set out to drink the Seine," she said in a rare lapse from her usual high style. She did not withdraw, as she said, because she doubted her ability to sustain the fight but because she had "better and more pleasant things to do" (p. 111). She did, too. In the next three years she brought out three books; by the end of her career in 1430 she had produced fifteen volumes of prose and poetry, many of them dedicated to the defense and explanation of women.

Christine de Pisan resorted to chauvinist diplomacy because she was a woman alone in a male-dominated, male-oriented society. Realizing the disadvantages of her position in that society, she bowed to male authority even as she challenged masculine prejudice in intellectual debate. She must have realized the contradiction and compromise inherent in chauvinist diplomacy, because she eventually abandoned the tactics which only evoked further insult and ended in frustration. Twentieth-century women should have the sense -- and the courage -- to follow her example. Chauvinist diplomacy is a dead end; we can and must create an uncompromising feminist diplomacy based on individual and communal strength. As individuals we can create, through art and criticism, unprejudiced images of women; through organization, we can acquire the economic and political strength to fulfill our ambitions now. We cannot afford to wait another five centuries for intellectual and moral equality.

A WAY OF LOOKING AT DORIS LESSING

by Nancy M. Porter

I spent part of this past summer cabined with Doris Lessing; that is, with her writing. I must say I was not altogether happy with the way the affair went, with Lessing's insistent refusal to iron out the wrinkles in our commonality as women. We had the usual monogamous couple's domestic quarrels. I wanted her to make political commitments she could not make. I do not know her side of the story, beyond what she will say in her writing; but for my part I have begun an accounting of Children of Violence[1] from the perspective of silenced history because such is the history of the twentieth century to which she has given voice.

The kind of history Lessing is concerned with in the five novels that comprise Children of Violence is individual biography intersecting in social structure[2] and with events in the larger political world. The novel form, with its traditional emphasis on social relations, seems particularly adaptable to Lessing's purposes. In The Golden Notebook Anna Wulf characterizes the kind of novel she wishes to write: "a book powered with an intellectual or moral passion strong enough to create order, to create a new way of looking at life" (p. 61). Reading Lessing has changed the way many women understand their lives, in part because Lessing gives us a "re-vision" of the silent history of women. In the first three novels of Children of Violence the focus is on Martha Quest who is trying to connect her sense of self with what parental and other forces in her world tell her about her past, present and future. As Martha seeks to locate herself in time, so do the others she shares space with: her parents and the other colonial Zambesian emigres; Martha's lover Thomas Stern and the other Europeans displaced by war to Southern Africa; the native Black Africans whose silenced presence surrounds them all literally and as a metaphor for their own silenced history.

---

1   Doris Lessing, Children of Violence, Martha Quest, vol. I, A Proper Marriage, vol. II (New York, 1964), A Ripple From the Storm, vol. III, Landlocked, vol. IV (New York, 1966), The Four-Gated City (New York, 1970); The Golden Notebook (New York, 1971). Further references to these editions will be included in the body of the paper.

2   C. Wright Mills, The Sociological Imagination (New York: 1959), passim.

Personal histories in these novels, as in The Golden Notebook, are developed by the structural use of the characters' sense of time and place, understandings that are at variance one with another and often with temporal event. In the following pages I propose to carry the perspective of time, place and history through Martha Quest, A Proper Marriage, A Ripple From The Storm in sequence, then consider briefly the formal experimentation of The Golden Notebook in which the various aspects of a woman's life -- each aspect embodying a different experiential time scale -- are dissociated and displaced into a conventional novel and five notebooks. Discussion of Lessing's experiment there provides an aesthetic bridge to the interconnections of time, history and biography worked out in Landlocked. Because I have limitations of space, I will not discuss The Four-Gated City, although I will suggest how time and personal history also figure in that novel to provide a new way of understanding life.

At the opening of Martha Quest, two generations jockey for position in the isolated world of the African veld. The Quest's "temporary" rough mud-walled house is set in the center of a vast basic, surrounded by mountains with an opening to the north, the "hinterland of the imagination" and the route by which comes news of happenings in the larger world. The sense of place is important in understanding the kinds of social relations of which it is expressive, relations that are three-quarters rigidly self-enclosing, one quarter open and diffuse. The Quest's house is fronted by a verandah: at one end sit Mrs. Quest and Mrs. Van Rensberg, "seasoning the dull staple of their lives -- servants, children, cooking -- with a confinement or scandal of some kind;" at the other, Mr. Quest and Mr. Van Rensberg, talking of "crops and the weather and the native problem," their backs firmly planted against the women in a gesture which suggests the effect women's culture has on men. Martha sits on the steps, her "fate" arranged on either side of her, provocatively reading Havelock Ellis on Sex, a subject the older people have absorbed enough through the newspapers to know is in the "spirit of the times," but one which they find nonetheless discomforting.

Martha's "time" is adolescence, and Ellis' "interesting collection of facts," useful as a power play in the generational warfare, seems on the whole to have little to do with her problems as a fifteen year old woman. Martha vigorously resolves "not to be like Mrs. Van Rensberg, a fat and earthy housekeeping woman . . . not be bitter and nagging and dissatisfied, like her mother," grubbing out bare subsistence on a farm remote both from her dreams of English respectability and from the promise that emigration to Africa once held. Martha wonders who then she will be. The unreality of the heroines' lives in the older novels she reads provides nothing for her to identify with, such seems "the gap between herself and the past." The sternly objective accounting of herself she derives from the contemporary books the Cohen brothers lend her hardly encourages her. If

adolescent, and therefore bound to be unhappy;
British, and therefore uneasy and defensive; in
the fourth decade of the twentieth century, and
therefore inescapably beset with problems of race
and class; female, and obliged to repudiate the
shackled women of the past [,]

with all that known and named, Martha wonders why she must go through
"the painful business of living it?" The question is, of course,
tautological; but the kind of history Lessing writes suggests these
stages must be lived through, a kind of time that needs to be lived
through her. Additionally, for a young girl, seeking recognition and
guidance for the inchoate perceptions she has about her feelings,
the question signals the silence abroad in the world of parents, neighbors, and books (pp. 11-20).

When Martha is not abandoning herself to resentment, her imagination paints from her reading visions of social justice on the blank
canvas of the landscape: the stately, ancient, fabulous four-gated
city in which all colors of children play together under the approving
eyes of their elders. Martha's golden age vision contrasts sharply
with her encounters with the real society of the district. She sees
well enough the divisive nature of the social system, the criss-
crossed lines of prejudice and national pride, invisible until broken,
and the immense effort of imagination it takes to break down the cata-
gories. The land and the people are "dreamlocked" in splendid isolation from their past and from the great political events in the
outer world, like the patients in Mann's sanitorium, isolated from
the processes of time. On the farms that dot the district, time
is measured by the yard stick of the cycle of the seasons. In the
political talk of the district the approach of World War II is debated.
For Mr. and Mrs. Quest, the argument over the war is fuelled less by
contact with temporal event and more by the memory they preserve of
World War I as the time in which they really lived, happy in the service of Britain, Mr. Quest as a soldier who becomes wounded, Mrs. Quest
as a nurse, roles they continue to play out in attenuated form in
their marriage of ironic complicity. For others -- the Afrikaans,
the Jews, the Greeks, the Welsh, those more attuned to military displacement -- the subject is treated cautiously. For Martha, war,
particularly World War I, is the "great Unmentionable," an implicit
although inadvertent discrediting through silencing of what her parents
remember from their past. Still Martha feels implicated in the past,
although she protests that she cannot locate herself in what she knows
of it, any more than she can establish herself in the future as she
sees it take shape in the persons of her mother and Mrs. Van Rensberg.

The sense of the present and the future as attenuations of time
past Lessing contrasts to an incandescent state of mind which Martha
achieves when she is alone. On the road from farm to station, and suspended in purpose from either of the two social poles of her narrow

world, Martha approaches a species of consciousness that simultaneously uses and transcends place. Conditioned as she is by her fit-
ful understanding that she already has a past history, not entirely of
her own making, as well as an uncertain future with which she must
struggle in her cry for new departures, Martha experiences a moment
that demands her reception, not her habitual analysis. The "great
wheels of movement" that catch up as in a dance the scurrying small
animals, the moving grasses, the trees, the underground rivers that
force themselves through Martha's swelling veins, make her flesh like
the earth, the sheer physicality of the flow excluding the human, the
personal, in no part the idea of herself important, nor the sound of
her voice even heard. The futility of her ego is not the point,
however:

> What was demanded of her was that she should accept
> something quite different; it was as if something
> new were demanding conception, with her flesh as host;
> as if there were a necessity, which she must bring
> herself to accept, that she should allow herself to
> dissolve and be formed by that necessity.

Alert to the quick silver scattering of the integral moment of pro-
jection, the perception of time as process, the sliding of process
back into the calcified memory of a longed for state of timeless being
and happiness, Martha understands that this was not ecstasy she
touched and lost, only "difficult knowledge" not fully grasped (pp. 60-63).

With the triumph of hindsight one might say that what was demanded of Martha is a change in how she views the world, a view which,
like the world itself, is dominated with forces lift over from the
past. But within the great wheels of indifferent matter necessarily
turn the smaller wheels of human history. Martha contracts pink eye
which develops into an attitude that prevents her from taking her
university matriculation exams; and in her eighteenth year she takes
the lesser passport to freedom, striking out from the timeless land
to the time-bound city where she becomes "Matty" the young secretary
who is sucked half-willingly into the whirl of social event, social
relation. If one aspect of Martha's quest is to locate a world in
which her sense of personal time harmonizes with the external reality,
life in the city specifically fulfills her needs on one level, frus-
trates them on another. In the world of movie going, sundowner
drinking and Sporting Club dancing until dawn, Martha comes to play
the role this playworld expects. She is the feminine young woman who
joins in the conspiracy to disavow the past and the future, to live
for the moment, a "timeless" group suspended on a slim thread in time
which will bring on the war. Sooner than some, Martha rebels against
the shallow, amoral and ahistorical society of the Club by having an
affair with a Jew who is the Club musician. But if the white middle
class rulers have no sense of past and future to offer, Adolph has
only too much past carried around in him, a past that he parodies as

the price of acceptance by his new masters. When both the affair
and the Club begin to pale, Martha and the others of her set move on
to become the "young marrieds," a logical progression in a society on
the brink of war.

Martha Quest ends with her marriage to Dougie Knowles; and A
Proper Marriage begins with her immediate desire to break the hold
which had made it "impossible for her to say no at any stage of the
process." Even as Martha with increasing self-irony turns from one
social form to the next, so in this second novel emerges the image of
a great ferris wheel, part of the equipment of the "fun fair" that
visits the town annually. The wheel, visible from the Knowles' bedroom window, its moving chain of colored lights garishly reflected
on their wall, catches up like a clock the locked-in rhythms of Martha
and her marriage in the mechanical round of sundown parties, dances,
loves and lovemaking that characterizes the social life of the young.
The approaching war is viewed as both an extension of the cycle and a
way out of the dimming excitement of "fun city," particularly of the
new marriages. While the men wait for their orders to go North, they
talk solemnly of the technology of modern warfare which will affect
their lives. But the dances continue, the band plays World War I
songs, and the young, catching the stavistic spirit, become "self-
dedicated worshippers of what their parents chose to remember of 1914."

> Their days and work, their loves and love-making,
> were nothing but a preparation for that moment when
> hundreds of them stamped and shouted in great circles
> to the thundering drums, felt less as sound than as
> their own pulses; this was the culmination of the
> day, the real meaning of it, the moment of surrender.

> (Page 327)

Martha herself, now pregnant through a conspiracy of silence about
the operations of her own body, contributes her cycle of the flesh
to the masculine rhythms of war, as she settles with the other women
into the lethargic round of preparing for, bearing and rearing a child,
her time of surrender to the next logical social role, motherhood.

In Lessing's technique, fictional time is foreshortened in the
early part of Martha Quest and lengthened gradually in the rest of
the novels.[3] The effect of this manipulation is the altering sense

---

3 Part I of Martha Quest encompasses three years; Parts II, III and
   IV occur over a period of a year. Martha marries within a few months
   of her arrival in town, and the fictional time of A Proper Marriage
   begins within a few weeks of her marriage and occupies about three
   years duration. A Ripple From The Storm takes up the narrative
   three months after the ending of the previous novel and spans a two

of the density and thinning out of psychological time for Martha.
Lessing also uses density of detail to build up the very different
time worlds the characters inhabit. Time is seen as the function of
social position, particularly notable among the white women in the
town. In A Proper Marriage, Martha likens the cyclical and backward-
looking time of the middle aged colonial women to the schema of a Victorian novel, with the rounds of afternoon tea and talk of the in-
gratitude of servants who do not understand the dignity of labor. The
young married whites have their own notions of order and time as
expressed particularly in the social patterns of the women. Martha's
new house provides the spatial equivalent. "The house was in the
older part of the city, at the corner of a block. From its gate one
could see a mile in four directions along tree-lined avenues . . . .
Everything was straight, orderly, unproblematical..." (p. 506). The
view from the new house, one of many in repeating order purchased on
time-installments as the men begin to return from their terms of service, contrasts the open prospects from the old farm house in the
pre-social land. Martha's relation to the house and to the life it
suggests is one of both living and criticizing. Inside the Knowles'
house, and similar ones, life settles into a cycle of time-buying and
"security," the great war and post-war ideology of the bourgeoise.
"[T]he great climax of their lives would come at fifty or fifty-five,
when their houses, gardens and furniture would be their own, and the
pensions and policies bore fruit" (p. 510). The men go off to their
offices, and the women to morning teas where they discuss their babies
and exchange tips on how to economize by remaking old clothes and
doing their own food buying. Although the culture of these women is
not officially recorded in any history book, Martha sees that it is
of the greatest economic importance in maintaining the white capitalist
domination. "It was," she notes, "the time of these women which
supported the whole edifice; their willingness to sink their youth
in acquiring multifarious small talents, which softened the road to
that great goal, comfortable middle age" (p. 511).

Martha does not need a Marxist analysis to see that the dominant
ruling culture rests on the time of the women, silent and unrecognized.
Martha, caught up in and yet critic of the times, makes her first
tentative break with the cycle, the institutions of marriage and the
family, because she begins at last to make contact with a version of
the past which makes sense. In the awareness of politics opened up
by the Battle of Stalingrad, Martha begins to piece together what
she has read and heard of Marxism from various sources and declares herself the child of the Russian Revolution who has been denied knowledge
of her birthright and history. At the same time she begins to make
contact with the past in another way. Her realization that she infan-
talizes Dougie even as her mother plays nurse to her father's war-
connected ailments, complements her understanding that in her relations
with her daughter Carolyn she repeats the same guilt-binding practices

year period of intensive political activity. Landlocked, with its central
image of waiting on a high plateau for time to pass and with it passage by sea to England, stretches the narrative over six years of
chronological time.

employed by her mother with her. Martha attempts by leaving her husband and daughter and joining the radical political circle of the community to establish herself in time with a past and a future other than her mother's. As always, however, with the young Martha, her motives connect political with sexual possibilities. Thus her break with the social institution of the family is accomplished as much by personal attraction to a potential lover in the new social grouping of the Party as it is by agreement with the Marxist view of the deleterious effects of the bourgeois family on the future.

From the time Martha first enters into social relation she seeks for masculine stability, a disease at least as debilitating in its effects as pink eye. Successively, her father, the Cohen brothers, her various boyfriends, her husband, her lovers let her down. In A Ripple From The Storm, Martha's need for the male presence and her growing sense of social responsibility lead her ironically into a mundane and fruitless marriage with one of the Party leaders, Anton Hesse, the German alien in need of the protection afforded him by Martha's British citizenship. The third novel details the histories and rhythms of the individuals who make up the progressive alliance that seeks involvement with the Africans and the Coloreds. The class-oriented approaches to African unity betray the very different time senses among those in the Alliance. The young European communists (like Anton and Athen the Greek), the Zambesian young Jews (like Jasmine, Solly and Jose Cohen) displaced by war, nationality and, in the cases of Martha, Jasmine, and the other young women, by sex from the colonial rulers, look to the immediacy of revolution to ring in the new form of the future. The trade unionists of the Alliance look to the slow time gain of economic parity between Blacks and Whites, hardly to equality in the tight job market threatening the post-war world. The Black "spokesmen" look to the even slower evolution of the Black economy through publically supported education for the natives. The middle class white liberals, with their ties to the ruling elite, look to rotting with the ebb and flow of the "spirit of the time" (Russia is an enemy, a friend, then again an enemy), on-again off-again social engineers who for the most part march to the major drum of expedient self-interest. By the end of the ripples that spread out from the storm of war, the disintegration by attrition and defection of the Communist group that has been Martha's primary social and political involvement cuts her off from the struggle for justice spread by the Russian Revolution, the struggle that feeds her imagination. Significantly, as the Social Democratic Congress splits over the issue of the feasibility of African education, Martha is not at the Congress but with her friend Masie who is giving birth to a child.

From the perspective of the first three novels of Children Of Violence, Martha's biography is the exemplary one of a woman whose energies are displaced into and drained by one social institution after another but who never finds more than temporary fulfillment in any, indeed never makes the vital connection among the sexual, the social,

the political aspects of her life. In <u>Landlocked</u>, the twenty-four
year old Martha waits for her life to begin, a position Lessing treats
with some of the homey irony she displays at the end of the previous
novel when the birth of a child takes precedence over the abortion
of social justice. Martha in the fourth novel sees herself as
divided among protean responses to different people. In a dream she
is charged with keeping separate the rooms of a large townhouse. In
another dream the house divided is the old mud hut on the kopje. The
price of not keeping things divided is the disintegration into dust
of the townhouse, the return to grass and bush of the Quest house on
the veld. Somewhere in the "shell of substance," which is her flesh,
the shape of her dream forms and reforms, moves back and forth in time
to build a house that is different from the other two: a dwelling "tall
rather than wide, reached up, stretched down, was built layer on layer,
but shadow above and below the shallow mid-area comprising (as they
say in the house agents' catalogue) 'comprising six or so rooms' for
which this present Martha was responsible, and which she must keep
separate." The price of such housewifely preservation of order, of
keeping separate the people and rooms of her life, is the "defeat,"
or "holding at bay, what was best in her:" the building of bridges
between rooms, connections between people. connections in herself.

Between the publication of the third and fourth volumes of
<u>Children of Violence</u> comes <u>The Golden Notebook</u> with its formal experi-
mentation of displacing various aspects of a single life which both
prepares for and illuminates what happens to Martha in <u>Landlocked</u>.
From one perspective, <u>The Golden Notebook</u> strikes the reader as an
uneasy alliance between a journal about the process of not writing a
novel, on one level, and a novel about the limitations of "free women"
on another. The chief protagonist in both is Anna Wulf who decides
to divide what seem the separable parts of her life into separate
notebooks: Black is reserved for discussions of her professional life
as a writer; Red for her involvement in the British Communist Party;
Yellow for the novel she is writing about the surrogate novelist Ella;
Blue for the intermittently kept diary of her every day life and psy-
coanalysis with Mrs. Marks.

In the Black notebook we learn that Anna has written a novel
"'about' a colour problem" in Africa during World War II, a novel that
makes its appeal to curiosity, Anna says, in a world in which groups
of people share physical space but are utterly ignorant of one another's
experiences. Anna tells us she suspects both the level in herself
from which the novel arose and its effect on art. Tormented by her
"inability to enter those areas of life [her] way of living, education,
sex, politics, class bar [her] from," she believes this malaise may
reveal a "new sensibility, a half-conscious attempt towards a new
imaginative comprehension;" but it both leads her away from the
writing trestle and feeds on an unhealthy attraction to formlessness
which she disguises by making up "stories," either response one fatal
to art. The novel Anna would write, if she would but exorcise her
devils of destruction, the novel "powered with an intellectual or moral

passion strong enough to create order, a new way of looking at life,"
seems irretrievably lost in her personal diffuseness (pp. 61-64).
The paradox in the Black notebook is the paradox of the business of
living in "Free Women:" one sees what one needs to be as in a blue-
print, but one cannot generate a form to sustain the idea.

The dilemma of the Black notebook appears again in the Blue,
which recapitulates on a psychological level the insights of the writer.
In this notebook, Anna tries to capture truth by a detailed accounting
of what happened on a certain day in 1954, then by a "terse record
of facts." Both fail.

> [A]lthough in life things like going to the lava-
> tory or changing a tampon when one has one's per-
> iod are dealt with on an almost unconscious level,
> I can recall every detail of a day two years ago
> because I remember that Molly had blood on her skirt,
> and I had to warn her to go upstairs and change before
> her son came in.

Anna notes that this is not a literary problem. In a remembered dialogue with Mrs. Marks, "Mother Sugar," the apparently Jungian analyst
Anna consults about her writer's block and her inability to feel,
the distinction between living and story is furthered. Psychoanalysis,
Anna says, takes one back into the repressed physicality of childhood and out into folk lore and myth.

> Look, if I'd said to you. . . Yesterday I met a man
> at a party and I recognized in him the wolf, or
> the knight, or the monk, you'd nod and you'd smile.
> And we'd both feel the joy of recognition. But
> if I'd said: Yesterday I met a man at a party
> and suddenly he said something, and I thought:
> Yes, there's a hint of something -- there's a
> crack in that man's personality like a gap in a dam,
> and through that gap the future might pour in a diff-
> erent shape -- terrible perhaps, or marvellous, but
> something new -- if I said that, you'd frown.

Mother Sugar, the female Marx, is satisfied if Anna casts her encounters
with people in the deterministic form of myth or story, for to see
one's life as the "reflection of that great archetypal dream, or epic
story, or stage in history" frees the individual from the pain of
uniqueness. This is to Anna the invention of story: "Because I'm
convinced that there are whole areas of myself made by the kind of
experience women haven't had before. . . ." One cannot write of the
new because it is formless, and people cannot stand chaos. "What is
happening is something new in my life. . . a sense of shape, of unfolding
. . . the beginning of something I must live through." Anna's sense

of "something I must live through" recalls Martha Quest's sense of having to live through the times. Perhaps in five years Anna will be able to say: "I was stuck fast in an emotion common to women of our time, that can turn them bitter, or Lesbian, or solitary" (pp. 467-480). In the present, however, the female's sexual sense of the temporal duration of love is sharply affronted by the male's sense of its transiency. Yet Anna's attachment to psychic unfolding, to revolutionary consciousness, leads her to seek out men and causes whose commitment to her is at best intermittent, at worst destructive, although they embody the attractive sense of living on the cutting edge of history where permanency is not an issue.

In the Blue notebook, Lessing gives clear voice to the silent rituals of women's culture. In the Yellow notebook, Ella illuminates the gap between a woman's emotions and social institution. Her "real" emotions have to do with her relationship with a man. "One man. But I don't live that kind of life, and I know few women who do. So what I feel is irrelevant and silly" (p. 314). Anna's increasing perception that her, and her surrogate's, personal psychological time is at variance with the social world they inhabit divides her, and this division is increasingly reflected in the notebooks. These notebooks end in disillusionment and disintegration. In the fifth notebook, the slim golden notebook, Anna strives for integration of herself with the spirit of the times. Her personality invaded by the alien one of her mad American lover Saul Green, Anna spends days in the timelessness of her room -- significantly, Anna's daughter, her one attachment to on-going time, is away at boarding school -- recovering in conversation and dreams the small painful gestures of human endurance that lie beneath the shimmering layers of her invented story worlds. Some of these gestures record the silent history of women: the set of Mrs. Boothby's shoulders, her daughter June's face when she is about to experience her sexual initiation in the uprooting of war. Close to the end of the notebook, Saul gives Anna the first sentence of her new novel, which is also the first sentence in The Golden Notebook: "two women were alone in the London flat," "the two women," Saul tells Anna, "you are" (p. 639).

The notebooks form the thematic center of Lessing's novel, each with a different time scale. The structural frame, the five "Free Women" chapters, transmute the raw materials of the notebooks into conventional form, into "story," which is the antagonist of the interlarded notebooks. Lessing's emperiment in form forces the reader to synthesize and synchronize the separate entities and times, particularly the division between structural and thematic time. "Free Women" begins in the summer of 1957 with a meeting between Anna and her friend Molly, two women who are divided on the value of "emotionally living from hand to mouth," proceeds through an autumn of tragedy when Molly's son blinds himself in a suicide attempt, a long winter of grotesquerie (Tommy dominates Molly and a male gay couple torment Anna) to a spring of comic resolution as Anna and Molly go

their separate ways, integrated into the mainstream of British life,
Anna into the Labour Party, Molly into a second marriage. The events
in the fictional time of "Free Women" at points parallel the happenings
in the time scheme of some of the notebooks, and conform to the general curve of each notebook, descending from the hopeful beginnings
(Communist Party membership, love affair, psychoanalysis, the keeping
of a journal, the start of a novel) through the nightmare of parody
and inversion to the ultimate dissolution of the bonds. The events
recorded in three of the notebooks, however, take place over the
seven years preceding the action in "Free Women" narrative; all notebooks conclude before the conclusion of the main action; events
and characterizations in the notebooks at certain points contradict
those in the main narrative; and in other ways the notebooks establish
their own time scheme which opposes as well the unconventional "I"
of Anna's psychological time to the conventional story-telling time
of the "Free Women's" omniscient narrator.

In Landlocked, Lessing uses the insights she evolves into the
complexities of recording an individual's history in The Golden Notebook.
There Martha, like Anna, is determinedly both dividing herself and
viewing this division from an outsider's perspective that annuls the
sexual whole. Anna's alternate attempts to keep a terse record of
fact and an expansive exploration of the effect of small physical details, such as the rituals surrounding menstruation, have on memory
appears as the writing of two kinds of history. Her final solution,
withdrawal into an insular room where sex, politics, art intersect
in madness and dream, is echoed in Martha Quest's addition of another
room in her dream house, which becomes the life she shares with her
lover Thomas in the loft above his greenhouse. In the little golden
notebook, Lessing, like Thomas Mann whose novels she obviously admires,
finds a way of linking the "past with the future, the future with
the past"[4] by the leitmotif of madness, the individual room suspended
in time in which the processes of time are yet concentrated.

With Thomas Stern, Martha's sense of her flesh as a shell is
met by his sense of living "inside his body as if it were an always
dissolving reforming shell or shape with many different names and
times," to quote Martha in The Four-Gated City. Even as Anna Wulf
struggles with the diverse times and personalities of Saul Green, sc
Martha struggles with the time world of Thomas as part of the struggle
to locate herself amidst shifting roles. Thomas states the problem
in a species of teaching story that focuses the time problem in
Children of Violence.

---

4   Thomas Mann; "The Making of the Magic Mountain" in The Magic
    Mountain (Random House: New York, 1969).

> I tell you, everything's changed and only a few
> people really know it....It was once like this:
> a child was born in a house that had a tree out-
> side it. It was an elm tree. His grandfather
> had planted it. The child grew up while the tree
> shed its leaves and grew them again.

All the important transactions of a person's life took place with
reference to the tree -- quarrels with the father, love-making, birth,
burial -- until "as an old man, he stood at his gate and looked at
the tree and thought: That tree has been with me all my life, I'm
smaller than that tree." Now the time scale has changed in the human
political world, and with the change the way of looking at the meaning
of a life. "That star over there," he continues, "that star's got
a different time scale from us. We are born under the star and make
love under it and put our children to sleep under it and are buried
under it. The elm tree is out of date: it's had its day." We are
left to understand that we are "midges compared to the star" (p. 386).

Lessing explores extensively the lives of those who measure
time by the elm tree but who have suffered dislocation in geographical
space and hence a crippling of the continuity from their past. Particularly this is seen in Mr. and Mrs. Quest who are successively
displaced from Britain to the African veld and from the veld to the
city. In Landlocked, as they wait out the dying light, Mrs. Quest and
to a certain extent Mr. Quest recapture in dream and reverie some
of the missing links to their formative pasts. Lessing also follows
those who, like Martha and Thomas, burn under a different generational
dispensation, try to make sense of their lives in the time scale of
the universe. The distinction is less between pre-Copernican and
Einsteinian physics, although that is the distinction Thomas remembers
his old Polish schoolmaster made when he advised him to understand
one before the other, and more of the social origins of a character's
thought. Martha comes to understand that she and Thomas are, as
he suggests, children of violence, the military violence of two world
wars in the twentieth century.

Thomas, however, differs from Martha in several important respects.
Both have lost contact with their pasts but in different ways that
illuminate one another. Thomas' dissociation comes first in terms
of his marriage to Rachel. Thomas, the son of a Jewish peasant family
from Sochaczen marries Rachel, the daughter of a university professor
from Cracow when Rachel and Thomas are students. Thomas describes
compellingly what he as a peasant had "to forget" of his life and
experiences in order to be "liked" and accepted by Rachel of the
bourgeois intellectual class. The price for her approval is silence
about all he knows from experience, from the past (p. 436). Thomas,
as a Marxist university student, predicts the advent of the Nazi
regime and convinces Rachel, but not her family, to flee to Africa,
"tossed out of Europe and into Africa by a movement of war," as Martha

notes in The Four-Gated City. Thomas' family cannot afford to leave
Poland, and both families are exterminated in the Warsaw Ghetto,
the final silencing of their history (Martha wonders if their names
were even recorded).

Martha, as we saw in Martha Quest, is also dissociated from her
past, cannot link past with future. In Landlocked she learns what
her parents, her novels and her books of history, sex, and social
science never told her. With Thomas off pursuing an historic revenge
against the British who are blocking the ports of Israel, Martha
stands, ironically, under a shade tree and argues with Thomas. "'But,
Thomas, what's the point of it?'" she asks. "'So, Martha,' she heard
him say . . . 'So, you don't believe in violence. . .'" "Martha was
the essence of violence, she had been conceived, bred, fed, and reared
on violence." In Thomas and Martha turn the millions of people dead
and dying from which they cannot dissociate themselves. Thomas has
literally lost his past, but the past still revolves within him,
unrecognized except by Martha. Martha herself, conceived with one
parent "in shellshock from the war, and the other in a breakdown from
nursing its wounded," is "as much a child of the 1914-1918 war" as
she is of her parents (pp. 462-463). They are the children of violence
and of time and of silenced history.

Former medical corps man and greenhouse grower, Thomas returns
from Israel to work with the native Africans whose lot is clearly
defined in the novel. The Africans who are invited into another one
of the progressive circles in Zambesia are treated to the history
of the Europeans in Africa. When they ask for a look at their own
history, Mrs. Van der Bylt scurries around, makes inquiries and reports back that, unfortunately, their history is not officially
collected:

> It was all there, but scattered over the world
> in old records and archives and bills of sale.
> There was no single book, or even pamphlet in
> existence in 1945 which Mrs. Van might order and
> make the basis of a study group on the 'History
> of Africa before the coming of the white man.'
>
> (Pages 390-391)

The thousands of years of silence, the silence of imperialism,
affects the Blacks profoundly. Thomas, whose own dislocation in place
makes him responsive to the relocation of the natives from their
original groupings to government reservations, ends his exile in
Africa by going off to live on one such location on the banks of the
Zambesi River, there to record the lineage and personal histories of
the people whose own silence matches his own, whose history, as his,
has been systematically disrupted by the movements of imperialism,
silenced by the dominant culture.

Thomas dies of fever among the Africans, leaving a manuscript that

Martha seeks to decipher. The sodden pages, as Martha works on them, at first obscure, begin to form a pattern, a leitmotif that connects the past with the future, for himself and for the Blacks who, as we learn in the last novel, are about to be again displaced for the building of a dam.

> A paragraph about life in Sochaczen was followed
> by poetry, in Polish. Translated it turned out to
> be a folk song. Then, how his mother cooked potatoes.
> Then, across this, in red pencil: If these people
> could be persuaded to grow potatoes -- but what use,
> if the salt has lost its savour? A great many Jewish
> jokes, or rather Yiddish. . . There was a long ar-
> ticle about how to run a carp farm. . . and the carp
> [could be] used to supplement the Africans' diet.
> Or for fertilizer? said the red pencil, across this.
> Stories: 'Once there was a man who travelled to a
> distant country. When he got there, the enemy he had
> fled from was waiting for him. Although he had
> proved the usefulness of travelling, he went to yet
> another country. No, his enemy was not there.'
> (Surprised, are you! said the red pencil.) 'So he
> killed himself.'

Embedded in the phantasmagoria are "stories of the people in the village, a history of the tribe, facts, figures," above all, obituaries. In the end, two versions emerge: one, written on heavy paper, "consisted of the short biographies and the obituaries and the recipes and the charms and the tables and the anecdotes;" the other, written on flimsier paper, insertable over the original, "made a whole roughly like the original -- more or less common sense, as a foundation with a layer of nonsense over it" (pp. 533-536). The nonsense is, of course, trenchant irony, the writer's cosmic perspective of the futility of even this recording to stop the flow of history and time imaged by the building of a dam that floods the tribal lands.

With Thomas dead and the concommitant rise of Communist China and the shaking faith of Stalanist Russia, Martha prepares to leave for Britain, the shoreline of her mother's past. There, in The Four-Gated City, her search for the link between past and future culminates in an excursion into madness through which she passes to prescience: in a world gone literally mad, the culminant of technological vio-lence, the destruction of the Victorian past, she at last achieves harmony between her inner psychological state and the mutated time of future history. The "times" literally catch up to her, even as she catches up to the times.

The significance of Children of Violence, its concern for per-sonal biography and history as these intersect in social structure and

political event can best be demonstrated in the light of the connection between time viewed as historical sequence and social structure. All "corporate" groups, the social scientists tell us, must
"by definition" possess continuity, which, in a "stable and homo-
geneous society," is expressed both in continuity of lineage (time)
and in continuity of place (space). The stable society is kept in
existence by, "and is at a given time, an expression of the forces
that determined its structure in the past and will do so in the
future." Time in this perspective is correlated with change within
a frame of continutiy: space or place -- the ordered arrangment of
spatial relations that shape structure -- suggests controlled movement that represents change also within the frame of continuity. In
the unstable society, in the society in which "military invasion,
conquest and alien settlement on a large scale" result in the creation
of a population of diverse origins forcibly brought together," dis-
continuity is exemplified.[5] In such a situation, for which Africa
is the microcosm, vital contact with the past is lost and with it
the ability for the individual and the group to determine the future.
In this context, Lessing's recording of the histories of those
dislocated in time and space parallels Thomas' efforts to record and
comment on the histories of the tribe and his own history -- captured
in jokes and recipes, in details as basic to him and his culture as
Anna's menstruation is to hers -- in both instances the giving of
voice to the silenced. Finally, Lessing's aesthetic creation of time
and place in these novels suggests that links between oral and written
traditions and a sense of place and time are extremely important.
If indeed we are to create, alter or nurture a sense of the future,
it is to the past we must look first, to the recovery of the silenced
lives, values and meanings that have been dislocated.

Finally, too, I must return to my quarrel of the summer with
Lessing. Martha, submerged in domestic cycles of violence, is a
woman and the child of social violence, doubly the child of violence
for being a woman whose work, whose loves keep the whole damnable
system going. Martha's passage to Britain lands her in London and
in a quest for understandings other than those of the past, she
lives her life out among the various groups of people whose sense of
function has been warped by the dislocations of war. Ultimately,
Lessing seems to capitulate to the dominant culture and makes a kind
of virtue of its distortions, those mutant children on the island
who know more and differently than we ever can unless we, as she
suggests, project ourselves into the future history of the last years
of the twentieth century. These children on the island form the
final leitmotif: the institutionalized madness and violence of the
twentieth century produces the ultimate heir whose mode of telepathic

---

5 Meyer Fortes, Time and Social Structure, (London, 1970), p. 2.

communication renders social organization as we know it obsolete, who within themselves connect the past with the future, the future with the past in an utter revision of both. My quarrel with Lessing is not that she writes a Marxist description of social structure over time, the requiring of things in a certain order, so marked in the progression of Martha Quest, but that her heroine's displacement itself destroys social vision, is the outsider's perspective that annuls the social whole. Frustratingly, Lessing implies that radical change to save the human community from exterminating itself is accomplished not in direct political action but in madness and mutation: the final product of institutional violence is schizophrenic individuals and, as lessing claims in Briefing for a Descent into Hell, the only place to go is within, or, as she suggests in "Report on the Threatened City" the only not-schizophrenic creatures capable of life preserving actions come from outer space. Having recovered in the images of time and place in Children of Violence and The Golden Notebook large portions of my past, as a woman and as a child of violence, I would like to think that the recovery will be of use in determining the shape of the future. In a world dominated by institutions, by forces left over from the past -- war, marriage, the single cell family -- Lessing's history suggests the need for radical change in these institutions, in fact their abolition would seem the logical next step. We who have recovered our understanding through Lessing's understanding see possibilities she does not see, and we are disappointed that she does not share our sense of possible change with us and help us clarify our own vision now as she has in the past.

FEMINIST STYLE CRITICISM[*]
by Josephine Donovan

In A Room of One's Own Virginia Woolf argues that the great women
novelists of the 19th century suffered from a lack of a feminine tradition in style.   The sentence which was given to the Bronte sisters,
Jane Austen and George Eliot was a sentence forged by male sensitivities.
The women writers had, in short, to deal with a stylistic tradition that
was fundamentally alien to their own way of thinking.   It was almost
as if they had to write in a foreign language.

To illustrate her thesis Woolf gives an example of "the sentence
that was current at the beginning of the nineteenth century."   I cite
it here:

> The grandeur of their works was an argument with them, not
> to stop short, but to proceed.   They could have no higher
> excitement or satisfaction than in the exercise of their
> art and endless generations of truth and beauty.   Success
> prompts to exertion; and habit facilitates success.[1]

Woolf says that this "is a man's sentence; behind it one can see Johnson,
Gibbon and the rest."   Moreover, she states it is a sentence that is
"unsuited for a woman's use."[2]   Charlotte Bronte and George Eliot tried
to use it and failed; only Jane Austen managed to ignore it, devising
instead her own authentic sentence style.

The fundamental assumption Woolf is making in this analysis is
two-fold: one, that there is a female "mind," and, two, that there is
or ought to be a feminine style tradition appropriate to that "mind."
In this paper I would like to explore some of the ramifications of
Woolf's thesis.   My suggestions will be highly tentative; indeed, my
primary purpose is to elicit discussion of the topic, rather than to
come to any definitive conclusions.

I might begin by looking at the hypothetical "male sentence" which
Virginia Woolf has set up, so as to determine exactly what characteristics she is atributing to a male style.   The first observation one
might make of the sentence is that it is of a certain rhetorical complexity.   The first sentence concludes with balanced antithetical
phrases: "not to stop short, but to proceed."   The third sentence
also reveals a sophisticated sense of rhetorical balance.   The semicolon provides a delicate causal hinge between the two segments of the
sentence.   Is it this rhetorical sophistication which Woolf is label-

---

[*] Reprinted with permission of Josephine Donovan and Bowling Green
University Popular Press from Images of Women, Feminist Perspectives, ed. Cornillon, 1972.

ing male? Probably not. The sophistication of the rhetorical art of
a Jane Austen or of Virginia Woolf herself precludes such a thesis.

But there is also in the passage another, more subtle, tonal characteristic which may be more to the point of Woolf's thesis. Clearly
whoever is speaking in this passage betrays a certain lofty arrogance,
a certain sureness, indeed smugness, which may be what Woolf sees as
alien to the female author (who after all was something of a newcomer to
the experience of writing in the early 19th century, and therefore, unlikely to be making the kind of bold, unchallengeable assertions as are
made in this passage).

The tone reveals the author as one who is quite confident of his
own authority. One can indeed picture Samuel Johnson making this kind
of declaration. Only a member of a ruling class in a ruling nation--
in this case a European patriarch at the height of European ascendancy--
could write authentically in this way. Its author shows himself to be
the heir of generations of secure "insiders." Only such a mind could
utter pompous aphorisms of the kind, "Success prompts to exertion; and
habit facilitates success."

It is clear that this tone would of necessity have been foreign to
a woman writing in the same period. For women were not, and are not,
the dominant class, and their assertions could never have had the lofty
air of authority of, say, a Samuel Johnson.

It is interesting to note parenthetically that Mary Ellmann, one of
our foremost feminist critics, has isolated "the sensation of authority"
as a primary characteristic of contemporary male, as opposed to female,
prose style.[3] In Thinking About Women Ellmann analyzes three prose passages from recent magazine articles written by men. In each she remarks
the tone of "confidence, reason, adjustment, efficacy . . . firmness,
directness . . . . " The passages are, she suggests, "fair examples of
critical prose now in this country, of an established masculine mode of
speaking competently on aesthetic issues."[4]

Dorothy Richardson, a late 19th, early 20th century English writer,
who pioneered the use of the "stream of consciousness" technique in her
lengthy novel Pilgrimage, made an observation about male style that is
similar to Virginia Woolf's. In criticizing what she called "masculine
realism" she pointed to the "self-satisfied, complacent, know-all
condescendingness" of the omniscient (male) narrator found in Conrad and
James.[5] ". . . Bang, bang, bang, on they go, these men's books, like
an L.C.C. tram, yet unable to make you forget them, the authors, for a
moment."[6] Richardson proposed to produce in her own writtings "a feminine equivalent of the current masculine realism."[7]

Leon Edel in commenting upon Richardson's theories suggests that her
primary criticism was that "male realism" was defective because it left
out whole areas of "reality."

What [these] novels left out, if we are to judge by what
Dorothy Richardson put in, are whole areas of feeling, the
self-absorbing reverie, combined with acute perceptual experience.[8]

Virginia Woolf has suggested that Richardson was able to forge a
prose style appropriate to this "feminine realism."   Indeed, in attempting to describe what would be a "woman's sentence," Woolf pointed to
Dorothy Richardson's accomplishment:

She [Richardson] has invented . . . a sentence which we
might call the psychological sentence of the feminine
gender.   It is of a more elastic fibre than the old,
capable of stretching to the extreme, of suspending the
frailest particles, of enveloping the vaguest shapes . .
. . Miss Richardson has fashioned her sentence consciously, in order that it may descend to the depths and
investigate the crannies of Miriam Henderson's [the
heroine's] consciousness.   It is a woman's sentence. .
. .[9]

Richardson and Woolf are, of course, part of the larger literary
movement against 19th century realism which was to dominate early 20th
century literature as "Modernism."   However, more to the point of our
concerns is the fact that they both suggest in their critical comments
as well as in their own prose fiction that there is such a thing as female consciousness and that women writers must evolve a style appropriate to that consciousness.[10]

They further suggest that the female consciousness is primarily
aware of--or concerned with--psychological events, rather than with
abstract philosophical assertions or with external, dramatic happenings.
The style most appropriate to such a consciousness would naturally be
some sort of "monolog interieur."

Another literary theorist who suggests directions complementary to
those offered by Woolf and Richardson is Nathalie Sarraute, the contemporary French "anti-novelist," who Ellmann sees as a descendent of
Jane Austen.[11]   In her essay "Conversation et sous-conversation" in
L'Ere du soupcon Sarraute argues that novelists must concern themselves
with the "subterranean" reality which underlies everyday surface
conversations.   These "sub-conversations" are, she says, really
interior dramas made up of attacks, triumphs, recoils, defeats . . . "[12]

In another context Sarraute illustrates what these psychic happenings are by calling them "Tropismes," the title of her first novel.
Tropisms are the involuntary instinctive movements made by animalcules,
like the amoeba, to external stimuli.   The psyche responds involuntar-
ily to other psyches or to external stimuli in an analogous fashion.
It is the artist's job to capture this preverbal reality.

Moreover, Sarraute insists that the novelist must resist the temptation to classify and analyze this reality. Rather he or she must capture the tropisms as if at the moment they occur. The reader and the author must experience them with the character. The continuity of this experience must not be broken.[13]

Now, while Sarraute does not make any claims that an awareness of this subterranean level of reality is the province of the woman writer, it is clear that her theory complements those of Richardson and Woolf in that she is rejecting the authoritative, objective, analytic mode of the male prose writer. Instead, she is arguing for a fictional technique, a prose style, which will effectively eliminate the objective narrator, which will plunge the reader in the midst of the psychic drama that is taking place in the pages of the novel.[14]

Although it is primarily the new French novelists--Sarraute included --who have tried to follow up on these precepts, it is a British woman novelist, Ivy Compton-Burnett, who Sarraute singles out for having devised the most effective style to the purposes sought. Sarraute points out that Compton-Burnett uses dialogue in such a way as to reveal the "sub-conversations" which are going on underneath. "The interior movements of which the dialogue is only the end result . . . try to insert themselves into the dialogue itself . . . . There is something present which is constantly threatening to break through."[15]

Mary Ellmann corroborates Sarraute's judgment by suggesting that Compton-Burnett's style is a "mode congenial to feminine talent [probably because] . . . women have had ample opportunity to learn the underlife well."[16]

What all of these remarks tend to be saying is that a female prose style is or should be one which enables the writer to deal with the psychic, personal, emotional, "inner" details of life in a way that is neither analytic nor authoritarian. What, then, specifically, is such a female style? Can such a theory be "proven" by analyzing existing specimens of female prose style?

To answer this would require a much more extensive study than I can document here. But to illustrate how such a study might proceed, I will analyze somewhat cursorily five specimens of female prose style drawn from the following major novelists: Jane Austen, George Eliot, Kate Chopin, Dorothy Richardson, and Virginia Woolf.

The first passage is from Pride and Prejudice:

Till Elizabeth entered the drawing-room at Netherfield, and looked in vain for Mr. Wickham among the cluster of red coats there assembled, a doubt of his being present had never occurred to her. The certainty of meeting him had not been checked by any of those recollections that

might not unreasonably had alarmed her. She had dressed
with more than usual care, and prepared in the highest
spirits for the conquest of all that remained unsubdued
of his heart, trusting that it was not more than might be
won in the course of the evening. But in an instant a-
rose the dreadful suspicion of his being purposely ommit-
ted . . . .[17]

While the author's style here is extraordinarily elegant (which
might lead us to conclude an authoritative distance from author to
characters), it is clear that the author is depicting the "inner"
reality of a moment in Elizabeth's experience. Briefly, it is the
moment of embarrassment/disappointment that occurs when she hears that
her "conquest" will not be present that evening. A gentle irony is,
of course, conveyed in the fact that she had hoped the conquest would
take no longer than an evening. This irony relates to the implicit
irony involved in the notion of conversations/subconversations. For,
Austen here relates a subterranean drama which in effect undercuts the
conventional surface ritual of the would-be femme fatale entrapping the
male.

It is significant also that the narrator, while distanced from the
character and thus a "third person," nevertheless "gets inside" her,
such that the point of view in this passage is primarily Elizabeth's,
undercut only by Austen's delicate irony. There is nothing assertive
or heavy-handed about the narrator's description of the event.

The following passage is from The Mill on the Floss:

But the constant presence of her mother's regretful
bewilderment was less painful to Maggie than that of her
father's sullen incommunicative depression. As long as
the paralysis was upon him, and it seemed as if he might
always be in a childlike condition of dependence--as
long as he was still only half-awakened to his trouble,
Maggie had felt the strong tide of pitying love almost
as an inspiration, a new power, that would make the most
difficult life easy for his sake; but now, instead of
childlike dependence there had come a taciturn hard con-
centration of purpose, in strange contrast with his old
vehement communicativeness and high spirit; and this
lasted from day to day, and from week to week, the dull
eye never brightening with any eagerness or any joy.
It is something cruelly incomprehensible to youthful
natures, this sombre sameness in middle-aged and elderly
people, ...[18]

There is no question but that Eliot is having problems with her
sentence in this passage. Note how she rephrases sections of the
sentence in passing, as if dissatisfied with the first phrasing and as

if wishing by a cumulation of aspects to overpower the reader with the truth of the situation. In the second sentence this occurs three times: first, the opening phrase "As long as the paralysis was upon him" is broken by the parenthetical observation that the illness may be extensive and repeated with a slight variation in "as long as he was only half-awakened to his trouble." The next instance is where "inspiration" is rephrased as "a new power," and the final example is where "from day to day" is extended to "from week to week."

I believe Virginia Woolf is correct in diagnosing Eliot's problem as being that she has tried to use a "man's sentence" to her own purposes. The length and cumbersome structure of the sentence suggest an attempt at rhetorical distance, but it is an attempt which fails because it lacks the emotional disengagement which stylistic distance must entail.

Austen's irony enables her to achieve distance and yet she does not err into the pompously assertive tone of the "man's sentence" Woolf cites. Eliot's tone does not allow for distance; the narration is clearly engaged in the event being narrated, and yet the sentence structure would be appropriate for a pompous, assertive "male" (in Woolf's conception) style. That the passage here cited concludes with a lengthy, ponderous assertion about human nature suggests Eliot is trying to effect the pose of the "know-all" male narrator decried by Woolf and Richardson. Perhaps the above analysis proves some insight into the question of why her prose style is so turgid, uncomfortable, and inappropriately suited to her content.

The following selection is from Kate Chopin's The Awakening, an American novel published in 1899, which deals with the vain attempts of a woman to free herself from an unhappy marriage:

> That lady was still clad in white, according to her
> custom of the summer. Her eyes beamed an effusive welcome.
> Would not Mrs. Pontellier go inside? Would she partake
> of some refreshment? Why had she not been there before?
> How was that dear Mr. Pontellier and how were those sweet
> children? Had Mrs. Pontellier ever known such a warm
> November?[19]

In this passage the main character Edna Pontellier is being greeted by her friend Mme. Lebrun, referred to as "that lady" in the passage. Edna never responds to these questions in the narration, as the focus changes to other characters in the next paragraph. One may, however, conclude that she did answer them in actuality but that the answers (and indeed the questions themselves) are of no consequence, being simply a part of a surface social ritual.

Here as in the Austen passage one has a sense of a gentle "decollage" between the surface and the "underconversation." It is clear that the essential or inner Edna is not "there" during the above exchange of surface niceties. Chopin's handling of the narration gives us a strong feeling that the heroine is operating on two levels: on the automatic level of social ritual, and on another many times removed, at a depth far below the surface. This impression recurs through the novel, and helps prepare the reader for Edna's final submergence below the surface in the death-by-drowning scene that concludes the work.

Whether one wishes to characterize Chopin's sentence as "feminine" or not, it is clear that she has fashioned a style that is an appropriate vehicle for the conveyance of the psychological depths of her heroine's inner life.

Virginia Woolf in the passage cited above says Richardson's sentence is "feminine" because she consciously fashioned her sentence

> in order that it may descend to the depths and investigate the crannies of Miriam Henderson's consciousness. It is a woman's sentence, but only in the sense that it is used to describe a woman's mind by a writer who is neither proud nor afraid of anything that she may discover in the psychology of her sex.[20]

It would seem that Austen and Chopin fashioned their sentences similarly.

Let us conclude our summary survey by looking at passages from Richardson herself and from Virginia Woolf. The following selection describes a scene where Miriam, the main character in _Pilgrimage_ is waking up:

> Miriam lay motionless while Emma unfolded and arranged the screens. Then she gazed at the ceiling. . . . She felt strong and languid. She could feel the shape and weight of each limb; sounds came to her with perfect distinctness; the sounds downstairs and a low-voiced conversation across the landing, little faint marks that human beings were making on the great wide stillness, the stillness that brooded along her white ceiling and all round her and right out through the world; the faint scent of her soap-tablet reached her from the distant washstand. She felt that her short sleep must have been perfect, that it carried her down and down into the heart of tranquillity where she still lay awake, and drinking as if at a source. Cool streams seemed to be flowing in her brain, through her heart, through every vein, her breath was like a live cool stream flowing through her. [21]

The following passage is from _To the Lighthouse_:

> . . . the whole bay spread before them and Mrs. Ramsay could not help exclaiming, "Oh, how beautiful!" For

the great plateful of blue water was before her; the hoary Lighthouse, distant, austere, in the midst; and on the right, as far as the eye could see, fading and falling, in soft low pleats, the green sand dunes with the wild flowing grasses on them, which always seemed to be running away into some moon country, uninhabited of men.[22]

In both these passages it is clear that the primary content has now become the inner, under-the-surface life of the heroines. No longer is it a question of pointing to the ironic distance between the surface and the inner depths of the characters' lives as it was in Austen and in Chopin; rather it is taken for granted that the surface is of little consequence. What matters are the inner lives.

In Richardson, however, the narrator enters into the flow of the characters' thoughts in a way slightly different from Woolf. There is little or no distance between the narrator and the character, even though the thoughts are still being indirectly narrated.[23] The emphasis in Richardson is on the sensual experience of Miriam: her feeling, smelling, hearing, etc.

The effect of her style is one of a hurried accumulation of impressions. Richardson's disregard of conventional punctuation is quite evident in the sentence which begins, "She could feel the shape . . . ." One has to ask why the semicolon after "limb" instead of a period. It can only be that Richardson wanted to suggest a close connection between Miriam's feeling the weight of the limbs and the sounds. In other words, the shift is one that takes place in Miriam's consciousness: she is aware first of the limbs, then of the sounds. The semicolons used in the sentence suggest that all of the "events" described in the sentence are part of one continuing moment of awareness in the mind of the heroine. Periods would have suggested breaks too abrupt to effectively connote the continuing mood of a span of mental awareness as is conveyed in this sentence.

The last sentence also gives a sense of emotional flow: phrases "through her heart," "through every vein" seem to give the sentence itself a rhythmic fluidity. It is apparent that Richardson has devised a sentence appropriate to her own purposes, which are to express the inner reality, the inner stream, of her character's consciousness.

In the Woolf passage, however (and I do not presume here to do a thorough analysis of Woolf's magnificent style), it is clear that while the eye of the narrator and that of Mrs. Ramsay appear to merge, it is not the narrator who loses ground to Mrs. Ramsay, as the narrator in Pilgrimage does to Miriam. The distinction is perhaps subtle but may explain why To the Lighthouse remains a masterpiece and Pilgrimage does not. Woolf's style remains the controlling voice in the episode here described; whereas Richardson's style "gives into" the pressure, the flow of the experience being related.

However much we may feel that the eye which is observing the scene in the Woolf passage is that of Mrs. Ramsay, we nevertheless never sense ourselves (through the style) lost in her experience. Rather the experience and the view become subsumed to a greater vision, which is that enforced by the style itself. The impeccable design of the sentences, that not a word could be changed, creates an aesthetic control over the "events" narrated that makes this great work more like a poem than the series of dramatic encounters of the traditional novel. One might wish indeed that had anyone attempted Flaubert's great ambition, to write a novel about nothing, it might have been Virginia Woolf.

And yet, the aesthetic control is not the pompous authoritarianism of the male sentence she herself cited as unsuitable for womens' uses. Rather--and this I believe is one of the unique attributes of Woolf's genius--she manages to create the effect that the world she is describing is a world of the "inside" where no assertive authoritarian distance could possibly exist. Follow the rhythm of the sentence fragment which begins "and on the right." "As far as the eye could see" suggests anyone's eye, an unidentified eye, and yet also Mrs. Ramsay's personal perspective is included in the sweep over the horizon. "Fading and falling, in soft low pleats, the green sand dunes . . ." is a sentence which creates a rhythmic effect in sounds which corresponds to the rhythm both of the eye observing the dunes and of the dunes themselves. The rhythm of the observing mind (inner reality) and that of the outer reality coalesce in the controlling aesthetic rhythm of the sentence, the "inner mind" of the novel itself. In the last phrase the word "seemed" suggests that we are back in the mind of Mrs. Ramsay and yet the image of the desolate uninhabited moon country universalizes the vision beyond her particular mind.

In this inadequate way I have hoped to show how Woolf manages to retain stylistic control over a passage while still entering within and universalizing the experience being narrated. If one accepts that this "tropismic" level of awareness--that is, the awareness of the underlife or the inner mind of the world's reality--is one which women and/or women novelists have to a high degree, then it is perhaps Virginia Woolf who has fashioned the most effective sentence style to the purposes of transmitting this reality, while not in the process losing the sense of aesthetic control necessary to great art. She is able to do this because the psychic rhythms conveyed in her style are her own.

The final question I would like to leave with the reader is whether close stylistic analyses such as we have attempted here on an extensive number of women writers would lead us to make further conclusions about "feminine style." Would we continue to find recurring traits? If we did, could we reach conclusions about the female mind in the way Erich Auerback, for example, was able to characterize the Homeric and Hebraic minds through his close stylistic analyses of The Odyssey and Genesis.[24] Surely such an approach is worth further exploration.

Notes

[1]Virginia Woolf, A Room of One's Own (New York: Harcourt, Brace and World, 1929), p. 79.

[2]Ibid., p. 80.

[3]Mary Ellmann, Thinking About Women (New York: Harcourt, Brace and World, 1968), p. 150.

[4]Ibid., p. 154.

[5]Dorothy Richardson, Dawn's Left Hand, as quoted in Leon Edel, The Psychological Novel, 1900-1950 (London: Rupert Hart-Davis, 1955), p. 74.

[6]Ibid., p. 74.

[7]Dorothy Richardson, Forward to 1938 Edition of Pilgrimage, as quoted in Edel, p. 73.

[8]Edel, p. 74.

[9]Virginia Woolf, Contemporary Writers, pp. 124-25, as quoted in Ellmann, p. 172.

[10]The issue of whether there is or is not a female consciousness is not one which can be settled here.   For further enlightenment, however, I refer the reader to two articles: David C. McClelland, "Wanted: A New Self Image for Women" in Dialogue on Women (Indianapolis: Bobbs-Merrill, 1967), pp. 35-55, and Meredith Tax, "Women and Her Everyday Life," Notes from the Second Year: Womens Liberation (New York: 1970).

[11]"Jane Austen's minutiae are liminal, Nathalie Sarraute's are subliminal, but they are alike in refusing to bypass detail."   Ellmann, p. 222.

[12]Nathalie Sarraute, L'Ere du soupcon (Paris: Gallimard, 1956), p. 118.   Translations of passages from Sarraute are mine.

[13]See Sarraute, L'Ere du soupcon, p. 124.

[14]Sarraute, p. 140.

[15]Ibid., p. 144.

[16]Ellmann, p. 227.   It is only fair to note, however, that Ellmann generally tends to resist the thesis that there is such a thing as a

emale "mind" and/or a feminine literary style.

[17]Jane Austen, Pride and Prejudice/Sense and Sensibility (New York: Random House, 1950), p. 75.

[18]George Eliot, The Mill on the Floss (New York: Pocket Books, 1956), p. 294.

[19]Kate Chopin, The Awakening and Other Stories (New York: Holt, Rinehart and Winston, Inc., 1970), p. 273.

[20]In Ellmann, p. 172.

[21]Dorothy Richardson, Pilgrimage, Vol. I (New York: Alfred A. Knopf, 1967), p. 149.

[22]Virginia Woolf, To the Lighthouse (New York: Harcourt, Brace and World, 1927), p. 23.

[23]For the latest discussion of the issue of what to label "stream of consciousness" see Paul Hernadi, "Dual Perspective: Free Indirect Discourse and Related Techniques," Comparative Literature, 24, No. 1 (Winter, 1972), pp. 32-43.

[24]See Erich Auerbach, Mimesis (New York: Doubleday, 1957), pp. 1-20.

ALICE AND GERTRUDE

by Cynthia Secor

"As I said Fernande was the first wife of a genius I was to
sit with. The geniuses came and talked to Gertrude Stein and the
wives sat with me. How they unroll, an endless vista through the
years. I began with Fernande and then there were Madame Matisse and
Marcelle Mraque and Josette Gris and Eve Picasso and Bridget Gibb
and Marjory Gibb and Hadley and Pauline Hemingway and Mrs. Sherwood
Anderson and Mrs. Bravig Imbs and the Mrs. Ford Madox Ford and endless others, geniuses, near geniuses and might be geniuses, all
having wives, and I have sat and talked with them all all the wives
and later on, well later on too, I have sat and talked with all.
But I began with Fernande."

I began the autobiography uncertain what attitude I would take.
It was unsettling in the age of androgyny to face up to Alice and
Gertrude and Gertrude's having written about herself the autobiography
of Alice B. Toklas.

I kept waiting for Alice to emerge, which she both does and she
doesn't. The conversational rhythms might belong to either or both
of the ladies in question, but the strong, recurrent assertions of
judgment would seem to be Gertrude's. The narrative problem is fan-
tastic, in retrospect. But it works. By the end I like them both.

I like them both and I believe in their joint presence. The
tonality is curious because it intentionally combines two voices --
Alice's and Gertrude's. The solution to the problem of an autobiography written by someone else is ingenious. Worthy of these two
ladies. It works because in good marriages of long duration the
partners do in fact begin to think and sound alike and in the areas
that stubbornly remain outside this circle of shared identity they
become ever more finely complementary.

Their amused agreement that Alice is indeed the wife is a pleasure. They both so keenly enjoy the tasks they have taken for their
own.

The brilliance of the book is that it asserts two facts about
female experience that are simultaneously true. It is fine and fulfilling to have success and recognition in the world of male activities
and it is fine and fulfilling to have a beautifully functioning and
delight-giving domestic establishment. Our contemporary women's
movement faces two of its problems, less successfully, often dealing
with them confusedly. How to get women good jobs. How to make it
common knowledge that the creative aspects of women's work are every

bit as creative as the creative aspects of men's work.

Gertrude and Alice, Alice and Gertrude create for us a fictional world in which this latter perception comes gradually to dawn on us.

Their life is at once exciting and spacious. Their union from that of the happily married heterosexual couple differs strikingly. In the latter the women may be happy and fulfilled, but it is clear that she is in her place and all is well in the world. In the former Alice is in her place and Gertrude is in hers, and either might have chosen to be the other. The message of freedom is implicit. They are free women, the identity sought unsuccessfully by the heroines of Doris Lessing.

I would be loath to separate them now, in retrospect. Had I known them when they had a present moment, into which I might have entered, I might have known them as individuals. It is too late now and not very important for any of us. I think there is in reality no question of what Alice contributed to Gertrude's writing or aesthetics or what Gertrude contributed to Alice's gardening and editing. They are and were a single field of energy and experience. It is the weakness of our male defined histories and literary critiques that we fail to see that the writings of Gertrude survive as artifacts, interesting in themselves, but that at the time they were but the excrescences of a fuller field of activity.

Gertrude's conversations with Picasso. Were they any more important than Alice's conversations with Fernande. We cannot tell from the evidence of the autobiography. Both are treated as having happened. Perhaps this is what is meant when Alice says that Gertrude is democratic.

Gertrude is writing the autobiography, so she quite naturally gives more attention and space to her interests and her contacts. Had Alice been bothered to write her own autobiography would she not have given a fuller catalogue of her conversations and of the opinions and experiences shared of cooking and gardening and editing, with occasional excursions, of course, into aesthetics. Whereas, Gertrude, of course, is distracted primarily by autos, and pictures, and dogs. Gertrude's central theme is writing, and Alice's, had Alice bothered to have one, would have been pleasure and harmony.

One wishes to do tapestry; one wishes to write. It is a strange world that chooses between them.

CHARLOTTE BRONTE: THE LIMITS OF HER FEMINISM

by Carol Ohmann

On August 11, 1836, when she was 20, Charlotte Brontë wrote in
her journal:

> All this day I have been in a dream, half miserable,
> half ecstatic, -- miserable because I could not
> follow it out uninterruptedly, ecstatic because it
> showed almost in the vivid light of reality the
> ongoings of the infernal world. I had been toiling
> for nearly an hour with Miss Lister, Miss Marriott,
> and Ellen Cook, striving to teach them the distinction
> between an article and a substantive. The parsing
> lesson was completed; a dead silence had succeeded
> it in the schoolroom, and I sat sinking from irritation
> and weariness into a kind of lethargy. The thought
> came over me: Am I to spend all the best part of my
> life in this wretched bondage, forcibly suppressing
> my rage at the idleness, the apathy, and the hyper-
> bolical and most asinine stupidity of these fat-headed
> oafs, and of compulsion assuming an air of kindness,
> patience and assiduity? Must I from day to day sit
> chained to this chair, prisoned within these four bare
> walls, while these glorious summer suns are burning
> in heaven and the year is revolving in its richest
> glow, and declaring, at the close of every summer day,
> the time I am losing will never come again? . . . .
> I felt as if I could have written gloriously . . . .
> If I had had time to indulge it I felt that the
> vague suggestions of that moment would have settled
> down into some narrative better at least than any-
> thing I ever produced before. But just then a Dolt
> came up with a lesson. I thought I should have
> vomited . . . .

Charlotte Brontë was at the time a teacher in a school where she had
earlier been a pupil for a year and a half, in 1831-32. This was not
the school, Cowan Bridge, that figured so notoriously in Jane Eyre
under the name of Lowood; at Cowan Bridge, Charlotte had been a child,
only eight years old. Her later experiences at Miss Wooler's School,
first located at Roe Head and then at Dewsbury Moor -- all in Yorkshire --
were comparatively benign. Miss Margaret Wooler, the head of the school

was intelligent, sensible, good-tempered. There was no burnt
porridge, no unheated dormitory, no undue coercion, no fire and
brimstone at Roe Head.

And yet it is clear from the passage above that Charlotte
Brontë perceived her situation there in extreme terms. Her service
as a teacher was, to her, nothing short of "bondage"; she felt
"chained" to her chair and "prisoned" in the four walls of the school-
room. She is unrestrained in her condemnation of her pupils: Miss
Lister, Miss Marriott, and Ellen Cook are "fat-headed oafs," "scrubs,"
and "dolts." Tied to that place and that company, Charlotte Brontë
could at least imagine others -- except that she was continually interrupted in her pursuit of her "dream." The evening of that same
day, her "dream" did recur as, alone at last and at leisure, she lay
down on her bed in an empty dormitory. The dream came back of itself
and unfolded with such vividness that she saw a hallway in which a
beautiful woman dressed in muslin held up a candle for illumination
and she heard the front door open; without the house moonlight fell
on the lawn and the lights of a town were visible at a distance. Two
or three men arrived and entered, one of them a doctor, and so on
and on -- scene succeeded scene and imaginary personages one another
on that evening and on other occasions noted down in the Roe Head
journals. It is possible to parallel a number of these scenes with
passages in the novels Charlotte Brontë wrote 10-15 years later.
Moreover, the nature of her imaginative experience in the journals
tallies with what she said later of her creation of her novels. For
her, creation would have its beginnings at least in "dreams" and
"visions", which would come apparently of themselves and which could
not be bidden. She had, always, to wait on her imaginative powers;
she could not command them.

To return to August 11, 1836, the moment was right for creation
and for creation, Charlotte Brontë felt certain, more mature than
any she had managed in a long apprenticeship that had dated from her
twelfth or thirteenth year. Teaching -- so much spelling and grammar
and geography and French -- kept her, on August 11, from writing.
But lack of time was not all that frustrated her will to create,
and the fact is worth remarking. To the objective "bondage" of her
work in the classroom was added a further constraint. She not only
spent her time teaching; she assumed "on compulsion" a personality
other than her own; she had to play the governess -- kind, patient,
and painstakingly interested in teaching her students.

The Roe Head journals are the most outspoken expression we have
of Charlotee Brontë's youth; indeed, among the personal documents
that have survived her only a few letters, some written to her lifetime friend Ellen Nussey and some to Constantin Heger, whom she
loved, are equally frank. The journals unmistakably show her will
toward creation in collision with the accommodations she felt obliged
to make to her circumstances. No other document records her rage;

it is an emotion, very probably, that her reserve or her sense of propriety did not later allow her to admit to and, probably, in the last years of her life, even to feel. It is an exaggeration, and yet a useful one, to say that she spent the rest of her life becoming what on August 11, 1836 she could only pretend to be -- a governess, and then a daughter, a sister, a wife, kind, patient, painstakingly interested in others. Or, to put this without exaggeration she actually struggled to subdue what was original in her and to nurture those impulses and attitudes that eventually accomplished her conformity to a Victorian ideal of womanhood. By her life's end, her will to create had diminished while her sense of conventional responsibility had grown increasingly peremptory. At her death, the obituary in the Manchester Guardian acknowledged her accomplishments as a novelist and, equally, celebrated her homemaking skills. The memorial tablet placed on the wall of Haworth church told that she was Charlotte, the wife of the Reverend Arthur Bell Nicholls and the daughter of the Reverend Patrick Brontë.

What has passed as a religious crisis in Charlotte Brontë's life at the time she went to teach at Roe Head should, most probably, be viewed as a crisis caused by the necessity of conforming to an uncongenial pattern of work and of personal identity. She left home in 1835, not happily but resolutely, to begin a career as a governess and found, as her journal shows, not only that she could not "dream" let alone write but that her work as a governess was tedious, unrewarding, wholly unsuited to her. Two later positions as governess in private families brought her the further intelligence that her work was also humiliating socially; lodged at one point on the third floor with servants, ignored by her mistress, she wrote to Ellen Nussey, "A governess is nothing!" She originally thought, and continued for a few years to think, that there was a relationship between knowledge or learning, which she liked -- she was a diligent student, and teaching or governessing. She assumed that the more she knew the better she would succeed in her career. But after she was done with the Pensionnat Heger in Brussels, which proved to be her last teaching position, and after she was back at Haworth Parsonage for good, she wrote to a father whose daughter was about to become a governess that a governess did not need elaborate or extended schooling; what a governess needed was patience and physical endurance. Charlotte Brontë's earnings from all four of her teaching positions totalled, apart from room and board and free tuition for first one and then another of her sisters at Roe Head and for herself at Brussels, her earnings almost certainly totalled less than ₤100.

Although she had set out resolutely to teach in 1835, Charlotte Brontë still hoped to write. The first time she came home for Christmas she sent to Southey a letter that has not survived, but that, to judge from his reply, asked if he would advise her to pursue a career as a writer. He replied that such a course was "perilous" even for young men. And he added:

The day dreams in which you habitually indulge are
likely to induce a distempered state of mind; and,
in proportion as all the ordinary uses of the world
seem to you flat and unprofitable, you will be un-
fitted for them without becoming fitted for anything
else. Literature cannot be the business of a woman's
life, and it ought not to be. The more she is engaged in her proper duties, the less leisure will
she have for it, even as an accomplishment and a
recreation ....

Charlotte Brontë was grateful, indeed pathetically so, for Southey's
attention and she wrote him again. In part, she said:

My father is a clergyman of limited though competent
income, and I am the eldest of his children. He ex-
pended quite as much in my education as he could
afford in justice to the rest. I thought it therefore
my duty, when I left school, to become a governess.
In that capacity I find enough to occupy my thoughts
all day long, and my head and hands too, without having
a moment's time for one dream of the imagination. In
the evenings, I confess, I do think, but I never
trouble any one else with my thoughts. I carefully avoid
any appearance of preoccupation and eccentricity, which
might lead those I live amonst to suspect the nature of
my pursuits. Following my father's advice -- who from
my childhood has counselled me, just in the wise and
friendly tone of your letter -- I have endeavoured not
only attentively to observe all the duties a woman
ought to fulfill, but to feel deeply interested in
them. I don't always succeed, for sometimes when I'm
teaching or sewing I would rather be reading or writing;
but I try to deny myself; and my father's approbation
amply rewarded me for the privation.

And on Southey's letter, Charlotte Brontë inscribed the words,
"Southey's advice to be kept for ever. My twenty-first birthday.
Roe Head. April 21, 1837."

It would be possible to pause and elaborate on all these experiences in Charlotte Brontë's youth. But I hope I have said
enough to indicate that both as a young writer and as a single woman
determined to earn her living, Charlotte Brontë came into contest
with a set of social, economic, and cultural conditions that can
fairly be called discouraging; indeed, I think they can fairly be
called oppressive. Her reactions to those conditions are ambivalent.
On the one hand, there is her youthful rage; on the other, there is
her own reverence for convention; she internalized custom's demands

upon her and strove to be a dutiful woman: "Southey's advice to be
kept for ever." I think it would be possible to trace a pattern in
her later creative life, to find, for example, that at the times when
her "dreams" came and she wrote most easily and well, two conditions
were necessary: first, her own aggressive conscience had to be at
rest, without any reason to chide her for failing in "all the duties
a woman ought to fulfill"; and, second, she needed support morally
and emotionally, which she received from her sisters, and, after
their deaths, to a lesser extent from William Smith Williams, her
publisher's reader.

Without stopping longer with the details of her life, however,
I want to move directly on to the fiction, to move on, in fact,
to a particular locus of discussion in the history of Brontë criti-
cism, namely, the structure of Charlotte Brontë's third novel,
Shirley, published in 1849. At once G.H. Lewes, in the Edinburgh
Review, called it a "portfolio of sketches." Lewes' judgment,
that the novel is conspicuously lacking in unity, has decidedly pre-
vailed among the critics of Shirley. Janet Spens, for example, Lord
David Cecil, Fannie Ratchford, Robert Heilman, Asa Briggs, J.M.S.
Tompkins have all reiterated it. More recently, two younger critics,
Jacob Korg and Arnold Shapiro, have argued strenuously on the other
side, claiming, although from different interpretations of the novel's
meaning, that Shirley is unified and that its unity is thematic.

They are, in these two general respects, I think, right. Still,
it seems to me possible to bring into accord with their view at least
this much of the earlier tradition of opinion about the novel's
structure. The earlier critics obviously experienced the novel as
disunified. I think it did so, and this is to change their terms and
at the same time to attempt to do justice to their impressions,
I think it did so because it is hesitant or unfinished in the ideological sense. It moves toward a radical criticism of Victorian
England, but it pauses and does not complete that criticism.

A number of the earlier critics I mentioned had recourse to
Charlotte Brontë's life to explain what they have taken to be the
novel's unity -- Janet Spens may serve as illustration here. During
the composition of Shirley -- the facts are well known -- Charlotte
Brontë suffered bereavement three times over. Her brother Branwell
died on September 24, 1848, her sister Emily on December 19 of the
same year, and her sister Anne on May 28 of the next year. So the
composition of Shirley was repeatedly interrupted and by no ordinary
events. And Spens has argued that in her grief Charlotte Brontë
abruptly changed the course of her novel, determinedly writing in
a wish-fulfilling happy end for a heroine whom she had originally
intended to die. That seems to me to be a sentimental way of relating
the life to the novel. Yet there is, I think, an important relationship to be drawn between biographical data and the nature of Shirley.
The background for understanding the novel's hesitancy, its

incompleteness, lies not, I would argue, in the sudden tragic events
of 1848 and 1849, but in the years-old ambivalence of attitude to
which I began by calling attention. Charlotte Brontë experienced
oppression, and strove to accept it uncomplainingly. She was enraged
at her bondage, and yet she prayed to God to help her to humility.

I'm not going to do more than allude to the three curates and
the three rectors who figure in Shirley. And no more than allude to
the millowners and the Luddite machine-breakers. The treatment of both
the clergymen and the manufacturers and their workers is such as to
dramatize the novel's major theme. In Shirley, Charlotte Brontë is
consistently concerned with the right use and the misuse of power.
And she is consistently concerned with the responses of those who do
not posses power to the actions of those who do. The ambience of
Shirley is cultural, social, economic, political, all four.

It is, however, with the position of women, not just as individuals but as a class, that Shirley is most sustainedly concerned,
and it is in its treatment of this subject that the novel is finally
most nearly radical, most nearly thorough-going in its understanding.
Through her two heroines, Charlotte Brontë defines the boundaries of
experience open to women, or at least to gentlewomen, in nineteenth-
century England. Charoline Helstone embodies a conventional ideal
of womanhood. She possesses the best Christian virtues: faith,
modesty, steadfastness in love, sensitivity, patience, docility, indeed more than that, submissiveness. Caroline possesses the best
Christian virtues and she has need of every single one of them.
Charlotte Brontë's strategy is to drive Caroline to the fullest exercise of her qualities, only to demonstrate how little they matter
in this world. Caroline's qualities are presented as good, there is
never any doubt of that, but they are not sufficient for happiness;
they are not sufficient even for Caroline to wish to go on living.

The crisis she undergoes in the novel is one of lovelessness and
idleness; it is a crisis that all of her life and her social circumstances have prepared for her. If her cousin, Robert Moore,
whom she loves, would love her in return or would permit, for this
is a more accurate description of his state of mind, his inclinations
toward her to flourish, Caroline's life would be fulfilled; it would
be happy. But Robert, who is a millowner, fixes his mind, though
not his heart, on the heroine Shirley instead; as the war with Nap-
oleon continues, he needs Shirley's fortune to sustain his mill.
With Robert lost to her, or so it seems during most of the novel,
Caroline is left to sustain herself.

She reckons up her future bleakly enough and resigns herself to
it. She is ignorant. Her uncle, who is her guardian, has never given
a serious thought to her education; so writing, random reading,
needlework, a little French make up her intellectual stock. Someday
she must be a governess, and an ill-qualified one at that. When her

uncle dies, he will leave her no inheritance; he has spent his fortune to build a church in his native parish. For the moment, Caroline's Yorkshire world offers just two models of what she might be. She might be like Miss Ainley, or she might be like Miss Mann; both are spinsters who have spent their lives "doing" for others. The rewards Miss Ainley and Miss Mann gather from their efforts are clearly minimal in fact and in Caroline's eyes, although she whole-heartedly concedes that heaven will be more impressed with Miss Ainley and Miss Mann than their neighbors in Whinbury, Briarfield, and Nunnely are. Face to face with the emotional and intellectual poverty of her lot, Caroline wonders in desperation how she can fill the empty hours of the day and all the days and years that stretch between her and her death. She makes up a schedule; she reads, she sews for the poor, she pays parish visits, she takes walks, and her unhappiness is such that she cannot sleep, that she loses color and weight, that she becomes so severely ill that her life is for a time endangered.

While Caroline's experience testifies to the emptiness, the poverty, the indignity of the spinster's lot, two further characters in the novel bear witness to the keener griefs that come from marriage, on the one hand, to a man who is insensitive and self-sufficient, on the other, to a man who is willful, cruel, violent. It is only by marrying Robert Moore, whom she loves, that Caroline can achieve a life that will make use of her heart, her mind, even, quite simply, her time. And whether or not he marries her, is Robert's decision.

While Caroline's experience defines the boundaries of possibility for women who are, like herself, dependent, and who are, besides, or, possibly, in condequence, modest, patient, docile, obliging, and the like, Charlotte Brontë presents in Shirley Keeldar a significantly different set of circumstances and an altogether different character. Shirley succeeds at twenty-one to the estate of Fieldhead and a clear ₤1,000 a year. She is beautiful, intelligent; she possesses moral and physical courage. She has the means to do as she likes, and she has the will for it as well. She easily understands the particulars of Robert Moore's financial necessity and she is willing to risk the investment of a substantial sum in business. Neither does she hesitate to take charge of Briarfield Rectory on the night the Luddites finally march on Hollow's mill. Or, the same night, when it appears that she can give warning of the insurrection to shortcut in the darkness from the Rectory to the mill. She defies, besides, all merely practical incentives to marriage, refusing one by one and one the "suitable" offers made her by her neighborhood's "suitable" sons and its sole baronet. She keeps her own counsel on all these points and more, until close to the novel's end.

Still, and I think prompting her readers to this conclusion is one of Charlotte Brontë's chief intents in the novel, Shirley's fate is not all that different from Caroline's. Caroline thinks it is; to her, Shirley is gifted, charismatic, invulnerable. Shirley has

finally to tell Caroline about her inner life, for Caroline cannot
guess it. And what Shirley tells is revealing of the constraints she,
too, feels. The night the Luddites march, for example, their plans
are suspected by the clergymen and the manufacturers of Whinbury,
Briarfield, and Nunnely. But when Shirley quite deliberately asks
Robert Moore what event is gathering, he refuses to answer, excusing
himself with mere courtesy as a man in a hurry. Much later the same
evening, as Shirley and Caroline arrive at the mill, too late as it
happens to give warning of the rising, Shirley holds Caroline back
under cover. Caroline would announce herself, by rushing to Robert
Moore because he is in danger and, again, because he is wounded in
the exchange of shots that scatters the workers. Unlike Caroline,
Shirley is aware here of certain hard truths. The women have arrived
too late to give warning; Robert's wound, even, is slight. So their
presence can only be an unjustifiable intrusion into a masculine scene,
and hence an annoyance and an embarrassment to Robert.

A third instance in which Shirley feels bound by constraints
is Robert Moore's proposal to her. Robert has, first of all, seen
in Shirley not a person but a fortune, a guarantee of his solvency
no matter how long the Orders in Council continue to block his trade.
Worse still, he has mistaken Shirley's interest in his business as a
purely personal interest in himself; he has presumed to think that she
must love him. It is the only conclusion he can draw from her readiness to converse with him about business and politics and from her
willingness to lend her money.

In all these instances, Shirley either recognizes or learns by
experience what limitations her society places upon her potential
freedom of action. To take up the last instance once again, Shirley
may speak to Robert Moore on any number of occasions as a friend, as
a landlord, as a colleague in a business venture, as a neighbor, as
a fellow parishioner, only to find that these ways of relationship
are of her invention rather than his consent. He nonetheless imposes
on her the insult of his insincere proposal. And it is a considerable
insult. To Robert, Shirley has only one mode of being -- she is a
young woman of marriageable age. And young women of marriageable age
want to get married. Therefore, since Shirley pays attention to him,
since she enjoys his company, she must, he supposes, want to marry him.
Robert has submitted Shirley to a process of reduction and, reducing
her, has seen her as an appropriate instrument to his overriding wish,
his chief motive during most of the novel, which is to save his mill.

Shirley can, of course, defeat Robert's attempt to exploit her;
she can also, and she does, disabuse him of his interpretation of
her interest in him and his affairs. But she cannot -- and this is
where she reaches the limits of her power of action -- she cannot enjoy
with him the genuine friendship of which each is potentially capable.
And Robert is the brightest, the ablest, the most sensitive young man
in Shirley's daily world. Similarly, Shirley must let the execution of

a charitable plan that she has devised pass from her hands. Similarly,
she is excluded from the arrangements made to protect Hollow's mill,
which is built on her land and rented from her and sustained by her
funds.

It is in the attempt to overcome precisely the kind of limitation
sketched here that Shirley has invented a fictive self, Captain
Keeldar. For example, in the midst of a conference whose concern is
how to relieve the neighborhood's unemployed, Shirley suddenly says
to a rector who has suspiciously resisted a suggestion from her: "You
must regard me as Captain Keeldar today. This is quite a gentleman's
affair -- yours and mine entirely." Adopting her fictional self,
Shirley says in effect, do not treat me as you usually do treat women.
Rather, assume that I am, as I am, intelligent, resourceful, and
independent. Her fictional self is a device that enables her to carry
an occasional point, to induce men and women, too, to relate not to
their conception of her, which is a fiction in any event, but to
another fiction, to whom they are willing to grant more liberty. And
yet, to state the obvious, that Shirley claims exemption from under-
estimation and from inaction by playing a role, by putting on a
masculine identity is, finally, an insistent reminder of her constraints. Shirley claims freedom only by an act of alienation from
her genuine self and from her sex.

This is the farthest extent of Shirley's practical achievement
in the novel; it is the best she can do. It is, however, not quite
the end of her vision, or of Charlotte Brontë's. Just before the
Luddite uprising, and just before Robert Moore has refused to share
his intimations of it with Shirley, she refuses to join all the rectors, the curates, the schoolchildren, and many of the adults from
the three parishes in a service that concludes their annual school
feast. Shirley keeps Caroline Helstone with her, despite Caroline's
protests, and offers an alternative form of worship to the conventional one in progress inside the church:

> Nature is now at her evening prayers; she is kneeling
> before those red hills. I see her prostrate on the
> great steps of her altar, praying for a fair night
> for mariners at sea, for travelers in deserts, for
> lambs on moors, and unfledged birds in woods. Caro-
> line, I see her! And I will tell you what she is
> like; she is like what Eve was when she and Adam
> stood alone on earth."
>   "And that is not Milton's Eve, Shirley?"
>   "Milton's Eve! Milton's Eve! I repeat. No,
> by the pure Mother of God, she is not! Cary, we
> are alone; we may speak what we think. Milton was
> great; but was he good? His brain was right, how
> was his heart? He saw Heaven; he looked down on Hell.
> He saw Satan, and Sin his daughter, and Death their

horrible offspring. Angels serried before him
their battalions; the long lines of adamantine
shields flashed back on his blind eyeballs the
unutterable splendor of heaven. Devils gathered
their legions in his sight; their dim, discrowned,
and tarnished armies passed, rank and file, before
him. Milton tried to see the first woman; but,
Cary, he saw her not. . . .
    ". . . It was his cook that he saw; or it was
Mrs. Gill, as I have seen her, making custards in
the heat of summer, in the cool dairy, with rose-
trees and nasturtiums about the latticed window,
preparing a cold collation for the rectors --
preserves, and 'dulcet creams' -- puzzled 'what
Choice to choose for delicacy best; what order so
contrived as not to mix tastes, not well-joined,
inelegant; but bring taste after taste, upheld
with kindliest change.'
    "I would beg to remind him that the first
men of the earth were Titans, and that Eve was
their mother: from her sprang Saturn, Hyperion,
Oceanus: she bore Prometheus -- . . . The first
woman was heaven-born; vast was the heart whence
gushed the well-spring of the boold of nations;
and grand the undegenerate head where rested
the consort-crown of creation."

Shirley offers here a new mythology, a new scripture, a new literature all in one. The first woman was not, Shirley says in effect,
the Eve we have known in Genesis and in Paradise Lost, whose highest
skill was plucking and serving Eden's delicacies and who fancied a
forbidden fruit and took it being flattered by a snake. The first
woman was not, either, born of Adam's rib. She was born of God and
was Adam's equal. Although that Eve has passed from mind, out of
history and lost to culture, she lives still under the name of Nature,
and so denominated, receives praise instead of a scolding. Nature
has courage, strength, vitality. And she is not cast in the image
of man, like Captain Keeldar. Captain Keeldar is a fiction, but the
personification, Nature, is something else, something more, a way
of telling truth.

    To repeat, it is in its treatment of women that the novel Shirley
is most nearly radical, most nearly thorough-going in its understanding
of the uses of power and the responses of those who don't have it to
those who do. The novel proceeds relentlessly toward this conclusion: what women experience they experience as a class, even if they
have a clear ₤1,000 a year. They stand outside the corridors and
boardrooms of power, outside the testaments of religion, culture,
history. They need history re-written and a new mythology. They are
in want of a sweeping re-constitution of social, economic, and political
relationships.

The novel proceeds toward this conclusion, but does not reach it, nor does it close in a way that is adequately congruent with this conclusion. What we have instead is the kind of ending Henry James was later to term with some scorn a "distribution of prizes." What we have are Caroline Helstone married to Robert Moore, and Shirley Keeldar married to Robert's brother Louis Moore.

If the novel Shirley at the last recoils, as I certainly think it does, from a radical critique of the position of women in nineteenth-century England, its incompleteness is even more obvious in, for example, its treatment of mill-owners and Luddites. Ad E.P. Thompson has pointed out in his Making of the English Working Class, Charlotte Bronte offers in Shirley a "true expression of the middle-class myth" of the Luddite risings in Yorkshire in 1811-1812. She accurately represents shades of political opinion among Whig manufacturers and Tory clergymen, whereas she pictures the Luddites not as they were, a class of local workmen organized for the achievement of certain political objectives, but as a rag-tag lot led by a hypocritical itinerant Methodist preacher. Christopher Caudwell spoke to the same end when he said that Charlotte Bronte "revolts only within the categories of bourgeois culture." To be particular where Caudwell is general, Charlotte Bronte sees the privations caused by advancing technology, and by depression; she sees the hardness forced on even well-intentioned manufacturers bound to make profits in a laissez-faire system and she remarks that it is a pity and that men should be kinder to one another.

I might at this point seem to concur with the sentiments of Mary Taylor, who was a friend of Charlotte Bronte's at Roe Head and afterwards. Mary Taylor declared that, as for herself, she would not be "a governess, a teacher, a milliner, a bonnet-maker nor housemaid," and she made a voyage out to New Zealand, where she bought and sold cows, built a shop and ran it. The letters she wrote back from there blow into the Bronte papers like an off-shore breeze, brisk and saucy. After she had read Shirley, she wrote to Charlotte Bronte from Wellington: "You are a coward and a traitor."

I might seem to be siding with Mary Taylor and directing impatience toward Charlotte Bronte herself. It is certainly time to set that stright. My purposes have been to approach Charlotte Bronte from a feminist perspective, to point to certain of her personal statements, to isolate at once her youthful rage and her studied submission to convention, a submission enjoined upon her by many more voices that Southey's. And, further, to suggest that the very real limitations that circumscribed her creativity and her sense of self are highly relevant to our reading of her fiction, as they are, very probably, relevant to our reading of works by women in general. In the case of Shirley, Charlotte Bronte's own discouragement, or as I have termed it, oppression, is, to my mind, at once an impulse to the creation of the novel in the first place and a fundamental explanation of what I have termed not its disunity but its incompleteness. To have

had a confident and coherently central perception of what it meant
to have been born or placed irremediably powerless, would have required no less than a liberation from virtually an entire heritage.
That Charlotte Brontë failed to achieve so much alone, is an occasion,
I think, only for understanding. I admire what she did achieve.

IV   WORKING TOGETHER: THE WOMEN'S STUDIES AT PORTLAND STATE UNIVERSITY

INTRODUCTION

In her cover letter to me, Sandy Willow, author of "Rounding
Our Corners," the final selection of this volume, lists forty-two
women's names and asks if the editors might include them all as writers
of her paper. (They are included p.228.) She adds, "There were many
more references to you and Nancy (Porter), but the class thought them
too teacherly, so I took them out." The Portland State writers do
work collectively. Women students and faculty have become a community
in which faculty experience, authority, and knowledge are respected,
even admired, but in which finally the community as a whole holds
sway. Indeed, you will probably remark a tone or style -- personal,
political, poetic -- common to women in that community which dominates
these papers. You hear it even in "Diving Into the Wreck," an essay
in the early part of this volume written about Berkeley by Melanie
Kaye, a woman now teaching at Portland State. You hear it because
our whole lives have been brought to school, school taken into our
worlds, so that teacher and taught, authority and friend have fluid
definitions which do apply to each of us some times.*

Our common tone, our interconnectedness, however, is not coin-
cidental, but comes from several years of thinking, talking, rejecting,
constructing together, using our minds honestly and conscientiously.
We ask many questions, answer few; when unsure, we return to our own
experience. We are loyal to each other, not to the structures we
create -- "Nuts and Bolts," and "Rounding Our Corners" both describe
our evolving forms of governance. Leery of theorists, we have developed enough confidence in our own critical judgments to say that
some theories are unintelligible, not we unintelligent. Indeed,
Ginny Foster ("Women as Liberators") said to us early on that she felt
women should avoid a tone of victimization, should consider themselves
outsiders fortunately free of the dominant frame of reference, able
to create new models for thinking about the world. Drawing on a
distinction from Hannah Arendt's On Revolution between men of letters
and intellectuals, Ginny Foster suggests that we should become women
of letters, cultivating our minds at a calculated distance from the
dominant social and political realms; we ought not to become intellectuals on whose thinking has always depended the smooth operation
of that dominant social order.

I do not mean to imply that we eschew theory or complex, abstract
ideas, but rather that we are not ready to present a coherent theory

---

* I left Portland State after two years of living in that community,
  and am now teaching in Boston. I say "our" in writing because my
  ties to Portland women, my involvement in their lives, and they in
  mine, continues.

of our own, need more day-by-day working, and feel misrepresented by
the gulf between many male theorists' descriptions of the world and
our own experience. We would, however, agree that the following statement about socialist education might describe a hopeful vision of
the future:

> Knowledge begins with practice, and theoretical
> knowledge which is acquired through practice
> must then return to practice. The active function
> of knowledge manifests itself not only in the
> active leap from perceptual to rational knowledge
> but -- and this is more important -- it must mani-
> fest itself in the leap from rational knowledge
> to revolutionary practice.
>
> (Mao Tse-Tung)

Some theorists, those putting into words, conceptualizing the practice of women, the poor, a practice silenced for centuries, do make
sense: Ginny Foster, one of her mentors, Pa lo Freire; Juliet Mitchell;
Shulamith Firestone perhaps; the Virginia Woolf of Three Guineas and
A Room of One's Own; Phyllis Chesler; Mary Jane Sherfey; others.
We take these theorists very seriously, though they exist in a sense
prematurely for us and will be better used in the future. When our
practice has proven itself correct by changing the lives and aspirations of many women as it has changed Mary Ann Hoch ("Stumbling Over
A Threshold") or the women in the writing class whose voices are
heard in "Rounding Our Corners," then we will be able to give it a
name and an order, be unafraid to move, as Doris Lessing suggests,
through the "gap in the dam," for "through that gap the future
might pour in a different shape -- terrible perhaps, or marvelous,
but something new..." Something new, a revolutionary practice.

Judy Annus' story, "The Choice Between Dark and Light," orders
and names the something new in one woman's life, suggests the
inevitablity of a discordant, but propitious future. Kathay's poem
with its mellow harmony, "Sisters winds are heard blowing/ some
come sweeping and howling....," Ginny's and Irene's poems of relations
between women -- mother-daughter, sister-sister; Alice's poem of
relation to her body, are assertions of "I" and "we" voices in a different shape. In "Women All Our Lives," books by women read in community, serve to affirm a female experience of which few of us had
ever spoken, on which fewer of us had acted. These tell why we
write of experience at Portland State, why we read women writers,
why women's studies has flourished in the literature department. On
these foundations we have begun to construct our reassessment of
history, sociology, psychology, to create the new paradigms of knowledge which Ginny Foster describes. For we are aware that we must
acquire skills as thinkers, researchers, writers, and activists not
only for our own survival, but to refute partisans of an imperfect past.

In some ways, serving our own needs first has resulted in a slowness
to learn the traditional disciplines, to learn classical psychological theories, for example, basic economics, or historical methodology. If this is a danger, a misjudgment of priorities, the next years
should tell. We have just begun; we are close to the ground.

A female administrator once asked me, "What if the women's movement rejects women's studies?" At Portland State one would never think
to ask that question. There, women's studies does not oppose the
radical women's movement, or even distinguish itself as the movement's
academic component although such are the definitions in programs elsewhere. Indeed, Portland State seems unlike most other programs of
women's studies. At Portland State University no graduate programs
are in the works preparing women either to teach women's studies or
to qualify for jobs in fields accessible to new feminists (child care,
health care, affirmative action, administration). Unlike elsewhere,
no faculty has been recruited for women's studies alone, though no
decision has been made that women's studies will dissolve into the
curriculum in a few years. No high-powered conferences, no research
institutes, no battles for outside funding, no grantsmanship, no
female faculty moving into administration, little worry about educating
men, no definition of professionalism. Faculty and students show de-
fiance or unconcern when asked about the effect on a career of being
identified as a women's studies person, and although women practice
administration, develop organizing techniques, care for children, and
learn the law, learning comes from present need, and is only
incidentally stored up credit for the future. From this, I draw a
risky, arguable conclusion: Portland State's Women's Studies Program
represents the radical women's movement, using an institution where
women congregate, as a place for organizing, and learning. Here women's
studies is larger than an academic program, and continuous with a
feminist movement for significant social change.

A NUTS AND BOLTS VIEW OF WOMEN'S STUDIES

by Nancy M. Porter

I feel it presumptuous of me to write on the "how to's and what for's" of Women's Studies as if any of us from Portland State were special authorities on the subject of instituting Women's Studies programs. If we read the papers on individual programs and particular classroom encounters, on the general theory and practice of Women's Studies collected in Female Studies, we discover that a number of women and men have already made their experiences available to us. In these articles we learn that there is continuing concern to define the subject of Women's Studies and fear that even when defined the subject is too broad -- courses range from "Women in Medieval and Early Renaissance History" to "Auto Mechanics" and take place out in the community as well as within the university. We learn that legitimacy, discipline and perspective are lively issues; that classes do not always live up to the expectations of the participants; that with men in the classes, and with colleagues and administrators, relations are strained and in need of attention; that successes when they come are not easily measurable in traditional academic terms of achievement; that failures are, invariably, instructive. In short, we learn in all these documents of the differing conditions and emphases that obtain in the field nationally in what is now over eight hundred courses. We also pick up some helpful syllabi and bibliographies. If at this point there is anything that our Portland State experience can contribute to the banquet, it is perhaps a midstream perspective. Our program, University based, interdisciplinary and problem-centered in approach, has been evolving since the winter months of 1970, which makes us architects of the first such program in Oregon and one of the earliest in the country. I want to describe our experience and some of the philosophical and practical issues involved, but I would like initially to state some of the conclusions we have reached -- conclusions about which I shall be writing.

As a group of women, we range from late teens to middle age. Some of us are on Welfare, some are gay, some straight, some students, some faculty, some community women. All of us seem in one way or another to belong to the Women's Movement. To the extent then that Women's Studies is the academic component of the Women's Movement it might better be defined not as a subject but as an action: women studying our bodies, our selves, our history, our work, our culture and institutions with the goal of changing our ways of thinking, our lives and our society. This is our first conclusion.

Our second conclusion is that there is no one way to do this studying, no best strategy for developing a discussion group, a class, or a series of classes that we call a University program. Practically speaking, women who seek to launch Women's Studies need to assess their own strengths and weaknesses and to analyze the flow of power in the particular university, college, department or community, for it is in considering both the personal and the political constellations in existing programs that we find the context for the kind of program, the kind of approach that might be taken. The strategy developed at Portland State will not necessarily work at Clark College in Washington, nor will it necessarily be acceptable to the people at the University of New Mexico. The structure of power varies among institutions, and the individual's involvement in Women's Studies is often intermittent, contingent upon idiosyncratic needs, priorities and rhythms. Some of us from Portland State have described our experience and have been told that Portland State is truly a state of mind, arising from conditions that are virtually pastoral. We have also been told by more insurgent feminists that we have not been sufficiently political; that is, instead of setting up a shadow department, with little attention from the Administration, we ought first to force the University to confer legitimacy and money on our existence and hire a full time coordinator to organize and press our demands for more faculty and resources rather than to depend as we have on a loose consortium of people and energies, many of which have been volunteer. We did not imitate the tactics of Black Studies because such was not our reading of the situation and because the rhythms of the individuals who shaped the program seemed more in tune with "let's give ourselves something" and less with "let's make them give us something."

Our third conclusion follows from the others. Women's Studies is neither solely a political nor solely a curricular matter. When we achieve equal status with other programs in the University, when other courses regularly include feminist analyses along with Marx and Freud, classes for women will continue their separate development so long as women need a room of their own and so long as these rooms function as a vital irritant and model for new learning.

Finally, I would like to assert a personal article of faith. I believe women individually and in groups will find their way by going where they have to go. The imperative Teufelsdrockian commitment is to work -- whether on stating the problem of oppression or in replacing an oppressive culture with examples of what a free one might be like. We are in no position to determine before the fact which if any of our women's experiments will press up through the hardened crust and endure in a universe in which survival is at best random.

Perhaps some of these ideas that have informed our program will become clearer if I weave episodes from our history in with some analysis of events that have influenced our thinking about Women's Studies. In the Fall of 1970 Nancy Hoffman came to the English Department at Portland State with a background of work in the Peace and Civil Rights Movements of the '60's and with experience at the University of California Santa Barbara (in what she refers to as the bankburning season) where women students asked her help in starting a women's literature class. Also in the Fall of 1970 Nona Glazer-Malbin, with a background in sociological research on women and a Marxist-socialist perspective on politics, offered for the second time a course in the Sociology of Women, the students in which expressed strong interest in continuing the study. Nona had heard that money was available for research, and she was determined it should go to helping women. Nona and Nancy drafted a preliminary proposal for a research institute and program of Women's Studies and called a meeting of interested faculty and students. At this meeting, which I attended out of curiosity, I first heard of Women's Studies. It seems to me now that I was then on the verge of making some radical changes in my own orientation toward men, even as I had become increasingly uncomfortable with my role as a teacher of traditional literature, and that I very much identified with the students gathered who had themselves already begun to carve out some atypically feminine ways of being in the world, ways for which they sought support and about which they wished further to inform themselves. This conjunction of political awareness and personal need has inaugurated a number of Women's Studies programs and classes; our uniqueness, it seems to me, stems from the amount and kind of student enthusiasm and the direction into which it was channeled.

At that first meeting we decided to organize a weekly afternoon lecture series on diverse topics related to women and open to the University and city communities, and also to survey whether members of the faculty were interested in asking their department chairpeople permission to teach under omnibus members a variety of Women's Studies courses. The lectures were arranged through the University's Educational Activities Office: speakers -- faculty, students and community women -- shared the program. No outside "stars" were brought in, and the emphasis was on audience engagement, particularly in small groups after each presentation. Two students received academic credit for surveying the faculty. Response to the survey of faculty interest and to the lecture series was enthusiastic enough to ensure course offerings and takers for the Spring. During Spring registration we printed and distributed our own descriptive catalogue, as we have each term since. We had in effect begun to establish a shadow department of Women's Studies, genuinely student and faculty controlled. Now, a year and a half later, our forty some courses have attracted over 2,000 students, a head count that has cheered the Administrative heart in a winter of fiscal discontent.

During the summer of 1971 we decided we would like to build a
University institute that could provide funds for students, faculty
and community people to teach in the program, office space and supplies
adequate to our burgeoning needs, secretarial help independent of
established department budgets, and official course designations in
the University catalogue.

When we began consideration of an institute and resource center
for the University and the city of Portland -- an ambitious under-
taking -- our intention was to develop an experimental program.
Several academic deans to whom we talked suggested we become "legitimate" by applying for a Certificate in Women's Studies following the
procedure and form set forth by the Oregon State Board of Higher
Education. Although we worried whether calling attention to ourselves
would cost us our autonomy, we nevertheless convened as an Ad Hoc
Committee, and wrote and submitted a proposal for a Certificate in
Women's Studies, which is equivalent to an academic minor, reasoning
that it would take at least a year for our application to make its
way through the labyrinth of university committees up to the State
Board. Meanwhile we could go about our business.

As we worked on the proposal we began to work out our philosophy and the practical issues involved in expanding the program beyond single discipline offerings in economics, sociology, psychology,
philosophy, history and literature. Our Women's Studies program as
we saw it should be concerned with developing in women an intellectual
and activist consciousness of ourselves in the world. We proposed
scholarly research in the arts and sciences, with an emphasis on a
structural approach that would seek new paradigms of knowledge, the
development of new perspectives in teaching and classroom participation
and the encouragement of new feminist writing and criticism. Our
lecture series had sought to provide a mix of information and theory,
from both the private and the public realms; at that point in time
we had an intuitive understanding of how it might all fit together,
not an interdisciplinary methodology. Further, we knew that atten-
dance at the original lecture series had trailed off toward the end,
leaving about twenty of us talking to ourselves, and we supposed
that busy people needed the incentive of receiving course credit for
their activities and that we needed to learn ways to focus women's
anger into hopeful, purposeful work. We decided, therefore, to
present an Introduction to Women's Liberation Studies course in the
Fall of 1971, preserving our issue oriented and problem-centered
(as distinguished from "trouble"-centered) format, an hour lecture
followed by two hour small discussion groups, which would offer the
students and community people who had been involved in the program
before the chance to organize lectures, choose appropriate readings
and lead small groups.

I would like here to say some things about this Introductory
course that has now been running for four terms and has attracted over

350 people. Oregon is a rainy state. The rains begin in November and last until April or May, with the sun shining at best inter- mittently. So metaphorically our class has gone in a pattern that will sound familiar to those who have had contact with Women's Studies even in the driest of climates. The changes in emphasis over three terms in the kinds of presentations made, like the changes in who made them, are reflected in the course titles: Fall, Introduction to Women's Liberation Studies; Winter, Women's Studies and the Com- munity; Spring, Introduction to Women's Studies. Also our grading policy moved from the hopeful blanket A or Withdrawal to Pass/No Pass, reflecting our moral crisis over the options available under a con- ventional grading system and our fears of being ripped off for an easy mark. The pattern writ large in the Introductory class, a lower division 199 course offered under the generous umbrella of the College of Arts and Letters, obtains, theme and variation, in almost all of the upper division Women's Studies courses.

We are in the University but we want also to be in the Community and to serve community women's interests. We want through day and evening classes to reach out, yet we forget that providing drop-in child care arrangements is a prerequisite for many a woman's atten- dance. We want to give grades to mirror pride in accomplishment, yet we don't want to give grades in a system that uses them to per- petuate class distinctions and to create a new educated elite. Our classes are open to men -- we are, after all, a public institution -- but we become uncomfortable in their presence, both as students and as lecturers on female subjects. We want separate women's groups. We hope to establish separate men's consciousness-raising groups. More often than not, however, women who begin to realize how per- vasive the reference to man has been in their past activities and thoughts welcome the relief and newly lighted intimacy of an all women's group, whereas the men, some of whom enter the course to study women's responses, others to learn what women are thinking about, still seem to need the female referent, possibly to avoid intimacy with other men. We try also to mediate among levels of feminist awareness and between socio-economic-political groups as well as between those who, inspired by the readings and lectures, want to move on to do research, either on their own or with a few individuals, and those whose need is to explore their intuitions together in small group sessions. We question whether we are developing a genuine dia- logue between self and world, in which social myths and social origins of thought about women's reality in a radical educational model, or whether we are scaring people off in a muddle. In preparing this paper I asked a freshman who had been a group leader and organizer in the course what would prove we had accomplished anything. Her re- sponse was a simple "go read the class projects that are in the Women's Studies office." These projects, indeed, with a range from personal testimony through critical studies and reports of community action programs students organized or participated in, suggest we have made a difference in lives far beyond, and in a different way from, what one sees coming out of orginary university courses.

Another episode of history from the Fall of 1971. In addition to expanding our offerings to include an economics course -- "Women in the Market Place" -- and a "Women and the Law" course offered by a local woman attorney who had called us during the summer to volunteer her services, in November three students and two faculty cadged money from several sources to attend a national Women's Studies conference in Pittsburgh and returned with the conviction that student participation in decision-making and running the program ought to be extended.

From the perspective of the students, the Pittsburgh conference had been dominated by individuals more concerned to extend the influence of women and Women's Studies nationally, in terms of careers in the University and grants from Foundations, and less concerned with student and community constituency organization. At Portland State students had begun to feel that Nancy and I were using our power as faculty to make decisions arbitrarily and without their consultation. For instance, we had chosen the conference participants by no criterion other than who was standing in the hall outside our offices at a particular time when the decision had to be made; and I had invited a male colleague from the School of Social Work into the Introductory class to cover a last minute cancellation by the woman who was to give the Psychology lecture -- also on my own authority. The colleague came to administer a Thematic Aperception Test to measure achievement in women whose consciousnesses had been raised by the Women's Movement. Unfortunately, to preserve the purity of the results, he did not level with the class, and they, to a woman, sensing the deception, voiced their feelings of being manipulated, the upshot of which was an open confrontation that questioned not only my power but the power of psychologists and their middle class male-oriented assumptions.

In this restive atmosphere a general meeting was called with a specific agenda worked out by the "Women and the Law" class. We formed a seven person collective, responsible to a constituency of all people in all Women's Studies classes and charged with coordinating all Women's Studies activities in the University, with expanding our contacts with the community (particularly through running a Speaker's Bureau), and with hustling up money for the coming term. Our random method of selection, drawing names out of a hat from among those women who declared themselves committed to do this kind of organizational work, produced a cross-section of old and new, gay and straight, students and community women. Characteristically, even as we had not tried to refine our Women's Studies philosophy until six months after the program began, so we did not inquire too closely into what we meant by a "collective" when we formed one.

This change from the at large Ad Hoc Committee we had started
with to a specific student group effectively fulfilled its purpose.
It solved some old problems and created a few new ones. Students who
had felt Nancy and I had been making decisions based on our power
as faculty without student consultation, which was difficult at times
to attain because the students carried responsibilities that were not
centrally located around the Women's Studies office, began to understand some of our problems. In dealings with the administrative and
clerical staff the students on the Collective represented Women's
Studies; but a number of students not on the Collective felt disen-
franchised and rumbled complaints of elitism. This underground tension erupted over the issue of hiring two work-study students. The
Vice President for Academic Affairs at Portland State alloted us
$500 from an operations slush fund to hire coordinators and obtain
supplies for the office donated by the Philosophy Department. Deciding whom to hire created heavy weather. Women who had been doing
considerable volunteer work needed money and understandably wanted
to be paid in currency more immediately practical than academic credit
hours, our standard form of renumeration. How should we decide,
what would be our criteria? Was this going to be the issue that
would substantiate our fears that money corrupts by dividing?

If who shall be paid became the bone of contention, the bone
had already several hair-line fractures familiar to Women's Movement
people. We had what was diagnosed by the sufferers as a gay/straight
split, an academic/political split, a working/middle class split.
Eventually, we survived the crisis. That we did so happened not only
because the love and trust among all our women proved resilient, but
also because people began to sort out which commitments they had made
to their own needs and which to the needs of Women's Studies. Put
another way, women began to talk about what needs a program such as
ours could fulfill, where individual priorities lay -- inside and
outside the academic community -- and in turn how much energy and
time each one wanted to give the program, both organizationally and
academically. Additionally, we began to learn tolerance, all of us,
and the Collective found renewed cohesiveness as they grappled with
the need for, and problems attendant upon, leadership.

In the Spring of 1972 three women (two students and a woman with
a Ph.D. in physiology from the community) organized and presented a
course in the Biology of Women, and we added several new courses including French Women Novelists, Women in Film, Women through the Media,
an outdoor class and an education course (Women's Studies in the High
School). For the summer we included a Feminist Writing Workshop
and a course in Styles of Political Action in the Women's Movement.
Additionally, hearing that with University financial fortunes tem-
porarily improved our Certificate Program was at last to move through
the first of its several review committees, we rewrote parts of the
application to reflect our growth in the year that had elapsed since

the original writing. Pending action upon the Certificate Proposal, Women's Studies received a $3,000 allocation from student incidental fee monies, which we have used to restructure our program, broadening and equalizing its base of student participation by making the co-ordination of Women's Studies classes one work study group among a number of work study groups concerned with women's issues. At this point in time, the group charged with monitoring the progress of the Certificate Proposal is learning to define goals and develop strate-gies for both communicating and advocating a woman-oriented program in an environment that is proving less receptive to us than we anticipated.

It is obviously impossible to update the history of a growing pro-gram. There are, however, several trends and directions in our ex-perience with respect to structure, personnel and content which warrant discussion because the experience we have had carries implications for other Women's Studies programs.

As has perhaps been evident in my presentation, structure that would ensure smooth transitions within the program and promote ex-pansion beyond our class and organizational concerns has been a problem. Some of us are afraid structures take on lives of their own apart from the people they were created to serve, while others of us think there must be more structure to maintain continuity, growth and meaning. I believe we are ready now for more structure. Most importantly, however, we are ready to define our goals clearly enough so that we can distingusih between advocating Women's Studies as a program and using the controversy over the program as an occasion for attacking sexism in the University.

With respect to personnel, students and faculty both make inter-mittent and short-term commitments to the program for reasons of econ-omics as well as personal interest. Some students whose alliance with the University was marginal to begin with, who looked to Women's Studies as a last hope or even panacea for the sickness of our times, have been disappointed, on several counts, and have left the program and the University. They and the more numerous others not so for-lorn in the fields of academia have taken what they have earned in strength, pride and information and have gone on to other regular courses or out into the community to put their ideas into action. Not all women who take a Women's Studies course become involved in the operations of the program, although we try to set up communications networks to encourage participation. I know there are women who take Women's Studies classes who never realize they and their instructors are part of an on-going program. Communicating with these people is an absolute necessity for they are our basic recruiting ground. But those forty or fifty students who have been involved in adminis-trative and teaching activities in one way or another find that for all the practical experience one garners there is a certain undeniable

drain on intellectual and physical energy. One simply cannot hassle
with Welfare, run down the missing Pepper Schwartz tape for the Intro
class, attend a work group meeting, finish a paper for statistics
class and worry about the crying baby's earache in a single day and
summon the energy, the will to analyze Juliet Mitchell's arguments
in Women's Estate. Some of us, however, do survive and even go on
to law, medical or graduate school, a fact which brings me to an
analysis of the academic direction of our program.

The women from our program who are remaining at Portland State
for graduate work are, for the most part, involved in the English
Department and have gone there because of Women's Studies with a
commitment to continue Women's Studies. Outside the Introductory
course our program has grown lopsidedly toward the study of literature
and the production of writing -- poems, short stories, journals, position papers as well as critical articles. I believe this has
happened for at least three reasons. One, the values and energies
of the women faculty who have had the most guiding hand in the Women's
Studies program and of the three Teaching Assistants now assuming
their teaching obligations lie in feminist writing and criticism.
We have been concerned to open the study of literature from its traditionally self-enclosed compound to the questioning of a writer's
point of view and the effect on people's lives when sexual and other
kinds of stereotypes are fixed in literature and language studies in
such a manner as to promote their perpetuation. We have also taught
the most courses to date: fourteen regular classes through the English
Department which has also been cooperative in hiring women to teach
women's literature and writing. Two, the women on the Social Science
faculty have been concerned to give good courses but have had their
other major commitments to their own research and publication. These
Social Science faculty have also been the most disappointed in the
women who take their classes and the least communicated with, for
the purposes of interpretation and aid, by those of us involved in
running the program. Three, there are simply not enough women faculty in Social Science, none for instance in Psychology, although some
Teaching and Research Assistants in History and Economics are now
becoming interested in Women's Studies. Given all this, it seems to
me the third reason is of the greatest significance.

Students and even I find we are capable of valued work that
makes a difference to other lives -- we can create a poem as well as
a politics. In trying to decide what there might be intrinsically in
literature and creative writing that is more attractive to women now
than, say, research in the social sciences, I set aside traditional
notions (women go into English studies -- feminine -- not into
analytical sciences -- masculine) and contemplate where we find the
largest room for the development of the personal informed by the
metaphoric vision.

My progressive experience in teaching literature by women has suggested a trend. When I first began I selected works that state and develop the woman's "problem": our "otherness," emptiness, insanity, lack of purpose unless directed by male expectations or male-serving socio-economic structures and held to leash by the fulfillment of our anatomical potential for bearing children. We took our texts from women writers, no less. No man is an island, said John Donne; but we are women not men, notes Marie Buchanan. How can we work back from our angry and frightened individual islands to the poem or novel or piece of criticism we read and on out into the world of action and change? One solution has been to write our own literature, every woman her own creator; another, to search out women writers whose work offers patterns of literary and spiritual progression -- Doris Lessing, for instance, and Adrienne Rich. In so far as the other academic disciplines concern themselves at all with women, they tend to deal with images of what women have been which, given traditional methods of analysis, may be a deadening to the will as reading too much Sylvia Plath has been to some of us who look not just to upset old images but to find some new livable ones. Because many of us have been deprived so long of images and characters that have to do with us, we look at an artistic representation first of all for the personal message, and we need to learn how to stretch ourselves from the personal to the aesthetic appreciation even when positive patterns are involved.

The teaching and reading of literature seems to me essential in Women's Studies because it embodies a movement essential to change. I think this movement is suggested in the following two passages: the statement of the "women's problem" from Anima by Marie Buchanan; the statement of a new direction in a poem by Adrienne Rich.

> The glass is flawed. In the bottom lefthand pane is a small, irregular hole. If I put my finger there, into the tiny, flaked crater, I can feel a thin thread of wind blowing in. When I lean close, there is a minute, attenuated sound of stress.
> Apart from that one small contact, the world outside is completely gone. Perhaps there is nothing out there in the dark. The window affords only a reflection of the lighted interior. A small, narrow room. A Plaster wall. The tilted mirror; in it a face. The white face of a woman who looks up from writing, who writes in a small, narrow room.[1]

---

1 Anima (New York: St. Martin's Press, 1972), p. 9.

You're wondering if I'm lonely:
OK, then, yes, I'm lonely
as a plane rides lonely and level
on its radio beam, aiming
across the Rockies
for the blue-strung aisles
of an airfield on the ocean

You want to ask, am I lonely?
Well, of course, lonely
as a woman driving across-country
day after day, leaving behind
mile after mile
little towns she might have stopped
and lived and died in, lonely

If I'm lonely
it must be the loneliness
of waking first, of breathing
dawn's first cold breath on the city
of being the one awake
in a house wrapped in sleep

If I'm lonely
it's with the rowboat ice-fast on the shore
in the last red light of the year
that knows what it is, that knows it's neither
ice nor mud nor winter light
but wood, with a gift for burning[2]

2 Adrienne Rich, "Song," Aphra, 3, No. 2 (Spring 1972), 2-3.

WOMEN ALL OUR LIVES: READING AND
WRITING WOMEN'S AUTOBIOGRAPHIES

by Nancy Hoffman

I.   "Blue is the color I like best. Green follows and yellow."
Set in an orange cardboard folder, and typed on yellow-green paper,
those words introduce Paeaina Williams. Born in Hawaii in 1930,
sporadic student at the University of Oregon in the fifties, married
to a black man, and now a member of my English class "Autobiography
by Women," Paeaina changes to blue paper to begin the chronology of
her life. Its mother's title, "A Moment for Me," may be apologetic,
but the first sentences are strong: "My life and I are friends. We
seem to suit each other lovingly, in spite of all. Our kinship with
one another is like a strong tree." In the "Afterthought," the
yellow-green pages reappear: "After reading the twenty-seven pages,
I am still undefined...I wrote about everyone and everything and
very little of Me." In the pocket at the back of the orange folder,
I, the teacher to whom this work is dedicated, find old school papers,
notes from friends, even letters from Paeaina's children. Boo, the
nine year old, writes "what I think of my Mom. She lazy and sleepy
and the reason why I think of her is becuases she cares for me and
Loves me and I Love her very very mush..."

     In the winter of 1972, the English Department at Portland State
University offered a women's studies class -- Autobiography by Women.
Our syllabus was simple. In nine weeks we had read and discussed
The Diary of Anais Nin, 1931-1934, Anne Moody's Coming of Age in Mississippi, Maya Angelou's I Know Why the Caged Bird Sings, Emma Goldman's
Living My Life, and our twenty-two women's (and three men's) lives.
(See appendix for some additional bibliography.) The tenth week, com-
pleting our own autobiographies, we reviewed such questions as:
how does one make transitions from event to event? how does one
separate one's life myths from reality? is our audience the class
we now trust with our private selves, our critical, vulnerable families, or any reader at all? what happens when you insert a poem,
a portrait, or a sketch in the narrative? could the autobiography
take the shape of a series of short stories with an "I" narrator?
and what of an organizing principle, a conceptual framework such as
puberty, identity, socialization, rebellion, political activism, religion? is there a language for sexual experience that will not
simply confirm the tradition that women are read for their love affairs,
men for their ideas?

I had been teaching literature by women since 1969 at various universities, and for the past two years, with students and a colleague, had been nurturing a substantial student-run women's studies program at Portland State. Because I was no longer an incredulous participant in the feminist classroom, had already taught that year Virginia Woolf, Poetry and the Female Consciousness, and Introduction to Women's Liberation Studies, I decided to keep a chronicle of my women's autobiography class. I would be the class biographer, recording, as they touched other women, patterns of the feminist classroom that I had shaped, and that had simultaneously shaped my life. How do women's classes go in the teacher's third year of women's studies? The preceding notes and what follows describe our progress from two perspectives: reading the books, talking about living our lives.

It is an unusual class at the outset, for I, the teacher, am perceived as a feminist while most students have little experience of either the women's movement or the feminist classroom. Such a gap between teacher and students is significant. I cannot honestly say we're equals. Indeed, having moved on from the first round of anger, of startling revelation, of frenzied work to a confirmed and plodding feminism, I do see the world through a well-ground female lens, one which I candidly wish women to explore. But vital in my own growth was the grinding of that lens, the process of discovery, which indicates that I should augment choice in the classroom, encourage women to grind their own lenses. In class I accommodate failure, silence, flashy domination, literary analysis, or an inability to know the questions to ask about women, instead of feminist criticism. When a student complains, "We just talked about this book as though a man could have written it," I may answer, "Then let's figure out whether that's on account of us or the writer."

This essay, then, is mostly about women, including me, the feminist-teacher, using literature as a bridge between personal experience, each other, and the world; women becoming a feminist community of readers. That we read literature not psychology, autobiography not drama, is in one sense inconsequential, in another momentous and deeply symbolic. Autobiography, the literary form which describes itself as closest to unmediated, raw experience, not only licenses, but demands that we say, "As a woman, I think..." or "no, that won't be my life." Secondarily, autobiography, as any literature would, demands that we create a vocabulary for feminist art, a women's aesthetic which distances the book from life, helps us to see ourselves. Notice the questions we ask.

II. On the first day of class, we gather in a too large, sterile room. I suggest with some irony that we make a magic circle, and do feel that we've created a human island, twenty-five of us in a

circle among fifty scattered chairs. We introduce ourselves; Maria,
an activist Chicana whom I know from other women's classes says:
"I need some relaxation, a pleasure in this work of school. I want
to watch other women living their lives in books," words of which I
would remind her ten weeks later when, having written her chronicle
of childhood as a migrant worker, she tells me after class: "I'm not
sure I wanted the pain of remembering." Most other women, new to
women's studies, merely say, "I needed a class." or "I heard about
you."

On Monday we begin our discussion of Nin. My journal entry
suggests the literary tone of the class. Criticism is a form of communication we know, this subject -- the self in autobiography -- more
interesting than most. I write:

> Slow week with Nin. I'm asking most questions.
> Much curiosity about her Lesbianism. Was that
> what it was? Did her psychiatrist Allendy con-
> vince her out of it? In some ways, we're more
> caught up in what Nin, the journal-ist left out
> of her account. Sense of shyness in the class;
> can we really be personal without the teacher's
> censure? My comments largely unheeded when I
> point out that Nin completely obscures her his-
> torical moment -- the incipient fascism of the
> '30's. More a scepticism about Nin's personal
> honesty. Is this a diary? Rather, people think
> Nin's mask too well constructed, too artful,
> persona as persona. What of sex? Did her pro-
> testations of a non-physical relationship with
> June have "fact" validity? or was "non-physical"
> simply the self Nin chose to present to the world,
> a fact of her self-concept? Rita, Maria, Shelley,
> Linda, Judy, Paeaina, and Jim speak. One woman
> says she's gay, and doesn't return on Wednesday.
> Celina, from Brazil, asks why we make distinctions
> between blacks and people; the discussion goes on
> for an hour after class.

We encountered a problem with Nin immediately, one which my
notes happen to exemplify. The journal or diary, like many of our
lives before the women's movement, presents diurnal events, time as
it passes, not in retrospect. Although the mind thinking, feeling,
orders experience in the act of setting words on paper, no interpretation is made. The diarist simply has no historical perspective.
Nin's first diary begins, for example, with a lovely time-space
motion -- the history of her home at Louveciennes, then up to the
small gate, and in through each mood-painted room. We wrote house
descriptions ourselves, read them aloud at the first potluck dinner
the class held at my house. Nin's ancient, foliage covered domain
exposed a delicate sensibility, as our brick apartments, family farms,

and ramshackled boarding houses, exposed us, but to what end? Nin
gave little help to women who had not yet begun to spell out in terms
of their own sexual identities, the socialization that had created
them.

Uncomfortable with their inability to settle on a meaning for
Nin's life, the class recognized their anticipation of authentic,
traditional autobiography, a life recollected, given a conceptual
framework, presenting a case, loose ends tucked into the net, its
bounds and patterns prescribed, and most crucial, its meaning decided.
Anne Moody's Coming of Age in Mississippi, a black woman's saga of
growing up, fit such a definition, and I now took a strong role in
pressing the class into that recognition.

Unlike Violette Leduc's autobiography, La Batarde with its squarely
anti-conventional opening, "My case is not unique," Moody seemed full
of autobiographical particularity, dependent on the individual chronology we had expected. She is the loner, the outsider, the stigmatized black child who, understanding more than her fear-deadened
schoolmates, acts out of deep anger, rebelliousness, and inner necessity. Her epiphany is the murder of fourteen year old Emmett Till
by white men. Why the title, Coming of Age in Mississippi, I ask the
class? Mississippi is the antagonist, we agree; Moody defines herself
through the tension between her hostile, murderous white culture and
her black identity. She comes of age in her own foreign land. Nin,
we realize, had no such external antagonist. Had we?

Given the idea of a conceptual framework, the society as antagonist,
the blacks, the Chicana, the Chinese man have the vocabulary they
sought, but the white middle-class women, myself included, would not
write Coming of Age in Portland, Oregon. Many of us were at work
on journals of self-exploration; our conflicts were of id and ego, for
the social order had accommodated our growings up. And just that
smooth accommodation had shielded us from insight into power relations
between black and white, female and male, poor and affluent, which
the other women and men had always had to know. Once we had discovered
how Moody had been set in relief against her environment, the discussion became political, though not yet feminist except that we were
women engaged together in serious discussion about the ways in which
social forces and economic exegency shaped our lives.

Anne Moody's decision to continue working in a chicken factory
where she had discovered herself to be scabbing brought conflicts
about survival versus morality, race versus class, into the open. We
divided into two small groups, and examined a passage in which Anne
describes the factory assembly line:

> Now the rate of speed was doubled. I stood there
> moving as fast as I could blink my eyes. I was on
> the end of the trough which pulled the insides out...
> I stood there reaching up and snatching out those

boiling hot guts with my bare hands as fast as I
could. But I just wasn't fast enough. The faster
the chickens moved, the sicker I got. My face, arms,
and clothes were splattered with blood and chicken
shit...(165). I worked at the chicken factory for
about a month. Within that time I saw the entire
place. I shall never forget the slaughterhouse --
the men pulling feathers from the bloody chickens
by the neck and knifing them one after the other,
their eyes sparkling with what looked to me like
pleasure...
        But there was something even more sickening to
me -- those rotten chickens that came in with sores
all over them. I would see women take them, cut the
knots and rotten sores off and box the remaining parts.
These women would often have terrible rashes break
out on their hands from the hot blood and diseased
flesh. (p. 168).

I note in my journal:

The factory itself takes on symbolic value as the
festering, putrefying, but life sustaining organ of
the white economy. Maria, Paeaina, and Michael Lee
get visibly angry at the white women who suggest
that Moody shouldn't have betrayed union workers; she
could earn $9.90 a day instead of $8 a week, they
say; besides, the unions are simply another form of
white power. Wasn't Moody paying enough in unbear-
able drudgery to survive? I also point out that when
white racism gets too much to bear -- the Emmett Till
murder, the burning of the Taplin's house, Anne's
persecution because the white Burke boy sought her
out -- Anne simply gets a fearsome headache and goes
to bed until she's better. This behavior, I suggest,
is a non-introspective, unselfconscious mode of
dealing with psychological stress. Moody fights an
enemy external to herself, and will not acknowledge
the personal toll. Nin could write a diary about one
of Moody's headaches. Two notes: Michael Lee says that
as a Chinese child, he felt the all pervasive fear of
whites, the threat that Moody feels constantly; second,
Maria seems absolutely pleased, astonished, and embarrassed when I say I have been thinking of her
development into a movement woman over the last two
years I've known her. She's strong as Anne. "You
think of me?" she says. We also begin to talk about
not invalidating the experience of white middle class
women. I am, after all, one of them, and must watch
out.

By reading together, by accounting for our own race, class background, social milieu and experience in our response to literature, we were beginning to see the subtleties of our own socialization processes. In understanding Moody's acts against the external demon racism, and its supporting cast of institutions, we identified in the patriarchal power structure some external sources of our own frustrated anger, our lack of confidence, our feelings of powerlessness and emotional dependence. Now the white women began to identify some external antagonists in their own lives -- the romance of American girlhood, for example. The white women too began to feel that the web of social and sexual relations which created them often varied only in subtlety and degree from the web which bound women stigmatized by brown skin and poverty.

Our openness as a group had grown with political awareness. When I asked whether the class preferred to read next Lillian Hellman's An Unfinished Woman or Maya Angelou's "Caged Bird," a white woman said we had done "enough black books," and an emotional black woman said "no," then wrote me an angry letter. Her language indicates that our vocabulary for dealing with autobiography had intruded into students' lives:

> I have sat in many classes without saying boo for some 20 years and accepted it outwardly. Nancy, I'm not sorry for my negative response to X's feelings, but my ears got pierced by her remark. I have the feeling that X and others, because they cannot relate to nor dig Moody or Maya, feel uncomfortable with black literature. They and people like them will never understand non-whites if they must always judge and evaluate us caged birds with the white conceptual framework. In I Know Why the Caged Bird Sings, Maya's brother Bailey asked: "Uncle Willie, why do they hate us, They don't know us. How can they hate us? They mostly scared..." For pure provocation, I wish you'd assign another black or two or three. I've been crammed with white, white, white too, too many years, and no choice either.

The class voted to read Angelou. Now, half way through the course, they decided also to direct our discussions themselves. This, I think, partly because I had criticized Angelou for her fragmentation of time, her mix of memory, contemporaneous narrative, and moralizing wisdom. Three students led a discussion in which we tried to differentiate between Angelou's girl-child growth and her blackness, a step beyond Moody to confront the woman question. For the next meetings, womanhood took precedence over blackness -- the topics were Maya's relationship to her mother, and to her own body.

We questioned Maya's unselfconscious adulation of "Mother Dear," the woman whom brother Bailey thinks he sees in the movies as the white starlet, the dashing, card playing beauty Vivian Baxter who with her "lipsticked mouth, white teeth and shining black eyes . . . might have just emerged from a dip in a beige bath," (170), the woman Maya describes as "a hurricane in its perfect power, or the climbing, falling colors of a rainbow." We developed several explanations for Maya's perplexing awe of this idealized female beauty. Ironically, Vivian Baxter's perfection explains to Maya's satisfaction why she and Bailey had not been cared for by their mother: "She was too beautiful to have children." While Maya depends on Mother Dear's beauty -- it seems to represent a potentiality, a dream of the good, beautiful Maya within the everyday visible one -- Maya uses this beauty as a weapon against herself, a mode of isolating herself from her family. To build the case, she claims that her beloved Bailey resembles Mother dear, and she excludes herself. "They both had physical beauty and personality, so I figured it figured."

Against this "glorious" goddess, and against Bailey, Maya pits herself, carefully constructing an image filled with self-loathing, the adolescent ugly duckling. She is "a too-big Negro girl, with nappy hair, broad feet and a space between her teeth that would hold a number two pencil," a girl who is "big, elbowy, grating," who dreams of waking up white, blond, who describes her skin as "shit colored," who pees in her pants, whose laughter turns to uncontrollable hysteria, who grips a tear-wettened handerchief wadded up in her fist, who sweats through horrifying nightmares; the teenager who reads The Well of Loneliness, thinks she's a lesbian because in the mirror she sees "sadly undeveloped breasts," a straight line from rib cage to knees, who decides from painful comparison with other girls that boys would call on her "to be generous" only when pretty girls were unavailable. The women in the class had all known such a contorted self-image; many of us confessed to holding it still. This was Maya's womanhood, to which her blackness added a more complex dimension. I note in my journal:

> Sandy, Christi, and Shelley begin to talk about what
> Francis Beale in The Black Woman calls double jeopardy,
> to be black and female, for had there been no Mother
> Dear, no perfect Negro beauty, Maya would have been
> confirmed in her conviction that no black woman would
> ever compare with Ladies Home Journal whiteness, cer-
> tainly ugly Maya wouldn't. Blackness seemed to become
> the visible, external proof -- for white women it was
> always internal -- that Maya would never attain an
> acceptable womanhood, that the comfort, ease and grace
> tauntingly portrayed in the media's white female was
> impossible. Indeed, Maya's ability to appreciate
> Mother Dear seemed almost to rest on denying her black-
> ness. She describes her in the vocabulary of sleek

models from Vogue or teasingly sexy movie stars who
never get pregnant, care for children, or know the
repetitive drudgery of housework. In character,
Mother Dear, almost white, plays (gambles, drinks)
while Grandma Baxter works as a black woman should,
"And yet better mother's female strength, than none
at all. Black men don't have it," says a black
woman in the class.

Finally Judy, with the class, tried to persuade me that she, a
painter and weaver, saw Maya's book as a poem, a transmutation of
reality into humorous beauty. Maya had no need of transitions, used
rather rhythms and juxtapositions to maintain contact with the reader.
I could see that. "Another day was over. In the soft dark the
cotton truck spilled the pickers out and roared out of the yard with
a sound like a giant's fart. The workers stepped around in circles
for a few seconds as if they had found themselves unexpectedly in an
unfamiliar place. Their minds sagged" (p. 100).

Angelou's positive humor, her growing love for her body and herself, the satisfaction of the class at having convinced me of the
strengths of the autobiography touched many women. When we had a
chance to move from our sterile classroom to the worn out rugs and
sofas of a student services building, we settled in to discuss Emma
Goldman with a new kind of urgency, direction and commitment. The
synthesis, the clicking together of feeling, emotion, political insight, intellect, dream, fantasy, love and sexuality into a woman's
perspective began to come true, at least in the way we could talk about
a life -- Goldman's, or our own. And I, as teacher became less an
outsider. Indeed, class went on without me once when I was out of town.

But there were women who were still silent. Articles describing
classrooms, including the dialogue between student and work of literature, necessarily depend on the comments of the talkers. The silent
ones make us anxious. Heavy presences in class, they never come on
stage in such an account, unless invoked in perplexity and to no
apparent end. Our autobiography class had many silences, had students
who felt dumb, who said they had no sense of responsibility toward
the group, who were locked up in deep private pain. In fact, on the
day of our move, the group asked whether we might continue another
quarter together, a question I interpreted rightly to signal both a
certain dissatisfaction regarding silences, and a healthy concern for
confirming and maintaining our community. Indeed, the core of our
discussion had shifted again from the writer Angelou's womanhood directly to our own.

We decided to be tough on ourselves, felt relieved to be less
attentive to, less indulgent of "women's fears." We would talk aloud
by sheer will, if that's what was needed. Next class Winifred, a
woman working at the Women's Health Clinic in town who has never spoken

a word in class, indeed, says she does not want to, breaks her silence
by reading us a passage from <u>Living My Life</u>. She, through Emma, illustrates her own engagement in work by agreeing with Emma's priorities --
The Movement, a love relationship. Winifred's passage expresses
the crucial woman's choice. Emma, unlike most women chooses freedom
with its inevitable companion, loneliness.

Emma and her lover Ed Brady, in discussing an anarchist comrade
Maria, clash over woman's instinct for maternity:

> "Well, then, Maria should guard against having children
> if she wants to devote herself to our movement," I
> remarked. "No woman should do that," Ed replied,
> emphatically. "Nature has made her role motherhood.
> All else is nonsense, artificial and unreal."
> I had never before heard such sentiments ex-
> pressed by Ed. His conservatism roused my anger. I
> demanded to know if he thought me also nonsensical be-
> cause I preferred to work for an ideal instead of
> producing children...I had believed that he was diff-
> erent, but I could see that he was like the rest.
> Perhaps he, too, loved only the woman in me, wanted
> me only as his wife and the bearer of his children.
> He was not the first to expect that of me, but he
> might as well know that I would never be that --
> never! I had chosen my path; no man should ever take
> me from it...
> My life with Ed had been glorious and complete,
> without any rift. But now it came; my dream of love
> and true comradeship suffered a rude awakening...
> Yes, that's what it was, the man's instinct for
> possession, which brooks no deity except himself.
> Well, it should not be, even if I had to give him up.
> All my senses cried out for him. Could I live without
> Ed, without the joy he gave me?
> Weak and miserable, my thoughts dwelt on Ed, and
> on Maria... (151)

In a poem by Adrienne Rich called "At Majority," we had talked over the
tone of resignation in the line, "All choices made, or choice re-
signed," in reference to marriage. "This," said Winifred, reminding
us of the discussion, "is neither, but rather a decision to keep on
having choices. Emma's anger testified that she felt herself deceived
into the belief that she could have a love relationship and the movement, maintain choice rather than orbit in a sphere described by Ed."
Rita asks that I xerox Emma's article "Marriage and Love" from
<u>Anarchism and Other Essays</u> (1911); Michael presents a paper on an-
archism as a political philosophy, and Mickey, a constructive critic
all along, says that in our discussion of Anne Moody she had held her
tongue since we discussed the book as though a man could have written it,

but now she demands that we ask what qualities of womanhood permit
Emma to make a synthesis between passion and intellect, her revolutionary practice of free love, and her anarchist principles. I note
in my journal now:

> The class seems vibrating with flashes about female
> identity and work. Emma defines herself by work.
> Should we be able to say, I am a "something," a tea-
> cher, an artist, an engineer; work sustains my sense
> of a continuous self, my identity, not love first?
> Paeaina says "love is my work;" most of us says "no",
> and add with some self-mockery, perhaps self-love could
> be our work. Winifred is still talking. Also, Felicia
> (never involved politically) reads us a passage in which
> Emma says she longs for a friend of her own sex. Judy
> points out to me after class that Felicia had used the
> passage as a tacit admission of her own longing, her
> new awareness of women. I think she's right for two
> reasons -- F. has begun to move from the world of her
> close Polish family to relationships with some of us;
> also she's still reading about the women's movement,
> standing behind a book, using a sentiment such as
> Emma's because it's safer than venturing on her own.
> It's like the way Alice talks about her marriage by
> telling me at length about images of doom in Martha's
> relationship with her husband (Lessing's A Proper
> Marriage).

We had reached week nine of a ten week term, and I was beginning
to see significant changes in the way we thought and read, even in
our behavior, as though a continuity between the world of ideas --
words in a work of art -- and our own lives was natural. Literature
was beinning to be a provocation, a force which set our lives in
relief against the patterned, explicated life of an Angelou, Moody
or Goldman. Our final classes moved the focus squarely from literature to ourselves, the autobiographical writing in which we were then
deeply engaged. We identified the three most challenging problems
for a woman in the process of change: autonomy or sense of self; work;
and love in their intricately woven web. Emma's refusal to allow
Ed to obliterate her self-chosen course -- the Cause rather than
motherhood -- had been inauthentic, though painful act of self-love
which assured her the continued power to choose her own destiny. Perhaps her words seem melodramatic, one-dimensional today, but we as
women congratulated Emma, knew the energy needed to resist the
charming lover who says: "Come live with me; I will support, protect,
help live your life." Inevitably, his work shapes his life and yours
too. Emma admits Ed "had roused the old yearning for a child," held
out the prospect of security. Her refusal, still startling, must have
been heretical in the '90's"

> But I had silenced the voice of the child for the
> sake of the universal, the all absorbing passion of
> my life. Men were consecrated to ideals and yet
> were fathers of children. But man's physical share
> in the child is only a moment's. Woman's part is for
> years -- years of absorption in one human being to
> the exclusion of the rest of humanity. I would never
> give up the one for the other. (153).

A sense of self without dependence on a permanent, primary commitment to a man, a hard goal for well-socialized women. A genuinely creative work life was one answer. Judy was among the few women in the class who, when asked for a work identity, answered immediately, unequivocally, "I'm an artist." For others, no work definition came, but a ready assent that at the first blush of love, or anticipation of it, a work definition became secondary. Only the end of a relationship, loneliness, revealed the hidden void. But what of love? Of course, we needed it, but our autobiographers had not been exemplery. Drama, chaos, contention hardly begin to describe Emma's love relationships, though Sasha, comrade and lover of the 1890's, in 1931 gives Living My Life its name. Neither Anne Moody nor Maya Angelou talk of being "in love." Angelou, twice divorced, today calls herself a lonely woman. Nin had perplexed us by the total absence from the diaries, at his request, of her husband of fifty years. Emma had set out a standard of mutual respect, of equality, of passionate intensity, but without possession of the other's soul. Such possibilities were being born between women, our class suggested. Could they also be between women and men?

When we met at Felicia's to read each other's lives, the final paragraphs of Spirit Flowers, Judy's autobiography, answered one way: "I can give most freely to women. There is no need to be afraid. I like men but I am wary. There are so many games involved. I don't trust myself either not to respond in a role playing way. When I am attracted to them, I get confused and don't honor my own feelings enough. Sometimes I promise more than I can give. Sometimes I'm very specific about who I am and they don't listen. I love affection. I love touching. It confuses me how varied my sensual responses are to men I like. I feel that my sexuality has a long way to grow and mature...I don't know what lies ahead."

III. The mood of my remarks represents living, active literary criticism, a criticism which starts from the meaning of a book, but moves outward to the reader's particular psychology, her class and caste, to classroom relationships, and political commitments. For me, such a relation to art must prevail because I, like some of my friends in the university, see much of literature -- the Western tradition -- as a source of oppression for students outside the dominant middle class culture, and as a reinforcement of inhumane values for those in the mainstream; thus, one cannot teach literature, particularly to women, as an objective, classless mode of preserving tradition at its best. But, precisely because literature embodies deep-rooted cultural values, teaching literature in schools is one way of understanding our lives in historical context, as women naming the ubiquitous male voice as only one voice while speaking aloud in their own. Thus women act to set art in the service of life.

Literary critics obscure subjective judgments by hiding behind the mask of the ideal reader, that responsive mind that constructs an environment mirroring, thus making understood, the world of the artist. The ideal reader of Anais Nin, our first autobiographer, for example, would have accepted the role of voyeur, would have pretended to over-hear a dialogue of one in which an inner, profoundly explored self sought her own strength against an engulfing world. In this ideal reader, psychoanalytic theory would bound the limited world in which Nin sorts out her multifoliate personality. But some of us could not assent to the psychoanalytic mode. Some were poor, politically active, and found a life goal of self-exploration not only a luxury of the affluent, but socially irresponsible. And some were middle-class, had already been told to mind their roles by a paternal male therapist. Our class had a choice. We could either bow to art silently, keep our values hidden behind the improbable but flawless mask of the ideal reader, an Ivy League male intellectual who is quite unlike a woman; or we could say, as we did, that our relation to psychoanalysis is as important as Nin's.

This account then has revealed the pace and scope of our exploration. I became a member of the class. We came to some conclusions about the genre autobiography, could recognize its conventions, archetypal patterns and fictions (literary analysis); having rejected our iden-tity as ideal readers, we evolved into a critical group, a supportive community which began to construct a poise between Nin's will for inner unity and Anne Moody's overt commitment to change the social order (political analysis); beyond literature, beyond theory, Paeaina or-ganized her classmates to protest a humiliating, authoritarian educa-tion class, spoke with women at a community college; Joy became a member of the coordinating collective of the women's studies program; others too began to shape women's history and their own (ACTION).

AUTOBIOGRAPHIES BY WOMEN (Some autobiographies appropriate for a women's literature class.)

Angelou, Maya
  I Know Why the Caged Bird Sings   Bantam

DeBeauvoir, Simone
  Memoirs of a Dutiful Daughter

Hellman, Lillian
  An Unfinished Woman   Bantam

Goldman, Emma
  Living My Life, Vol. I; II   Dover

LeDuc, Violette
  La Batarde   Livre de Poche

McCarthy, Mary
  Memories of a Catholic Girlhood Berkley Medallion

Marshall, Paule
  Brown Girl, Brownstones   Avon

Moody, Anne
  Coming of Age in Mississippi

Nin, Anais
  The Diaries, Vol. I-IV   Harcourt, Brace
              & Jovanovich

Plath, Sylvia
  The Bell Jar   Harper & Row

Stein, Gertrude
  The Autobiography of Alice B. Toklas

Woolf, Virginia
  A Writer's Diary   Signet

STUMBLING OVER A THRESHOLD

by Mary Ann Hoch

At the time I enrolled in a Women's Studies class at Portland State University, I felt I was being an impulsive woman behaving in a juvenile manner. After all, I had just passed my fortieth birthday, and it had been eighteen years since I graduated from college. I had enough to keep me busy at home. There were four children to feed, clothe, help with homework, and oversee in their many activities. There was a five bedroom home to keep clean. There was a large yard with many trees and plants to nourish and many weeds to pull. There were soap operas and quiz shows to watch on my color T.V. There were books to be read. There were women's magazines exhorting me to re-decorate my home and try their luscious new recipes. There was a husband who needed me to do all these things and more. There were bridge games to play, women's Christian clubs to attend, friendly neighbors with whom to gossip.

It seemed to me at the time that I had made a hasty decision to change a way of life in which I was increasingly wasting time instead of using it wisely. When I look back now, I feel that a seed had been germinating within me for some time to return to a classroom situation -- a learning, sharing, teaching, experiencing, feeling situation. But my indoctrination into the great middle-twentieth-century American ideal of wife, mother, homemaker had been so complete that I felt that any decisive action to the contrary had to be impulsive and juvenile.

Over coffee cup and cigarette on a typical March Portland morning, I turned to the women's section of my Oregonian. When I started reading the lead story, I thought that I was being treated to another dose of "Julie Childishness," because her picture also appeared on the page. But after hastily perusing the first two paragraphs, my mind and reading slowed down. I was reading about an important event. Time magazine had just published an entire issue devoted to the American woman. I finished the article, donned my raincoat, sped to Safeway, and bought a copy of Time. Although I had been reading articles in the women's magazines about the new woman's movement, and becoming increasingly dissatisfied with myself, I feel that on a rainy day in March, the Oregonian and Time changed my life by transporting me from an existence of mediocrity in America's suburbs to a more meaningful life as a participant in a moving force.

This issue of Time magazine is important. It **is** especially important because it brought to light the fact that here in Portland, Oregon, women were working toward something for themselves for a change on the campus of Portland State University, an institution which is in easy access to any woman in this area. My anaesthesia was erased when I read quoted words of Nancy Porter, English professor at Portland State. I thought to myself, "I would like to meet her."

About a week later on a hot Thursday afternoon while my children were home for spring vacation, I dialed the number of the registrar at Portland State. I was told that I was welcome to register as a special student, with no matriculation, at a mere twenty dollars per quarter hour. After a long ride through spring fields and hills in abundantly beautiful Oregon and a talk with two of my sons, I decided that I would enroll as a special student at Portland State. My youngest son shouted, "Hurray!"

To a novice resident of this city, newly immigrated from a small town, an enrollment at a large university can be a traumatic experience. It was to me. It was the first thing I had done completely on my own in many years. Upon walking into the gymnasium on Monday night, I almost **turned** around and went home, because the large swarm of people sent a certain terror through me. But my newly determined conscience kept saying to me, "You've got to do it, you've got to do it!" Because of full classes, faltering indecisions, and a completely new environment, it took me three days to complete my registration. It is paradoxical that all of my stumbling blocks led me to take the class on Doris Lessing, the class I should have wanted to enroll in in the first place. I had never heard of Doris Lessing until I read the special issue of Time magazine. I learned that Nancy Porter was the instructor and felt the class would be something special. Nevertheless, I hid my anticipation and simply told my family and my friends that it was a literature course. Such an explanation is acceptable for forty year old women who graduated from college in the mid-1950's with a major in English. Despite this excitement, I very furtively approached the class on that Thursday afternoon.

Perhaps the casual reader will believe it impossible that one could approach a class with terror. If you know the terror of pounding adrenalin throughout your body, you know how I entered the Lessing seminar. If you, at forty, fear today's youth, today's intelligentsia, you know how I entered the Lessing seminar. Perhaps the casual reader will believe **it** impossible that one can walk into a college classroom and be as shocked as I was about the way the people looked and the things they discussed.

During my college days, I always went to class in skirt and
sweater with a single strand of pearls or a neat little silk square
scarf tied around my neck. I always wore white ankle socks, with
either saddle oxfords or penny loafers. My classmates and I were
careful to wear what society had prescribed for us. Our professors
did the same.

I knew that times have changed, but I was not quite prepared for
a class that met in a lounge, with the instructor sitting cross-legged
on the floor in blue jeans and tennis shoes. We called our instructor
Nancy. Nancy has long auburn hair which falls to her waist. She
wears no make-up. I thought at first she was a student. It was a
surprise to me to discover that she is only four years younger than I.
She has such a tremendous respect for young people that she has remained young herself.

Most of the younger women in the seminar surprised me because of
their willingness to talk about themselves, their world, and their
feelings with fluency and clarity. Some of them were more quiet,
but their silence was often more expressive of their feelings.

The class looked so comfortable and open, but I was in a state
of terror from the moment I literally stumbled over the threshold.
When the class began to read The Golden Notebook, one member wished
aloud that Lessing had written about a lesbian so she'd have a
character to identify with. I was taken aback because I didn't
think Lessing should have to cater to special needs and interests.
But I was too scared to speak up. Communism was talked about in the
novel and not criticized. I went home thinking, "They are all a
bunch of lesbians! It's a communist cell!"

Recently I told a group of people this story. A young woman
asked me, "They why did you stay?" I replied, "Because, scared as
I was, I felt I had something to contribute." I at least knew what
literature was. Gradually, we all began to see that each of us
wanted a mirror from The Golden Notebook, but that the novel stood
on its own merits, not on what we as individuals needed to see reflected of ourselves and our experiences. As importantly, I found
that these young women and Doris Lessing had a whole world to bring
to me. At first, their "unconventional" clothes and hair styles
amused me, but I soon realized how much more they were expressing
their individuality than my classmates and I had done when we were
in college. I soon learned to respect them for their attitudes,
philosophies, and outlooks; appearances became unimportant. I have
since learned to appreciate their appearance because of the time,
money, and energy they save to devote to important tasks at hand,
a necessity for today's feminist students.

It was difficult for me to assimilate into my structured, scheduled, organized life a women's class that was devoted to a non-hierarchical, student-contributing, non-assignment oriented procedure. Nancy seemed to be more interested in her students' views than her own. She gave no written assignments. For a few classes I felt as if I were in a foreign country. I was afraid to speak.

One day after class I mentioned to Nancy how intrigued I had become with Mrs. Quest in the Children of Violence pentology. Nancy asked me to talk about it in class. I was so happy to be given an assignment! It was childish of me, but one doesn't break the traditions of a lifetime in a few weeks. Because of thoughtful preparation, and a new found conviction that I did have something to contribute, I presented my thoughts about Martha Quest and her mother. (I had carefully written it all out in advance.) I was apprehensive. Would these young women take me and my work seriously? This experience was a real turning point in Women's Studies for me. I found that I could talk to the class; they were interested in what I had to say and were eager to hear my views. Once the ice was broken, I started to settle in, relax, and contribute. Because I was accepted and appreciated, I started to look at myself and all women with a new perspective. I am satisfied. I am gratified. I found out that I could shed years of hidden guilt concerning my capacities as a woman. I found that I am an individual, but that what I thought were unique experiences in my life are shared by many women. For the first time in many, many years I realized that my individuality, my egocentricities had worth. I would like to see more women like me confirm their secret convictions about themselves.

Some of my friends in the Doris Lessing seminar started encouraging me to join a feminist perspective writing class that would be taught at Portland State during summer term. I met Sandy Willow, the instructor, a petite little woman of twenty-four with nut-brown skin, and wispy long dark hair, a mixture of lighthearted gaiety and deep serious concern blending in her face. If I took the writing seminar, I was afraid I'd have to re-orient myself again. Stubbornly determined, I faced the challenge and enrolled in the writing seminar. After one hour of class, we were all beginning to be friends. Women of varying ages met together for an hour each day, sharing their creative efforts, openly criticizing, sharing their innermost thoughts, shedding tears together, laughing together, and growing together. It no longer bothered me not to be given assignments. I found that learning is more valuable when it isn't forced. Because this class became so important to us, some of us are still getting together, even now, to share our writing and to talk about writing.

Because Sandy, Nancy, and my many women friends on the campus have consistently been encouraging and sensitive to me, I have become more involved with Women's Studies here. I started attending the Women's Studies meetings, learning how we function in this large university. I have helped to write orientation material for incoming freshwomen. An essay I wrote about myself and other mid-twentieth-century American women was used in a protest pamphlet. I served on a personnel committee. Because I have positive feelings about Women's Studies, and wanted to communicate this to local women, an article similar to this one was printed in the Portland Scribe, a community newspaper. In October, I was selected by the Women's Union at Portland State to appear on a local television program to talk about Women's Studies. Responses from community women to these two experiences have been rewarding on a personal as well as collective level. I have been encouraged to speak up and give my views. I have received support for my life and have been told that I have value. I have written this article because my friends realized that my experiences as a student are just as valid as theirs. To be met by others with such confidence is an overwhelming experience, especially considering my earlier self-conscious attitudes toward the college scene of today.

In closing, I would like to quote to you some passages from my diary. I believe that these glimpses show more deeply my personal insights reached about myself through Women's Studies:

June 26, 1972

". . . I am no longer constantly making apologies for myself, although I still do it more than I should. I really need to succeed . . ."

July 1, 1972

"It is so good to go to Portland State where I'm not looked upon as some freak of an old woman. Why did I ever allow my self-image to become so low? I am amazed that I allowed myself to fall for all the phony propaganda. Is there some way that I can help others?"

ENG. 448, VIRGINIA WOOLF, THURSDAY, FEBRUARY 3, 1972

by Rowan A.E. Muirden

Kate and Ellen are doing The Waves. Betty was going to help,
but she missed the meeting yesterday morning in Nancy's office. When
the class started, though, she said she'd read the novel and had
things to say. Will she say them? Who knows? She's always smoking.
Nancy gives the class structure, otherwise we would talk about images
without connecting them. Carolyn and I, who talk most of the time,
took vows of silence today -- there are a lot of silent women in
this class. Nancy might have been silent too, talked about being so --
but isn't. Why? Because the waves are difficult. . . because her
friend the Woolf scholar is coming on Thursday and she wants us to
know something about the novel so we'll make a good impression. Nancy
is the mirror -- she reflects both images, the learner and the learned.
Silence is just too hard for Nancy -- she can't wait for the silence
to speak. (For all these reasons -- partly and wholly -- she can't
be quiet. She doesn't wait to be asked -- she feels silence as an
inconvenient luxury neither the class nor she can afford.)

Carolyn is writing too. What else can you do to fill the gap
caused by a vow of silence? Other people would day-dream, and we
would too -- only, we can't. There's too much to do. We feel less
time to submerge in the passive portions of our minds. We spend less
time staring into space -- the soft-eyed looking out that's a front
for looking in. Sometimes Carolyn and I look up from our writing at
Kate, Ellen or Nancy, who now and then read aloud passages from the
novel -- but we're not listening. Well, I'm not listening, though
I hear the words. I'm thinking about what's going on. . . about what
I'm writing. . . how to do it. . . which words to use, and why.
Carolyn, what are you thinking? Are you listening? You're smiling
now -- there's a question on your face. Why? You might be thinking
about the Women's Press in Eugene, or the Collective. Who would
know? Who ever knows what we're thinking, even when we aren't doing
our duty to silence. . . .

Kate looks intelligent, but she also looks tired, from waking up
after sleeping too long. She doesn't stick out of herself -- not
at all. Ellen looks intelligent -- not shiny bright -- softly bright,
a frosted light. Betty smokes and stares and flaps her mouth like
one of those fish, kissing fish -- but who wants to kiss Betty. . .
Pink blouse, blue deck shoes, black glasses -- who knows what Betty's
thinking? She's not frightening, but she's noticeable -- the times
have made her twitch. Is she insane. . . are we. . . Would we be
classified so, if they could catch us. . . . She's fine in class,
but she looks like a fish thrown up on shore, choking in the atmosphere.

The man at the end of the table talks, but not much. He's
the only man in class. There was another man, but he doesn't come
any more. He used to come, and he used to talk. We scared him, or
wore him down -- probably both, first one and then the other. Most
of us didn't like what he said -- what he said was strange. He was
strange. We didn't like him. The man sits at one end of the table,
Nancy at the other -- symbol or fluke? Nancy puts distance filled
by women between herself and the man. Is that how she's married?

Mistake: the woman I thought was Phoebe, isn't. Phoebe isn't
here. This may be the first time I've seen Alice without Phoebe.

Not enough time -- too many people. I'll never make it all
around the table. I'll never get to the wall.

One comment about women's classes: the women in them eat -- they
eat in them, the classes. It's nice, so I judge. . . (?) -- no,
just a comment, like everything else. It takes away from the sterility.
We take away from the sterility. We are non-academic. For this,
at least, we must also be intelligent. There are other reasons
why we are strong.

TWO WOMEN

I trust my daughter to pierce my ears.
She has the sure steady hand of a girl
who climbs mountains and bakes bread.

But as her hand advances
with the slow circumstance of ritual,
the kitchen table becomes an altar
spread with implements of sacrifice,
alcohol fumes rise from the basin
and the needle glitters in the light.

Her long hair falls about her face --
she has become an ancient priestess
inflicting scarification to mark a handmaiden,
the midwife who ripped Caesar from his mother,
even the farm women who can wring a chicken's neck --
these rites of women.

I see in her eyes primeval knowledge
of pain given and endured, prescience
of that to come. And with a ruthless thrust
she commits us both to being women --

one nun scourging another.

                                    Ginny Foster

OUR BODIES

i haven't burned my bra

i haven't got one to burn

and won't have, either

      i like my body.

      it moves,

warmly.

      it breathes

inside

      and it's firm

      and there's a bump

      right there, and

a red spot on my ankle.

      and it's mine.

      a woman's.

    *   *   *   *   8

the frizzled

stubs

of hair under my arms

got soft, when

i stopped scraping them

off

                 Alice Donaldson

MAYDAYS

all morning we drove around in the van
you were angry
we drank coffee in the co-op
you cursed all the past years
you demanded your name back
you said you'd take your baby on your back
    and head back east alone
but somewhere the shape of your tornado
    got changed around
        looking too long at him across the table
caught up now in his pale blue eyes the blonde curls
the hands you knew so well
    gold-banded
        around his wooden cane
and the storm settles back down   seething
    and rolling   clawing   at the nuclear box
but listen now andi
in brooklyn and seattle
and i've heard in pine bluff too
sisters winds are heard blowing
some come sweeping and howling
    some lie moving beside your bed at night
        just barely sighing
but the day is coming
when some giant mother hurricane
will sweep us all up
    now and forever
    sisters all
toward a strong new freedom

                        Kathay

MY SISTER

My sister is a cowboy
She rides a golden mare.
Through fields and fields
Without going anywhere.
She says there are others out there
They serve tea from a thermus jug,
Candied apples from Safeway.
There are quilted blankets to lie on
That leave patterns on her back.
She practices songs that help her remember
What she wants to say.
She has stretch marks on her arms
From passing back and forth
Notes,
Which she awoke in the night to write.

                  Irene Grudzinski Townsend

THE CHOICE BETWEEN DARK AND LIGHT

by Judy Annus

I dreamed that the house we sold two years ago was vacant, and I had to stay in the house to protect it from intruders. I was afraid to stay alone because the lock on the front door was broken, and the door, when I tried to close it, would open again.

When I told my husband that the lock was broken, I expected him to offer to repair the lock. He said that he had to go to work and told me to take care of it. Feeling helpless, and wanting his advice, I asked if I should take the lock to a repair shop. He refused to tell me what to do and repeated that I could take care of it myself.

I managed, after much fumbling, to remove the mechanism from the door, and, as I drove toward the locksmith's shop, I saw my husband, wearing a dark blue policeman's uniform. He was standing on the sidewalk beside the busy street, and with him was a woman, his other wife. I stopped the car to ask him about the lock again, emphasizing the high cost, thirty-five dollars, of having it fixed. He told me to take care of it myself.

As I looked at my husband and his other wife, I saw that they were shadowy and dark. He told me that he was going to leave me and stay with her because they had their darkness in common. I looked at myself, light and pale, and felt hurt and alone. I was on my own. As I started the car to drive toward the locksmith's shop, the alarm clock woke me up . . . .

How does it feel to wake up from a dark dream?

I felt alone. I felt that everything was my responsibility, that there was no one to take care of me. I was angry with my husband because he had not fixed the lock. When he woke up I told him the dream, and although he was sympathetic toward me, he reacted against the policeman's uniform. He said that he did not want me to see him in that way. I was reassured after I described the dream to him, but the memory of the door and the broken lock was still with me.

What causes a dark dream?

Later in the morning, I decided to write the dream down on paper,

to get it outside of myself. I wanted to understand the dream, to
know the meaning of the dark and the light. I began by recalling recent
events.

The day before the dream we had a picnic with my husband's family.
The weather was warm and we spent the afternoon sitting in the shade,
watching the children and dogs play. Because there are few views that
we share with our relatives the talk remains safe, and to us dull.
Conversations that stray from recipes, plants, the weather, and babies
are considered controversial and unacceptable, unless minority groups
or political activists are under attack. Then the favorite family
platitudes and prejudices are expressed. On this afternoon in the
sun I was told that the Jews were taking over the world. I said
that the Jewish conspiracy, the Catholic conspiracy, the communist
conspiracy, and all the other conspiracies people dream up, are nonsense and that I did not want our children to hear such destructive
lies from people old enough to know better. I risked being considered
cruel, thoughtless, insensitive, and even worse, controversial. I
was expected to agree or to maintain golden silence. But my silence
is usually bright yellow. I want to be an adult, to speak as an adult,
but I want approval, too, as a child does. I want the security of the
role of dependent female. This is where the conflict lies.

What causes a dark dream?

The day of the dream my mother, who lives in the country, called
me on the telephone. Her relatives were visiting her and she decided
to ride with them to our house and go to her job from there. Because
my father, who drives my mother to and from work, a two hour trip, was
not coming, I knew that I would be expected to perform this duty. I
was irritated, because I knew that I was again in the middle of one of
my parents' silent quarrels. I decided to speak up and express my feelings about the destructive effect these quarrels have on our family.
When my mother arrived she said that she was afraid my father would
start drinking again and she would have no ride to work. My mother
says she is too nervous to learn to drive. I pointed out that my
father had not had a drink for two months. Mother cried and telephoned
my father to come get her. I knew that I was reasonable by refusing to
enter their personal quarrels, but I still felt guilty. I wanted to
speak out, but I wanted approval, too.

What is the meaning of the dark and the light?

I am the house. The house is my past, my childhood. My parents
are the intruders. If the intruders did not come, I would not have to
protect the house. I am grown now, and the house is vacant; the childhood is over. But when intruders come and want to get into the house,
want the house as a parent, I must protect the house of my past, myself,
all over again. I am vacant, vulnerable. The door will not close.

The door stays open. If I close it, it only opens again. The door is the way to gain access to the house. People always come in through the front door, even intruders come in the front. I only want to keep them out, not let them in. If the door would close, the intruders would stay out. Then I could protect the empty house.

What is the meaning of the dark and the light?

I am the door. I refuse to close. I slide open. But it is not my fault, not my responsibility, that I am open. The lock is broken. If the lock were fixed I could stay closed, and for good, too. I would keep out the intruders and the Jewish conspiracy that I don't believe. How could I believe in a conspiracy? Who could plot a week vacation without botching it? I am the door. If I had a lock that worked, I could keep out all the conspiracies, all the interminable afternoons in the sun with relatives who bore me. I could keep out my child-parents. The lock, if it worked, would keep out the intruders. Front doors have keys, if you have a key, and if the door is locked, you can come in anyway, it's all right, come in, use the key. But if the lock is broken, anyone can come in.

I am the lock. I am broken, expensive to fix, too, thirty-five dollars. If you want the lock to work, to keep out the intruders, you will have to pay the price. If you can get to the locksmith before the alarm clock goes off that is. Otherwise, maybe your husband can fix it. Husbands are good at fixing locks, at keeping out intruders . . . if they want to.

What is the meaning of the dark and the light?

Husband can say, tell your mother she can't come here anymore. That fixes the lock. And it doesn't cost me anything except I am dark and helpless, married to a man in a dark policeman's uniform. Husbands can be dark and heavy. The world expects, wants, dark men in dark uniforms. I can be dark and weak, a good daughter, devoted, and I would love to have you come, Mother, but you know how policeman husband feels about it. It's not my fault, Mother, not my responsibility. He fixes the lock. He closes the door. He protects the vacant house. He is the one, he is reponsible; see the uniform he wears. I am dark and Mother will know that is the husband who decides. My daughter would want me there everyday, but it is her husband, you see.

What is the meaning of the dark and the light?

We all know how husbands are, dark, in police uniform, ready to protect dark wife. Dark husbands need uniforms, to protect them, need wives who turn to men in uniform. The world expects dark men, expects dark women.

The dark me expects them, too. I need the dark. I am the other
woman who wants a policeman. I am dark, hidden, pushed into dreams.
I am there, in the darkest recess of the darkest dream, standing on a
busy street, wanting a policeman, wanting to be saved from the lock
in my hand.

What is the meaning of the dark and the light?

But thirty-five dollars is a lot of money to fix a lock. Is the
cost of freedom so high? Thirty-five dollars is high, all right, but
that is what freedom always costs.

The light husband says, fix the lock yourself, or don't fix it.
Either way you pay a price. That is what freedom is; you do it yourself.
I am light, says the husband, and I need a wife who can reach out, drive
the car, have the lock fixed. I don't wear a uniform. Look around,
there is no uniform anywhere. The closet doesn't have one waiting to
be worn. If you are afraid of intruders, have the lock fixed. Pay
the price. You can keep out your own intruders. Just don't put me in
a uniform. I am not the dark protector of your dark woman.

What is the meaning of the dark and the light?

Mother can't do it herself. How could she? She doesn't drive the
car. How could anyone expect it? Expect anything? It isn't her responsibility that she doesn't drive, she is too nervous. She can't
help that can she? Father drinks, can't help that. You certainly
don't expect your father to drive in his condition. You do it. You
know how to drive the car. You don't drink. You are strong enough to
carry us. The strong take care of the weak, that's what they say. If
you couldn't drive it would be different, then no one would expect.
Or if you drank.

But you don't drink. You push the child down   down   down to
the dark. You push the child under. The child-woman in the dark does
not want to pay the thirty-five dollars, to pay anything. You are in
the light; you drive the car. You take care of things. But you need a
lock on the door.

Is there a choice between dark and light?

My dream wants a dark woman and a dark policeman husband to protect
her. And my dream wants a light husband who says, reach out, fix the
lock. My dream says be dark and safe. And my dream says be free, pay
the price, you can afford it, you can afford everything. You'll feel
alone sometimes? On your own? All right. You can do that. Stand
alone. Pay the price.

In our neighborhood people fix everything themselves. That is,
the husbands do. It is dark in our neighborhood. Our old neighborhood
is dark. Neighborhoods are all dark. Policemen always live in neighborhoods.

The choice is between darkness and light.

The dream is over now, and the dark is pushed down. I never look
at it in the light. It belongs to sleep. I am light now. I can fix
the lock and close the door. The intruders will not come in. Intruders
stay out. It is necessary. Jewish conspiracy stay out. All child-
mothers, all conspirators who do not drive cars, who need policemen,
stay out. Stay away. I will pay, am paying, the price of freedom. I
will pay anything. I will be a free woman. My husband does not need a
policeman's uniform, and I do not need a policehusband. The vacant
house has a lock that works. The house can protect itself. I live in
another house now.

ANYONE CAN BE SANTA CLAUS

by Katy Annus
Age 11

Once upon a time a girl named Pam wanted to be Santa Claus.
"I would do anything to be Santa Claus," she said to herself. So
one day while she was gazing at the newspaper she noticed a ad that
said - "Santa Claus wanted, at J. K. Gills for $$ a hour." So she
went to apply for the job. They said she was just perfect but it
was not right to have a girl Santa Claus. She became very angry!
"I want to be Santa so bad!" she exclaimed. "Why don't you be
Santa Claus' wife?" they asked. "But I want to be Santa Claus!"
she yelled like Tarzan. Then she ended up with a job as a clerk
for $1.25 an hour!

The End

ROUNDING OUR CORNERS

by Samantha Willow

...BEGINNING

It's been a quietly constructive summer for feminists at Portland State University. Through a cohesion of energies generated in
a political action class, a women's writing workshop, and the re-
organization of our Women's Studies program, we've contributed time
and talents we didn't know we had. We've built reservoirs this
summer, with channelings for fall's flood energies. And our student-
initiated program has emerged more fully student-run than ever before.

Through our collective creation of writings, classes, meetings,
actions, and decisions, this summer's experiences taught us a fresh
trust, inter-connectedness, and tolerance for ourselves and others.
Like the edges of squares knocking against each other on the same plane,
the sharply differentiated corners of our school lives rubbed so
constantly together that they rounded and softened. In re-fusing the
identities the university system tends to separate, we learned a
greater cohesion. We learned how to lessen the isolation of one
course from another, one group of people from another, and eventually,
one person from another. With our corners rounded, our angularities
drawn, our focus as individuals seems sharpened. And like Adrienne
Rich (who became the inspirational muse of the writing workshop), we
can function each and together as:

> an instrument in the shape
> of a woman trying to translate pulsations
> into images   for the relief of the body
> and the reconstruction of the mind.[1]

---

[1] "Planetarium," The Will To Change (New York, 1971).

II

POLITICAL ACTION CLASS

At the start of the summer I believed in corner-rounding, but had little sense of how it might happen. Helen Cameron and I were beginning the all-women writing workshop (Feminist Perspectives: Writing) which was rapidly promising to be the least teacherly, most communal class any of us had been in so far. Some of us from this class were also "students" in 'Styles of Political Action: The Women's Liberation Movement,' which Amy Kesselman had finally convinced the political science department to let her offer, officially. Others in these two classes were beginning in their own ways to seek and create new directions for themselves as individuals, class members, movement women -- given the hopes and doubts we usually bring to the start of a new term. But the first sign that our separate pursuits shared common directions, that our corners were rounding, didn't come until the third week of school in the political action class.

It was already late. We were about to break up after a heavy, headachey discussion when some women in a rap group finally decided to share the rage that their previous evening's discussion had developed to the sticking point. A free introductory lecture to a $220 "femininity clinic" was to be held in two days. The pink advertising brochure promised connubial bliss through wifely submission to "Masculinity Deified." Their rage spread, and we scheduled a guerrilla theater meeting, a library research foray, a planning gathering... an Action.

Preparing and executing this Action had begun to unify us the morning before that night class. A woman of forty with four children had moved everyone in the writing workshop to quiet sobs or bitten-lipped silence with readings from her journal. When we heard that night about Dr. Watrous's femininity clinic, our concern as woman and feminists about the fate of other women, and our recognition of the causal relationship between Masculinity Deified and women's wasted lives brought us to the synaptic leap associating Mary Ann's[2] life wit that of Dr. Watrous's victims. And so it happened that the literature we gave to these women included Mary Ann's journal entry,[3] research into Living Dynamics' financial ties,[4] and an impressionistic response to the Living Dynamics' publicity pamphlet written by Eve[5] a special friend to Mary Ann and member of both the writing workshop and the political action class.

---

2 See Hoch, p. 192 of this volume.

3 See Appendix B.

4 See Appendix A.

5 See Appendix C.

I can best communicate how the Action itself completed the rounding of this first corner, connecting the political action class with the writing workshop, with an excerpt from my journal:

Tonight, the Portland headquarters of a woman-hating, Jew-hating, Black-hating love-management institute was quietly invaded by 20 to 30 freaky-to-straight, teenage-to-middle age, radical-to-conservative women-loving women. Prepared with three pages of library research and personal writings in hand and whatever outlined or fluid assumptions of the change she could effect in mind, each woman entered, signed her own name or a false one, and sat with one or two friends in the small, stuffy Living Dynamics conversion room.

The plump pink pamphlet that drew us there had indicated that by the end of Dr. Watrous's 3-hour lecture we would all see his light, prostrate ourselves before our husbands, and exist happily ever after in voluntary slavery. But before too long one and then another of us began asking hard little questions, interrupting his sermon in ways as varied as our personalities and political philosophies. We'd been a little nervous 'till then because this introductory lecture to the $220 femininity clinic was being attended by husbands too, meaning we wouldn't be able to talk honestly, personally to the women as we'd planned. So our cleverly innocent and earnest and sometimes "unladylike" questions forged a silent bond of laughter and pride among all of us uppity women. Politics was becoming fun!

But, though The Man continued congratulating his audience on its unusual brightness and energy, eventually his manly patience fizzled and he ordered first one, then several, then all the women to shut up for 45 minutes. Or leave. In keeping with the individuality of our common Action, some did (in disgust). Others of us stayed. But when Watrous's star pupil asked one too many questions, violating his misogynic moratorium, after he stood stiffly still for many long seconds slowly realizing he'd been royally had -- ah falsehood thy name is woman... ...but vanity they name is man! so RAGE and Call the Police! and Out With Them!!

The two identified rowdies were forced to leave, threatened with arrest for UNLADYLIKE conduct, and all but one of us left in support of them, reducing the poor "doctor's" audience by half. The women we came to reach got our literature, and one of Watrous's disciples risked getting his consciousness raised by guarding

the door we politely stayed on the Out side of.
And we brought with us a couple who'd come thinking
of paying $220 so the wife could become "Warm, Soft,
and Yielding" and the husband become "Masculinity Deified,"
and they were now leaving, supporting freedom of speech
and, yes, even unladylikeness.

After interrogating the doorboy and the cops for
a while, savoring our successes, some of us went to
savor some beer, reviewing the Action for the brilli-
ancies and weaknesses. And some stayed to support the
lone infiltrator remaining inside, and further heckle
the doorboy -- "Hey, does your wife have orgasms? Vag-
inal or clitoral? Or anal?"

We felt proud, pleased and exhilirated that with
only 2 days planning, community and university women
joined wits and worktime to develop a mass action in
which each woman could do what was comfortable and natural
-- ask her own questions -- and yet all of us together
could present some alternatives (like rap groups) to this
pseudo-religious, super-commercial rip-off. We combined
the personal with the political, creating a truly feminist
Action.

III

WOMEN's STUDIES

This Action probably had more long-range effects on WS than on
the Living Dynamics participants we'd come to reach. During the beer-
drinking evaluation session following, we became enthusiastic about
structuring into the WS program ways in which political actions and
corner-roundings could happen again. Even more women could be involved in the exciting and educational process it had been for us.
And we could all become better at it. To this end, we looked back
at the foundations of the Action.

Women had been in two concurrent WS classes before. Was the
corner-rounding between these two prompted by their activist orien-
tations? In the writing workshop, one of our major goals was publishing, sharing our writings with other women. In the political
action class, we were studying theories, goals, and strategies in the
women's movement in order to apply what we learned to WS and the community; our ad hoc WS program had been snowballing for over a year
towards an 800-woman constituency and a certificate program, without
the time or place that this class afforded to discuss our on-going
tactics and long-term goals. So, the classes converged at a time in
our WS history when theory was no longer stopping on the In side of
the classroom door, nor was action beginning only on its Out side. We

had to look back on the development of our program to see why.

The previous fall (1971), after WS teachers made a number of rushed, arbitrary decisions, we all realized that more students had to be involved, in "official" ways, in decision-making. Through the efforts of students and teachers, WS classes had been offered for several terms. And a certificate proposal had been written. But, the increasing visibility of our program was prompting the question: "Who's the head of WS?" Also, most of the women taking WS classes were as yet uninvolved in policy-making. We decided to draw from a hat the names of seven volunteers and two alternates to serve, for credit hours, on a decision-making, governing body called a "Collective." Students then had official means of using power collectively which would have otherwise reverted to our too visible, too available WS teachers.

At the first Collective meeting winter term the original members lighted upon the most pressing business, the schedule and classes, and decided: "Oh, that's our function!" and started happily to work. Spring term came, and to ensure continuity, the next Collective retained three of its original members. To prevent a governing elite, the four new members were chosen randomly again. But by then, only the old members were doing all the WS work; the new members weren't learning how to share in it; the constituency felt uninvolved and unrepresented. And still the only connection between the program and classes was that the Collective planned the classes. So, we all reached summer term with the somewhat demoralized decision that "whoever's around" would do the work.

So, at the time of the Action, three weeks into summer term, we should have been having the same problems of participation and communication that had been with us all year. But things were happening differently. A changing group of from ten to twenty women were meeting once a week to take care of business: determine the coming year's budget, choose new work-study people, and make the usual day-to-day decisions. These meetings began going on all afternoon long, as we brainstormed and theorized about those usually pressure-cooked decisions. We were finding that in order to settle the budget, for instance, we needed to get back to asking some basic questions: "What do we want to accomplish next year? How?" We began to recognize that this re-examination of our working assumptions and goals was accompanied by an increase in efficiency and in the number of new people involved. Things were getting done more as in the old, pre-Collective days: whoever was there made the decisions. But many different new people were "there." And we were all doing the work.

The birth of the Macho Box was the summer's first promise of growing involvement from people neither members of the Collective nor of an unofficial power elite. Helen and Chris (PSU English prof) and Marilyn (from the writing workshop) and I were driving back from the

Women On The Move conference in Eugene, and Marilyn was describing
the sexist practices of one of her instructors. We went from the
usual "something should be done" to "someone should keep records on
such teachers so women could be warned away, or take the class together," to "we should have...a Macho Box!" Then the leap from theory
to practice: "Well, Sandy, why don't you make one?" Well I couldn't
think why NOT, so I did! The next Monday the WS office was presented
with the Macho Box: red, shiny, beckoning, complete with sassy
lettering and three filled-out file cards. And so, without any further authorization except asking more people's opinions, and just
trying it out, a small step was taken by unofficial WS participants
toward developing a critique of the university and a resource center
for students.

Through this accomplishment and others (getting some feminists
into freshmen advising jobs, compiling childcare information for women
taking classes, and preparing a fall WS supplement to the school newspaper), we began to realize how exciting and easy it was to get things
done if we didn't first have to go through some "proper channel,"
our Collective, for authorization. It was exciting and easy because
we were functioning humanly, following the flow of an idea as con-
nectedly as rounding corners. So no wonder we were so efficient, so
productive! But it seems also human, natural to plan ahead. And
we did, yet without damming our flow. How?

In the WS meetings where we were getting back to basic questions
("How will we function next year?"), we noticed how well we were
working without an official Collective. In the political action
class, we were examining some of the problems that had arisen during
the previous year from not feeling represented by the Collective.
Between the meetings and the class, we discovered how we could both
flow and forecast.

One night in the political action class we role-played, choosing
delegates from our group to send to a hypothetical convention. The
process was exhilirating, the discovery startling: we didn't need to
cull our representatives blindly, from a hat; we could determine
what criteria they should meet, who they would be, what principles
they would represent us by. We needn't mistrust our differences! We
could acknowledge, not ignore them and work with, not around them.
And we realized a potential sense of representation that we'd never
had with our nearly anonymous Collective. Since everyone felt something in common with at least one of the "delegates," and considered
her most crucial concerns accounted for in them, we all felt we had
someone we could speak to about our special interests.

But what about our Collective? If representatives didn't need to
be drawn from a hat, how could they be chosen, not from a class of

fifteen, but from up to 800 participants?

This question sparked between the class and WS meetings, and circuited us into the concept of specialized work groups that will send representatives to a "collective" that will mainly coordinate the decisions reached in work groups. At this point we realized we already had a work group, and what that meant.

Bea had taken responsibility early in the term to see that WS had a 1 1/2 page description in the freshman orientation brochure. Several of us met a few times to plan and write some of the material. And the final drafting was done at one of the writing workshop's pot-luck with a new assortment of women. We'd formed, performed in, and disbanded a work group to meet a temporary need. New people had taken most of the responsibility. A product was created, a need met. We'd achieved some of our highest ideals about work groups while still in the process of formulating them. Finding our way by going there together.

So, that interconnectedness is why we can function smoothly while planning ahead. Although the Collective had helped decentralize power, it didn't distribute it equally. Within the Collective, the old members were more involved in consolidating their hard-won know-ledge and trust than in learning how to share it, and the new members didn't know how to "work themselves into" a structure that had no established entrance routes beyond the random hat drawings. And be-tween the Collective and its constituency there were no corner-rounding devices: its members represented no particular people, groups, courses. In fact, with the work group concept, even the problem of connectedness between the program and its classes found a potential solution. WS classes would not be just one of the work groups in the "Women's Union," equivalent to the speaker's, or counseling, or child-care work groups. And its representatives would meet regularly with representatives from those and other work groups, in a more collective "collective."

In all, we were functioning well because the answers to our basic questions had formed a reservoir of goals and plans which new people could tap and develop at their own pace. And because corners sep-arating those who theorize from those empowered to act, and WS classes from the rest of the program, were being continually rounded by the fluid interconnections in our new Women's Union paradigm.

IV

WRITING WORKSHOP

While WS activities were teaching us the interdependence of planning, sharing, and fluid functioning, in the writing workshop we were trying to use those means to pursue individual goals.

For an official class in the university, we were exceptionally communal from the beginning. Helen and I were interested in using the opportunity of being teachers of our first WS class -- I was the official teacher -- to restructure the burden of class-conscientiousness more evenly, so that everyone would teach each other. We were both "only" graduate students. We'd both had experience with the supportive, sharing atmospheres of feminist classrooms and consciousness-raising groups. And we were both eagerly looking forward to sharing our writing too. And perhaps primarily, "we" were not an "I". Unlike two opposing spotlights focusing on an authority figure and casting two huge shadows against a wall of students (like some team-teaching situations), Helen and I worked closely together and shared whatever light we offered. The class atmosphere, therefore, was unlike the stark light of an interrogation room and more like the diffused warming glow of a celebration where everyone takes part.

We discovered and strengthened this communality the first day when we were discussing our reasons for taking the class. There was a man in the room. Helen and I explained the greater focus the class could achieve by specializing on the writing styles and problems endemic to women at this time in our cultural history, using ourselves as part of the subject matter. We questioned the women about their probable openness in the company of a man: "Could you bring a menstruation poem?" And though I played a heavy devil's advocate, the class welcomed him. Fortunately, the very act of questioning his presence raised enough doubts in his own mind about how he could hamper communication and lend nothing but an outsider's view (and we were surrounded by that), that he never returned. By considering in advance his effects on us, those who hadn't thought about such issues before, and might not have 'till late in the term, approached the level of awareness of those who'd had previous experience in all-women, women-oriented groups.

By the end of that first session, we'd also learned that within our group unity as women was a broad range of ages and outlooks which, from the start, required elastic attitudes toward each other. This elasticity defined the bounds of our cohesion much as our shared goals defined the center. Each of us individually wanted to improve her writing. Collectively, we wanted to explore the writing of women. So in both cases "we" were the subject matter of the class.

We began by discussing theory (Shulamith Firestone's The Dialectics of Sex, Mary Ellmann's Thinking About Women, Virginia Woolf's A Room of One's Own), but it was soon punctuated with practice. Martha read a poem. Mary Ann wrote a story churning in her since spring term.

Donna printed up some of her photo-like poems. These punctuations became the rhythm of the class, the theory we practised; hardly a day
passed without fresh dittos from yet another of our heretofore unpublished group. And Joy said it all for us after her first sharing:
"I didn't think anyone would understand it...or want to." The isolated student-teacher-student paper route we'd traveled almost exclusively since we first wrote, except for brief brave flights in
letters to close friends -- and that wasn't serious writing (besides
they had to like it, they were friends) -- had pretty thoroughly convinced us our writing was peculiar, inarticulate, too simple, too
personal. Now each of us in turn was discovering that our writing
could excite empathy, admiration, response.

The isolation-breaking dynamic of sharing our writing with many
other women reinforced the unity we felt the first day. Could we
have felt so free to bring in the journals hidden under our mattresses
if we had shared our class with a man, symbol of the predominant
male standards of taste that had always made us doubt our natural
inclinations in writing? We already carried inside our heads a heavy
dose of male dictates ("Make it move. It must have action, events,
vigor. Don't clutter it with your own feelings. It must deal with
matters of importance!"). Our symbolic union against such forces
was an inevitable and necessary coherent.

Also, speaking as a composition teacher for a moment, rarely
did our writing suffer from the awkward affectations I've seen in
freshmen (and to be more fair than the language, freshwomen) writing.
Considering that writing affectations need not be shed with the label
"frosh," I suggest that, though many of us were no longer freshmen,
our elevated status was less significant than our improved environment.
We were feeling comfortable enough to be ourselves, trust each other,
and write from our instincts, not from internalized male values.

Beyond these general reasons for unity, some of the most specific ties binding us to common goals appeared in answer to our working
questions. For instance, why did we concentrate on poetry for so
long? Were we less familiar with its male-defined "shoulds" and
therefore less likely to expend energy ignoring them? And why did
we find it so difficult, so unsatisfying to write fiction? Were we
wary of departing from our own experiences because we had too recently and with such difficulty validated them in the face of the pre-
vailing male definitions of reality? Or, were we unconsciously
following cultural proscriptions that women should be truthful, obed-
ient, and respectful about "what really happened"? Lying was for men?
Or was it rather the greater penchant for relational, contextual
thinking that the psychological tests attribute to us; did we maintain
such awareness of "the field" in which something occurred that we
couldn't fabricate or prevaricate about a particle, realizing how it
could change the whole? Or was it, finally, a political matter? Perhaps

we could not afford the leisure of fantasy when our raised consciousness taught us that power over our own lives, not escape, was the
only release.

Many of the questions that arose as merely personal puzzles
found political answers. Judi wondered why she found it so difficult
to write when she was happy. It was so easy to pour out tears in ink.
Many of us agreed. Our pages filled with variations of "I am happy,
happy, so-o-o-o happy!" appeared so silly, saccharine and romantic
later. Were our articulate energies channeled only into depression-
and oppression-offing modes because of our oppression as women? As
long as we needed to be articulate in our defense, would Virginia
Woolf's "incandescent" prose elude us? Late in the term when one of
the women brought in a very happy, very communicative piece about an
episode in her growing love for another woman, we could see defense
and offense made irrelevant, as it is in the whole range of intercourse between equals.

This non-defensive type of communication that women have found
by sharing information to reach shared goals made the writing workshop
a special place for most of us. Sensitized to the difference between
our academic training and this womanly style, we found the class a
refuge from the polemical atmosphere men often set up. Questions were
for seeking not attacking. And cooperation yielded greater gains in
knowledge and camaraderie than competition could have.

So, the external standards we were reacting against helped to
unify us. The demon was pushed far away. When it came to internal
conflict, however, unity became a less theoretical, more personal
matter. The demon crouched between us, waiting for a yawn in our concern for each other.

Some people, for instance, felt intimidated by and estranged from
outspoken Eileen. They spoke of her "insensitivity." Eileen, in
return, found it increasingly difficult to be tolerant and accepting
of women who seemed so different from her, so reactive to her comments.
Then, the last week of class Eileen shared a poem she'd written and
sent to her church newspaper. It spoke of discarding the insulating
barriers of uninvolvement, of transforming tolerance to love. Only
then did any of us realize what she had been going through. The
elasticity our differences required was stretched, in her case, to
the bounds of tolerance where it met the demon of impersonality and
rebounded into love. With "the quiet women," however, the demon
stepped in a little closer.

Paula came every day, sat somewhat outside the circle, and said
nothing the entire term. If I'd felt more like a teacher in this class,
I would have done more than speak to her casually a few times about
"how's it going for you?" and probably would have made her so self-

conscious that my "encouraging" glances would have propelled her from the class into a less oppressively caring one. The demon, here, could have snuck into the teacher's role and threatened Paula with the impersonality of democratic concern. For, instead of respecting Paula as an equal capable of meeting her own needs in her own ways, and trusting the class to be responsive to those needs, the demon could have objectified her as a student in my eyes and made me feel "responsible" for her silence, as if it were a disease I the teacher could cure. Fortunately, I was too preoccupied with my own learning to objectify my role, and the demon was ignored.

The last day of class Paula handed me a critical paper and two poems to fulfill the suggested requirements; they spoke of her quiet, absorptive learning. She had spent more time listening to the less-labored words of those already involved in the women's movement, rethinking her former assumptions and considering new possibilities, than trying to articulate her own burgeoning consciousness. Summing up her experience with a statement becoming familiar in WS classes, Paula said: "I think I got more out of that class than anyone else in it." So much for my teacherly compulsion to push people to per-form!

It was not under- or over-concern for one person that caused our closest brush with disunity, however, but instead an over-extension of that concern. Many of us began inviting friends to the class. Each new voice delighted us, and we had something to offer her. But by the last week, with outside friends, outside speakers, and just outsiders, we weren't beginning to feel like in-siders, but onlookers. We were all in the audience watching the class and wondering where it'd gone to.

It was only a coincidence that Marilyn Hoff didn't come to sing her songs and talk about her novels until the second to last week, that Portland science fiction writer Ursula Le Guin couldn't come 'till the last week, and that one of the most recent "outside friends" had been coming regularly and talking too much. But these minor co-incidences were making the class come apart under the heavy influxes and constant onward flow. Since Helen and I didn't consider can-celing the last speaker, Le Guin, (though maybe we should have) we concentrated instead on the too-articulate newcomer, deciding her needs had to be subordinated to the groups'. After class one day Helen tactfully told her that certain people weren't finding the space to talk, as they used to. No effect. A few days later I reminded her before class that she should try to talk less. Nothing. Finally, five minutes into the next to last day of class, I sat by her, whis-pered another reminder, and she spoke considerately little. For those last two days, we felt like a class again. And now we know: no new friends or speakers the last week or two of class, and no regular new people after the first couple weeks.

Having learned some things about building and maintaining a
class, we decided to continue meeting once a week -- with a moratorium
on new people, more in-depth criticism, more one-to-one critiques
and written suggestions, and more time (we'd always felt the closing
of the hour like a rope 'round our throats, stifling dialogue). We'd
learned that a good class is a sensitive, collective creation. If
it tries to be more than a jumble of people constantly competing for
domination and the teacher's approval, then it must round the corners
between maixmal individual and maixmal collective growth.

V

ROUNDING THE LAST CORNER

During the class evaluation when the decision to continue
meeting was made, I learned how much people had been changed by this
class, which made me realize how I had been changed. I'd always know it was
a super class, but my ultra-feminine paranoia had made me fear it
wouldn't be "tomorrow." So my memory of our two months together
was an odd blend of actual successes and imagined failures. A short
verse I wrote in my journal one day after class typified my thinking:

Teacher

Hearing the 20 silences
over the 3 voices,
Seeing the 15 stares
around the 9 nods,
Feeling that 1 frown
on top of the 22 smiles,
Lying awake for 2 hours worrying
about the class which the next day calls itself:
"Terrific!"

Teacher?
no.
Taught.

I guess I've rounded a few corners myself since then. And, as I spoke
in part II of how two classes connected in an Action, in part III how
differing people got together for WS projects, and in part IV how
one class developed and maintained its cohesion, in this section I'd
like to express some of those personally integrating changes I've experienced this summer. They are common to supportive situations and
were shared by many other women.

After the writing workshop evaluation when I began looking at myself in retrospect, objectifying the summer's effect on me, I applied to myself for the first time a Joy of Cooking song I hadn't liked 'till then because "love" was in the refrain and title, "Let Love Carry You Along." Listening to the whole song, though, I realized the love spoken of was not the sappy romantic stuff that pop songs help the feminine mystique sell to all the lonely people, but instead a totally unprivatized "love and let love," exactly what this summer taught me. I feel more able now to lean back, take myself with a grain of salt, and love and trust the people around me. Somehow, through all the corner-rounding -- working with so many different people, getting into so many lives -- my emotional ties have been broadened and deepened so as to bind me less firmly to real or imagined negative feedback. I can take it more in stride.

I find I'm imagining it less, too, or at least recognizing when it exists only in my head. With so much personal feedback, much of it contradictory, I find I can't take it _all_ seriously; so I feel less threatened by it, less defensive, and I'm less likely to distort people's messages by first passing them through my expectations, fears, hopes. And I'm less likely to distort the people sending the messages, too. When I don't feel threatened by people, I needn't pass them through the judgments I apply to myself to organize and pattern a fearful, chaotic multiplicity. I can accept the friendly chaos.

Through writing this paper, trying to tell the stories of many people through the eyes of one, and seeking help with it from many of them, I'm realizing another part of that change: I'm finding it less necessary to see myself as special. Like dropping the mask of make-up, dropping defenses means no longer seeing myself as an objective, quantifiable reality whenever I feel inadequate to a task, whenever I feel bad. Allowing myself to be an amorphous schmuck is better than weighing, measuring and grading my schmuckiness. I can substitute the real pleasure of feeling ordinary, human for the perverse pleasure of categorizing my inadequacies. And I can seek help with this paper, with blue moods, because Hallelejah! I'm not everything I "should" be.

Structure and importance are related in another way, too. I felt less need for structure in the writing class as the term progressed because I was learning to rely less on external standards of achievement, more on an intuited sense of accomplishment. This wasn't based on whether or not a certain idea was carried through, but on whether whatever was done was done well -- an intuitive reality, _not_ a measurable one.

For instance, early in the term when lots of people wrote "waiting" pieces after we discussed this "woman's role," I felt good just because the idea had been carried through. By term's end, however, when everyone hadn't yet tried to publish their "mattress" manuscripts, to offset the much less moving, male-oriented stuff usually published, I wasn't disappointed. Because there had been changes. If everyone was not ready to submit her writings to unknown publishers, we had all learned to share them with each other. And we were all willing to have the school paper, The Vanguard, and the literary magazine, The Review, solicit our writings. And some of us have since ventured farther... In fact, the wave of writings generated this summer is only beginning to surface, in the WS supplement to The Vanguard, in the women's issue of The Review, in The Scribe, a small local paper, and in national publications like this one. So I feel good about what behavioral objectives would term a "failure."

When I experience accomplishment subjectively, trusting my feelings more than timetables and charts, I'm more in touch with a reality that agrees with the changes and feelings that others in the class experienced. And I'm sharing a power of definition with others, since everyone's feeling of accomplishment, not just the teacher's (the Authority's), determines whether a class is good...or a poem, an idea, a goal.

This "ideological democracy" explains another change I went through this summer. I bridged a long-standing gap in my perception of people. I no longer see people as either potential best friends or merely casual acquaintances. I see a sisterhood. And I feel a satisfaction in casual relationships that before I felt only from deep friendships or intellectual discussions. Trust, like sunshine, spreads over my ordinary world and rounds the corner separating thought from emotion. And tumbled, like a tall building, is the idealized concept of true friendship (or romantic love), so in the place of conceptual hierarchies I'm helping to build more people-oriented structures. And finally, as with replacing value hierarchies with an intuitive sense of accomplishment and a sense of self-worth independent of differing people's contradictory feedback, I feel more effective in rounding the corners between courses, groups, and individuals because my own corners are rounded.

VI

ENDING...

Since I'm making the final revisions of this paper late in November, I must indicate why corner-rounding can never be completed, how changes in time and place dislocate new edges to smooth.

In the Women's Union, for instance, we've found that the energies of new people didn't gush forth with the coming of fall, as we'd expected. We're finding it necessary to face the dangers of becoming a new power elite in order to activate the work groups. We're now planning regular "happenings" in the Women's Union meetings (a pregnancy counseling session, a lesbian rap...) so that the momentum of the work groups will be carried by an aggressively broadened constituency.

As for "place" changes, after a year and a half, our WS proposal is moving from administrator's desk to active consideration. We're fighting several battles at once: an informational struggle to involve larger numbers of students in its advocacy, a quicksand contest to function on the administrator's ground without getting absorbed in it, and a holding battle to preserve the essentials of the proposal (student control, an adequate budget...), without which it would be worse than useless to us. Moving into the machinations of an absorptive bureaucracy, we're struggling to maintain a corner-rounding paradigm which does not make our differences disappear or become divisive, but encourages their organic upsurge and productive interconnection.

APPENDIX A

<u>WOMEN</u>:   :<u>WOMEN</u>:   :<u>WOMEN</u>

<u>Take a course in the magic of self-hate</u>...

*Learn that everything bad that happens in your
 marriage is <u>YOUR FAULT</u>,

*Learn that freedom equals submission,

*Learn to hate your own body so that you will spend
 $$$ per week on make-up to hide your face, and
 underwear to change your shape,

*Learn that no one will love you if you are active,
 self-respecting, and independent,

*Learn that happiness is <u>easy</u> --
             -all you have to do is not think about
              your own <u>needs.</u>

*Learn to be a happy slave!!!

!! ALL FOR ONLY <u>$220</u> !!

$ $ $ $ $ $ $ $

?

Why must we pay $220 to be told who we <u>should</u> be as women? Women
know better than anyone else what it <u>feels like</u> to be a woman. By
exploring together what being a woman means to <u>us</u>, by reading and
talking together, by trusting and supporting each other, we can grow
and change.

?? <u>WHO PROFITS FROM LIVING DYNAMICS</u> ??

In this course you will be taught that you need to buy cosmetics and health food products in order to create your femininity.

The following men will teach you these secrets with the aid of those companies with which they are affiliated:

Bob Cummings, Vice President for Public Relations of
 Holiday Magic, Inc., a cosmetic firm

In a 1967 Newsweek article, this expanding business was predicted to net $100,000,000 in sales and clear a profit of $15,000,000. Teaching women that they have no worth except in appealing to their husbands is indeed a good public relations venture; they will then need and must buy Holiday Magic products.

He is also Chairman of the Board of the newly formed Bob Cummings, Inc., which will market natural foods and food supplements. You will not be taught that you can make yogurt in four hours, you can grow alfalfa sprouts in three days, or that some of the most nutritious foods are also some of the cheapest. You will be taught that you need to buy Bob Cummings' products.

Dr. Howard Watrous, President of Living Dynamics and
 Nature's Table

He is a business executive who specializes in creative selling. Living Dynamics is exactly that. Don't let yourself be used.

*** If you want to talk more about ways we as women can deal with our own problems, call us:

Helen Frazier -- 227-3064
Eve Simonsen -- 222-3484
Marcie Willems -- 281-6093
Women's Studies Office -- 229-4978

APPENDIX B

WAITING

For years, she had cleverly disdained her role as wife and mother by putting un-darned socks in drawers and by snatching a few moments reading time after breakfast. There were times when she waited until feeding time to prepare formulas. Once in a while she would saturate herself with gin; sometimes she'd sink herself into a novel until 2 a.m. She was able to do these things because she subconsciously knew that the myth was a lie. But the tragedy lies in that she was unable to confront the myth in an aggressive, self-assertive way by lending herself to activities that would be beneficial and contributive and constructive. Because of her training and her background she felt such guilt about her natural inclinations that she had to bury them with self-destructive actions.

This woman of mid-20th century America was educated. She grew up in a Christian home. Her rigorous and self-denying childhood was spent during the depression and World War II. Graduating from college in mid-1950's, she was thoroughly indoctrinated in sacrificing self for man-home-family. If she didn't have a man by graduation day, it became her duty to find one soon. And, above all, that man should also have an education. He must be able to provide for her and the children, because, of course, once the first child was born, she had to stay at home and become the perfect housewife and mother. She bore a large family. It was in.

Many of these women by clever manipulation were able to fit into the world that others had created for them. They played bridge, played on the floor with their youngsters, took over all phases of parenthood so that their husbands could work and even go to school if they wanted to. They read novels, gossiped over coffee cups with their neighbors, discussed their pregnancies and childbirth experiences and conscientiously strove to have a house as clean as their neighbors.

In the 1960's with the concentrated advent of Civil Rights for Black people, she became piercingly aware of the inequalities of life. She identified with these people so much that she shed open tears when Martin Luther King, Jr. gave his "I have a Dream" speech between the Lincoln Memorial and Washington Monument. While white men were guffawing at Selma, she was torn up so much that she said to herself, "That is me. That police dog is lunging and clawing at me." The swollen bellies of starving children in Biafra became her own children's bellies. Other people's children dying from overdoses became her own. After too many assassinations, too many riots, too many phony political platitudes, she saw Mayor Daley in Chicago

in 1968. Burning with rage, pain and frustration, the woman of the
'50's became the woman of the '70's. Because she could not condone
suffering anywhere, she began to see herself as a separate individual.
She no longer supported the war in Viet Nam just because her husband
did. She could no longer tell her daughter that she was the one to
do the dishes, and sent her out to clean the car or mow the lawn.
She started reading a new type of literature. John O'Hara was no
longer relevant to her.

This new awareness, this new acute objectivity, is more than
most women can cope with. To be able to turn her back on the weekly
TV propaganda and to spend her time in studying and sharpening her
awareness of our new age, has meant that many have had to leave their
husbands behind and seek a new life on their own. Other, more heroic
figures are struggling within their marriages to make their husbands
understand their new outlook. They are waging a daily battle within
the structure of marriage to gain the rights that they want and deserve. There is such a multiplicity of aims within these women,
that it staggers the imagination. They will keep working at all
levels and in all manner of activities, because most of them have
daughters, and young friends, and it is important to them that these
younger women grow up outside the myth.

Written by a 40 year old woman in
the writing workshop for women at
Portland State University.

APPENDIX C

WAITING?

I go into the bathroom, closing the door behind me. While
waiting, I file my nails and think of what perversion means: Is
it more perverted to assume the attitude that one has the right to
tell another how to be happy; or does perversion lay deeper in
those who seek happiness in beliefs not their own?

It is quiet in the next room. I am released from my self-
imposed exile. My cat is nowhere to be seen but there on the rug
lies the lifeless, twisted form of the baby robin I could not
watch her kill. And now I will read Woman's Estate, and wait for
her lover to come eat the body, leaving me with a severed head,
scattered feathers, and a pair of claws.

eve

APPENDIX D

WRITING WORKSHOP

Kate Ashmun
Nancy Bachman
Helen Cameron
Martha Cannon
Joy Graham
Mary Ann Hoch
Paula Jones
Carolyn Lavespere
Judi Laurel
Elaine Merryfield
Chris Ochs
Muriel Oliver
Eileen Opie
Linda Parra
Donna Pollach
Jan Schibel
Eve Simonsen
Lauren Sonik
Marilyn Sullivan
Anne Tallman
Barb Tuggle
Betty Wagner
me

POLITICAL ACTION CLASS

Helen Cameron
Martha Cannon
Joy Graham
Rusty Hale
Bea Johnson
Amy Kesselman
Andrea Lowenstein
Janet Lucas
Suzy Malool
Donna Pollach
Eve Simonsen
Tina Stevens
Mary Rose Wesley
Marcia Willems
me
Jane Wolfe-Lande
Kathy Ziegler

MSC. WS

Donna Brown
Pat Knott
Kathy Linde
Maxine Miller
Nancy Porter
Chris Thompson

SPEAKERS

Lesley Conger
Marilyn Hoff
Ursula Le Guin
E.G. White-Swift

WITH SPECIAL THANKS TO MY MERCILESS "EDITORS":

Helen Cameron, for demanding accuracy

Mary Ann Hoch, for a day of ink, sweat and tears

Nancy Hoffman, for inspiration and general
    suggestions

Melanie Kaye, for deflating my metaphors and
    teaching me clarity

Amy Kesselman, for political action and WS
    portions suggestions

Stevie Pierson, live-in critic

Nancy Porter, for the suggestion to write this
    at all, plus WS portion suggestions

Shelley Reece, for stylistic suggestions

WHAT IS WOMEN'S STUDIES???

A course, a program,
a pedagogical method,
a way of looking at
the world, a new dis-
cipline, a movement
for change, a critique
of male mythology, a
feminist cultural re-
volution... the experi-
ence of women thinking,
talking, working, and
being together.

"Every day is women's studies."
A Student.

History. In the late 1960's
women active in the burgeoning
women's liberation movement
discovered what had long been
true -- that we were absent from
history books, often misrepresented by male writers, an en-
igma to scientists, psychologists, and sociologists, and
of concern to anthropologists
only if we were from primitive
cultures. We realized that
women needed studying. In
schools we had two tasks: to
test the assumptions of a culture which either stereotyped
women or ignored them, and to
provide new knowledge about
women and their history through
discussion and research. As
early as 1966 women were teaching
university courses about women,
and by 1969 a debate similar to
that concerning the necessity for
ethnic studies heightened consciousness of the new field.
When in 1970 the MLA Commission
on the Status of Women published
a second volume of Female Studies,
it included 66 descriptions of

women's studies (WS) courses. In
1972 The Clearing House on WS
lists over 1200 courses at 400
institutions, and 47 programs.
There are women's commissions and
caucuses in most disciplines,
majors in WS at several
schools, and growing numbers of
high school WS courses.

"This was a university of male
studies." A WS Student.

Courses. The following titles
suggest the breadth of WS: The
Feminine Personality, Women and
the Law, The Female Labor Force,
Self-Defense, American Feminism
and Women's Rights, Women in
Cross-Cultural Perspective, Poet-
try and the Female Consciousness,
Women and Their Bodies, Auto-
mechanics, The Black Woman, Sex
Stereotyping and Social Work,
The Feminine in French Literature, Feminist Political Theory,
Sex and Politics, Women Writers
and Women Writing, Sexuality and
the Sacred.

"Help create writers, among them
yourselves!" A Woman Writer.

The Feminist Classroom. The
atmosphere is typically informal
with interplay between personal,
subjective experience and the
objective world. As distinct
from the open or non-structured
classroom, in the feminist class
the student tests ideas
against her own experience as a
woman using the acumen developed
as an outsider, alien from the
dominant male frame of reference.
There is an emphasis on acquiring survival skills, and on
building a community through

collective work.

"I never do anything alone any more." A Feminist Administrator.

Programs. Of the 47 programs now admitting students, all are multidisciplinary, share an administrative structure separate from the usual departmental organization, and have a commitment to function as a resource to the non-academic community. Programs tend to spring up where the women's movement is strongest. Beyond these characteristics, WS Programs vary in regard to autonomy, attitude toward academic tradition, degree of community involvement, menthod of funding, and administrative procedure. So far there are 5 graduate programs, and numerous women's community schools.

Spin Off from WS. At most schools having significant WS courses, women have initiated the following: child care programs for students, faculty and staff as well as the community; affirmative action regarding admissions, hiring, and retention of women and minorities; research into and action on the political and legal status of women in a specific community or state; community resource centers organized around such issues as sexism in high schools, women's health care, news about women in the media, and informal classes for women.

"It's August and my class is still meeting." A Feminist Professor

The Future. Here are the questions. Should WS grow as a distinct discipline, or should its concerns be integrated into the total curriculum, or both? Should there be a graduate degree in WS? Should we have WS departments, institutes, colleges, community schools? In what ways should WS break barriers between academia and the community? What are the ways WS should change high schools and primary schools, the professions? What part will WS play in movements for social change? How will WS affect the life patterns of and careers of women?

Resources.

Female Studies I, ed. Tobias, 17 courses, biblios., 10/70, 77 pp., $2.25
Female Studies II, ed. Howe for MLA Women's Com., 66 courses and biblios., 5 essays, 12/70, 165 pp., $4.25
Female Studies III, ed. Howe, Ahlum, for Women's Com., 54 courses, 17 WS programs, 12/71, 190 pp., $4.50
Includes New Guide.
Female Studies IV, ed. Showalter, Ohmann, Teaching About Women, 7 essays, anthology review, biblios., 12/71, 80 pp., $2.25
Above available from KNOW, Inc. P.O. Box 86031, Pittsburgh, Pa. 15221

College English, 6/71, A Case for Equity: Women in English Departments, ed. McAllester
Women Writing and Teaching, ed. Hedges, College English, 10/72. Both special issues from NCTE, 1111 Kenyon Rd., Urbana, Illinois 61801

Academic Women, Sex Discrimination, and the Law; An Action Handbook by Adrian Tinsley (updated 12/72) 50¢, available from MLA Women's Commission.

Female Studies VI, Closer to the Ground: Women's Classes, Criticism, Programs--1972, ed. Hoffman, Secor, Tinsley, 12/72, 235 pp., $2.50, 50¢ post. The Feminist Press, Box 334, Old Westbury, NY 11568.

The Guide to Current Female Studies II, (list of courses, programs), 35 pp., $1.00.

Women's Studies Newsletter, quarterly, sub. $5.00, ed. Howe, Ahlum, others.

Above available from Clearinghouse on Women's Studies, Box 334, Old Westbury, NY 11568.

FEMINIST PRESS PUBLICATIONS

Feminist Press Biographies, $1.50 Elizabeth Barrett Browning by Mary Jane Lupton; Elizabeth Cady Stanton by Mary Ann B. Oakley; Constance de Markievicz by Jacqueline Van Voris.

Feminist Press Reprints
The Yellow Wallpaper by Charlotte Perkins Gilman. With an afterward by Elaine B. Hedges, $1.25; Life in the Iron Mills by Rebecca Harding Davis. With a biographical interpretation by Tillie Olsen, $1.95; Daughter of Earth by Agnes Smedley, $2.50.

Feminist Press Books for Children
The Dragon and the Doctor by Barbara Danish, $1.00; Challenge to Become a Doctor: The Story of Elizabeth Blackwell by Leah Heyn, with illustrations by Greta Handschuh, $1.50;

Firegirl by Gibson Rich, with illustrations by Charlotte Purrington Farley, $1.95; Nothing but a Dog by Bobbi Katz, with illustrations by Esther Gilman, $1.50; I'm Like Me by Siv Widenberg, with illustrations by Claes Backstrom, (translated from the Swedish by Verne Moberg).

CONTRIBUTORS

Contributors were asked to prepare their own biographical statements, and to include their addresses if they wished correspondence.

Judy ANNUS says: I attended college and graduate school at Portland State University where I became involved in the Women's Studies Program, and began to write short fiction. I teach high school in Sandy, Oregon, and live at 10987 S.E. Tyler Road, Portland, Oregon, 97266.

Katy ANNUS says: My name is Katy Annus and I am 11 years old. I enjoy writing stories. The girls in my stories are going to be independent, strong, and smart. 10987 S.E. Tyler Road, Portland, Oregon, 97266.

Dr. Judith M. DAVIS is a medievalist who believes that her area of specialization -- early French romance and courtly love literature -- is highly relevant to modern feminists who are engaged in the hazardous descent from the pedestals on which women were placed during the Middle Ages. She is currently preparing presentations on courtly love poetry and on the couple in romance literature for the Medieval Conference in Kalamazoo, Michigan next spring; and she is active in the Wisconsin Coordinating Council for Women in Higher Education and Women for Equal Opportunity at the University of Wisconsin, Green Bay. 700 Karl Street, Green Bay, Wisconsin 54301.

Josephine DONOVAN is Assistant Professor, Honors Program, 233 Office Tower, University of Kentucky, Lexington, Ky. 40506. Ph.D., University of Wisconsin, Comparative Literature, 1971, B.A. Bryn Mawr College.

Ginny FOSTER has taught high school, and is presently employed as a ward clerk at the University of Oregon Medical School. She is working on a play about a woman who comes from another planet and successfully defeats the Messiah syndrome. 2163 N.E. Weidler, Portland, Oregon, 97232.

Phyllis FRANKLIN (A.B. Vassar College, 1954; M.A. University of Miami, 1965; Ph.D. University of Miami, 1969) is an Assistant Professor of English at the University of Miami. English Department, University of Miami, Coral Gables, Florida, 33124.

Mary Ann HOCH is a graduate of Monmouth College, Monmouth, Illinois, class of 1954. At present, she is a graduate student at Portland State University, Portland, Oregon. 12405 S.W. Foothill Drive, Portland, Oregon, 97225.

Nancy Jo HOFFMAN says: I was an activist in the civil rights and anti-
war movements of the 60's, and in 1968 began to use the political perspective and organizing skills I had learned for work as a feminist.
Women's studies has kept me in academia, and has renewed my interest
in Renaissance literature, my official field. I feel that women's
studies must be more than pro-woman, for women must learn to think politically, and to wield power humanely while finding new ways to teach
and write. I am Assistant Professor of Humanities at M.I.T., and a
member of the MLA Commission on the Status of Women. 41 Pinckney St.,
#3, Boston, Mass., 02114.

Melanie KAYE says of herself: After years of fragmented university
existence, split between my love of literature and interest in education on one hand, and commitment to political activism on the other, I
finally feel coherent and whole, thanks to the Women's Movement. As
a student of literature and a near-member of the McLuhan generation,
I know that form and content are one, and am intent upon finding new
forms, new kinds of classes, new ways of administering programs, in
which we can learn and teach the new content that makes up women's
studies. University Scholars Program, Portland State University, Portland. Oregon, 97207.

Rowan A.E. MUIRDEN says: After five years of bullshit, I found a reason
for being in college -- the PSU Women's Studies Program. Graduating
was incidental. I now work in a half-way house. 550 N. Main, Attleboro,
MA., 02703.

Alleen Pace NILSEN writes: Alleen works on the field of English education and is actively involved in improving the accuracy or presentation of both males and females in books for children and adolescents.
She is Research Assistant and writer in a new reviewing service, "Books
for Young Adults," at the University of Iowa where she is working on
her Ph.D. Her dissertation topic deals with one aspect of linguistic
sexism in children's books. Her home address is 919 W. 16th St.,
Cedar Falls, Iowa, 50613.

Judith NEWTON is an Assistant Professor at LaSalle College. She is
team teaching with Caryn Musil LaSalle's first course on women. She
also writes poetry. 108 Dudley, Narbeth, Pennsylvania, 19072.

Carol OHMANN is Associate Professor of English at Wesleyan University,
Middletown, Connecticut. She is the author of Ford Maddox Ford: From
Apprentice to Craftsman, and St. Margaret's School: 1865-1965, and
co-editor with Elaine Showalter of Female Studies IV, Teaching About
Women. She has written numerous articles on English and American fiction,

and teaches literature by and about women. She is a member of the
MLA Commission on the Status of Women, and its former chairwoman.

POETS

The poems of Alice Donaldson, Kathay, and Irene Grudzinski Townsend
first appeard in a PSU Women's Studies Newsletter called "Jane Sees
Red, So Run Dick Run." They may perhaps be reached through Women's
Studies Program, Portland State University, Portland, Oregon, 97207.

Nancy Maxwell PORTER's friends say: Nancy has been teaching women's
studies, and especially contemporary literature by women, at Portland
State University for several years. Having grown increasingly committed
to feminist political activism, she is presently a faculty participant in the PSU student and faculty administered Women's Studies Program, and has put her Yale literary training to uses Yale would never
have predicted -- writing feminist criticism, particularly on Doris
Lessing. Department of English, Portland State University, Portland,
Oregon, 97207.

Janet SASS is a dropout from the academic and establishment work
world. She's presently trying to work out some alternatives, exp-
ecially in the area of work humanization. 4800 Berwyn House Rd.,
Apt. 620, College Park, Maryland.

Cynthia SECOR is an Assistant Professor of English at the University
of Pennsylvania, She is an active member of Penn Women's Studies
Planners and is currently co-ordinating the twelve courses they are
offering through the College of Thematic Studies. 3901 Spruce Street,
#447, Philadelphia, Pa., 19104.

Ira SHOR says: I completed my graduate work at Wisconsin in 1971,
where over a period of five years I began to grow politically as a
new leftist. I studied literature, wrote creatively and critically
(still do), and learned the need for historical and theoretical knowledge in political work. I respond vividly to the women's movement
because it has matured our sense of revolution's totality. It has
made many of us conscious of how a personal, existential, insistently
humane and immediate ethos must be linked to ideology and to practical
politics. 52 Daniel Low Terrace, Staten Island, New York, 10301.

Adrian TINSLEY is an ex-English teacher (University of Maryland, College
Part) and a member of the MLA Commission on Women. Last year I wrote

Academic Women, Sex Discrimination and the Law and began to teach
women's studies. This year I am Dean of William James College (part
of the Grand Valley State College cluster in Allendale, Michigan, 49401).
I'm personally committed to developing women's studies outside as well
as inside the regular school curriculum.

Aleta WALLACH writes: Bennington College, A.B. 1968; University of
California, Los Angeles; J.D. 1972, University of California, Los
Angeles, School of Law; member of the California Bar; author of
articles on women and the law; presently law clerk to an associate jus-
tice of the California Court of Appeal. 9800 Easton Drive, Beverly
Hills, California, 90210.

Samantha (Sandy) WILLOW is working toward an M.A. in English (spring,
'73?) at PSU, where she earned her B.A. degree in 1970. Except for
Letters to the Editor and one small poem, this is her first publication.
2528 S.W. Ravensview Drive, Portland, Oregon, 97201.

THE MLA COMMISSION ON THE STATUS OF WOMEN

The MLA Commission on the Status of Women in the Profession was first appointed in 1969. It is funded on an annual basis by the Modern Language Association of America, whose members, approximately 30,000 in number, are one-third women.

The Commission has worked both to improve employment opportunities for academic women and to publish information designed to alter ideas of women, in courses and in scholarship in the modern languages and in women's studies.

Study I, fully reported in <u>PMLA</u>, in May, 1971, surveyed the status of women studying and teaching in the modern languages. (Fifty per cent of graduate students in the languages are women; as professors, they are clustered in the lower ranks and in the less prestigious institutions.) Study II, fully reported in <u>PMLA</u> in May, 1972, laid down guidelines for the improvement of the employment situation of academic women and surveyed progress toward affirmative action in departments granting the Ph.D. in the languages. Annually, the Commission has sponsored at the MLA Convention in December a Forum and a series of Workshops on women writers, on feminist criticism, on textbooks, on teaching women's studies, on children's literature, and the like.

The current Co-chairpersons of the MLA Commission are Nancy Hoffman and Elaine Reuben. The mailing address: c/o Elaine Reuben, 364 Bascom Hall, University of Wisconsin, Madison, Wisc. 53706.

FEMALE STUDIES VI. CLOSER TO THE GROUND: WOMEN'S CLASSES, CRITICISM, PROGRAMS--
1972. Ed. Nancy Hoffman, Cynthia Secor, Adrian Tinsley for the Commission on
the Status of Women in the Modern Language Association. (1972). Essays on
women's studies in the classroom, literary criticism from a feminist perspective, course materials. $3.50 plus $.50 postage

FEMALE STUDIES VII. GOING STRONG: NEW COURSES/NEW PROGRAMS. Ed. Deborah Rosen-
felt. (1973). Syllabi for over sixty recent women's studies courses; descriptions of twelve new programs. Introductory essay assessing recent developments
in women's studies. $4.00 plus $.50 postage

FEMINIST RESOURCES FOR SCHOOLS AND COLLEGES: A GUIDE TO CURRICULAR MATERIALS.
Ed. Carol Ahlum, Jacqueline M. Fralley. (1973). A selective guide to curricular
materials at every level from the elementary school to the university, for
teachers, students, librarians, and parents who want to challenge sexism in
education and create nonsexist and feminist curriculum. $1.00 plus $.25 postage

GUIDES TO CURRENT FEMALE STUDIES I, II, AND III. (October 1971, October, 1972,
Summer, 1973). Lists of women's studies programs and courses in women's studies,
arranged by institution. Available only until the publication of Who's Who and
Where in Women's Studies (See below). $1.00 ea. plus $.25 postage

HIGH SCHOOL FEMINIST STUDIES. Ed. Carol Ahlum and Jacqueline Fralley. (Forthcoming Spring 1974). A collection of curricular materials in women's studies
for and from the high schools, including essays, bibliography, teaching units.
                                                           $2.50 plus $.50 postage

WHO'S WHO AND WHERE IN WOMEN'S STUDIES. Ed. Jean Mangi, Tamar Berkowitz.
(Forthcoming Spring 1974). Complete directory of women's studies programs,
courses, and teachers, arranged by institution, department, and instructor.
                                                           $3.00 plus $.50 postage

WOMEN'S STUDIES NEWSLETTER. Quarterly containing articles on new women's studies
programs, innovative courses, teaching techniques, curricular materials, book
reviews, conference reports, bibliography, job information, etc.
                              Subscriptions: $5.00 a year
                                              $10.00 for institutions

        OTHER PUBLICATIONS FROM THE FEMINIST PRESS OF SPECIAL INTEREST:
        (Postage: $.40 for first two books,$.10 each book after two)

        LIFE IN THE IRON MILLS. By Rebecca Harding Davis. $1.95

        THE YELLOW WALLPAPER. By Charlotte Perkins Gilman. $1.25

        DAUTHER OF EARTH. By Agnes Smedley.   paperback $2.50
                                                   hardcover $8.00

        APPROACHING SIMONE. By Megan Terry. $1.50

        WITCHES, MIDWIVES AND NURSES: A HISTORY OF WOMEN HEALERS. By
        Barbara Ehrenreich and Deirdre English. $1.25

        COMPLAINTS AND DISORDERS: THE SEXUAL POLITICS OF SICKNESS. By
        Barbara Ehrenreich and Deirdre English. $1.25